Superior Court
of
Law and Equity
Mero District
of
Tennessee
1803–1805

MIDDLE TENNESSEE

Abstracted by *Mary Sue Smith*

HERITAGE BOOKS
2010

HERITAGE BOOKS
AN IMPRINT OF HERITAGE BOOKS, INC.

Books, CDs, and more—Worldwide

For our listing of thousands of titles see our website
at
www.HeritageBooks.com

Published 2010 by
HERITAGE BOOKS, INC.
Publishing Division
100 Railroad Ave. #104
Westminster, Maryland 21157

Copyright © 2001 Mary Sue Smith

Other books by the author:
Davidson County, Tennessee Deed Book H: 1809–1821
Davidson County, Tennessee Deed Book T and W: 1829–1835
Davidson County, Tennessee Deed Book Z:
Personal Property Deeds, September 5, 1835–January 2, 1838
Superior Court of Law and Equity
Mero District of Tennessee, 1806–1809, Middle Tennessee
Superior Court of Law and Equity
Mero District of Tennessee, 1810–1813, Middle Tennessee

All rights reserved. No part of this book may be reproduced or transmitted in any form or by any means, electronic or mechanical, including photocopying, recording or by any information storage and retrieval system without written permission from the author, except for the inclusion of brief quotations in a review.

International Standard Book Numbers
Paperbound: 978-0-7884-1861-7
Clothbound: 978-0-7884-8576-3

Superior Court - Mero District 1803-1805

This book is an abstract of the Superior Court of Law & Equity - Mero District of the State of Tennessee. [1803-1805] It has been microfilmed as Vol. 2, Circuit Court, Davidson County, Tennessee.

Volume A was copied by the WPA in the 1930's and the Tennessee State Library & Archives has the WPA transcription. The original Docket Book was lost for many years but recently found in the Davidson County Courthouse and is in the care of the Davidson County Archives. It has yet to be microfilmed.

The importance of this abstract is that both the jurors and the cases covered all of early Middle Tennessee in the years before there is a surviving Census. Many of the people named may not be found in other documents. Today it is hard to believe that in the early 1800's there were jurors who had to come over 200 miles to serve. The cases cover everything from murder to divorce and give the county of origin for the case to appear in the Superior Court and the jurors serving in the originating county.

We find Andrew Jackson here as both Judge, witness, plaintiff and defendant. It is truly a picture of early Tennessee history.

A History of The Courts of Davidson County

When counties were formed in the territory that became Tennessee, by the Legislature of North Carolina, they were first made parts of adjoining Judicial Districts in that state; but in 1784, the counties of Washington, Sullivan, Greene and Davidson were constituted a separate Judicial District in that state and named the District of Washington. This District covered the whole of the territory that now is the state of Tennessee.

The newly created Davidson County covered all of what is now middle Tennessee and covered an area of nearly twelve thousand square miles.

On the first Monday in November, 1788, a Superior Court of Law and Equity for Davidson and Sumner Counties met in Nashville for the first time. [There were 2 Superior Court Districts - one meeting in Knoxville - the other meeting in Nashville] *The Court had been set up by North Carolina and the Governor had appointed John McNairy, Esq., as Judge. On coming to the new area Judge McNairy brought one Andrew Jackson with him. Mr. Jackson was admitted to the Bar and was appointed Attorney for the State on the Law Side.*

In 1790, Davidson County was ceded to the Territory of the United States southwest of the Ohio River. Davidson County then came under the Territorial Government of the Mero District, and remained as such until 1796, when the State of Tennessee came into existence. In 1809 the Superior Courts of Law and Equity were abolished, and Circuit Courts were established in their stead. [1]

1. *A History of the Courts of Davidson County.* George L. Rooker, Circuit Court Clerk. [Handbook for jurors]

Superior Court of Law & Equity
Mero District of the State of Tennessee

District of Mero before the Hon. David Campbell and Hugh L. White Esquires on the second Monday in May 1803.

John Den lessee of Andrew Allison vs William Roper
  [In Ejectment]
Thursday, May 12, 1803   Heretofore in Nov. 1801, before the Judges of the said Court came John Den by H. Tatum his attorney, & brought a bill against Richard Fen of a plea of Trespass & Ejectment which bill follows:
  John Den complains of Richard Fen for that Andrew Allison, on 1 Oct. 1801 in the County of Smith, and State of Tennessee & District of Mero had let out to farm to the said John 640 acres, lying in the State, District and County aforesaid, formerly a part of Sumner County, on both sides of Goose Creek, bounded as follows: beg at a poplar on Capt. Martin Phifers N boundary, thence E 320 poles, crossing Goose Creek … to have for ten years ..[torn page] pltf John Den, Richard Roe pledges to prosecute.
notice ~ Mssr John Stone, David Vantress, Frederick Earick, Bassel Shaw and William Roper. I am informed you are in possession of a claim title to the previous mentioned in this declaration of Ejectment, or to some part and I being sued in the actions and having no claim or title to the same, do advise each of you to appear at the next Superior Court of Law to be held for the District of Mero, at the Courthouse in the Town of Nashville, to cause yourself to be made Defendants in my stead..Richard Fen Oct. 13, 1801.
  And it appearing by the return of the Sheriff of Smith County, that William Roper, Tenant in possession of the premises has been duly served, came into Court and was duly admitted Defendant; whereupon William Roper by Jenkin Whiteside his Attorney says he is not guilty and the issue was continued until this' Term
Jury: Joel Lewis, John Graves, Joseph Woolfolk, Robert Edmiston, James Frazier, William Hill, Mathew Alexander, James McMurry, Alexander

Kirkpatrick, James Roberts, Edmund Jennings & Kasper Mansker. Defendant found guilty [pp1-3]

Tues, May 13, 1803   Present David Campbell & Hugh White, Esqr, Judges

John Den Lessee of Andrew Allison
       vs
 Bazzel Shaw   [In Ejectment]
Continued from Nov. 1801 - Into Court came John Den by H. Tatum his Attorney, and brought his Bill against Richard Fen of a Plea of Trespass and Ejectment (same as the preceeding case) And Basel Shaw comes into Court and is admitted Defendant by his Attorney Jenkin Whiteside …
Jury - John Buchanan, James Andrews, Joseph [hole], William Donnel, John Coots, John Smith, Henry M. Truit, [hole] Hutchinson, James Crabtree, Chapman White, Isaac Roberts & Thos Clynton. Jury could not agree on the verdict and with the assent of the court John Buchanan is withdrawn and the rest of the jurors are discharged and the cause continued [pp3/4]

John Den, lessee of Andrew Allison vs William Roper
Motion of Deft by his Atty to show cause and a new trial granted [p4]

Matthew Lodge, Gent. Produced a license to practice as an Attorney at Law in the several Courts of Law & Equity, took oaths and admitted to practice as an attorney in this court.[p4]

Friday, May 13, 1803

John Den, lessee of Andrew Allison vs Frederick Earick   [In Ejectment]
[same as suit against William Roper] it appearing by the return of the Sheriff of Smith County that Frederick Earick, tenant in possession of the premises, has been duly served. Earick, by his attorney, Jenkin Whitesides, pleads not guilty.
Jury: John Buchanan, James Andrews, Joseph Hopkins, William Donnel, John Coots, John Smith, Henry M. Truet, John Hutchinson, James Crabtree,

Chapman White, Isaac Roberts & Thomas Clynton. Jury could not agree, John Buchanan is withdrawn and the remaining jurors discharged and the cause continued. [pp4/5]

John Den lessee of Andrew Allison vs David Vantress [In Ejectment]
[same as suit against William Roper]
Jury: John Buchanan, James Andrews, Joseph Hopkins, William Donnel, John Coots, John Smith, Henry M. Truit, John Hutchinson, James Crabtree, Chapman White, James Roberts and Thomas Clinton. Jury could not agree, John Buchanan is withdrawn and the remaining jurors discharged and the cause continued. [pp5/6]

John Den lessee of Andrew Allison vs John Stone & George Wilson [In Ejectment]
[same as suit agst William Roper] [same jury as above] case continued [pp6/7]

Banyon Dupriest vs Benjamin Davis & William Adams [Trespass]
The pltf by his attorney came into Court - intends no further prosecution Defendant Benjamin Davis by his Attorney and William Adams came into Court and assume the payment of the costs.. [p7]

Thomas B. Craighead vs John Duffield
[In Covenant]
John Duffey - Duffield was to answer Thomas B. Craighead of a plea of covenant broken - damage two thousand dollars. Craighead, by his Attorney Bennet Searcy, Nov. Term 1801, filed his Declaration - On 23 Nov. 1792, in the County of Davidson, John Duffee did sign a covenant ...delivered same to Thomas B. Craighead ... he, John Duffee would execute a lawful Deed to a tract of land containing 666 acres, being part of an entry of two thousand acres of land made in John Armstrongs office in the names of John Duffield and James Buchanon, being on the west side of Harpeth River, said 2000 acres to be divided into three equal parts, and the part to be laid off for said Thomas to be taken by lot with James Buchanan and Robert Weakley within two years.

[much argument over the writing of the name Duffey, Duffee, Duffield and case continued from term to term]
Jury: Joel Lewis, Joseph Woolfolk, John Graves, Griffith Rutherford, James McMurry, John Lancaster, Matthew Alexander, John Payton, Robert Shaw, Edmond Jennings, James Roberts & Alexander Kirkpatrick. Jury find for pltf to the value of nine hundred dollars and costs. [pp8-11]

Leonard Fite vs John Lancaster, adm of John Lancaster, deceased   [In Covenant]
Leonard Fite, by his Attorney, Overton, in May Term 1802, declares that Articles of Agreement signed 17 Nov. 1798 by John Lancaster, deceased, to deliver a General Warrantee Deed to a tract of land lying on Smiths Forks of the Cany of Cumberland River, the south end of the lower tract, which John, deceased, had from Micajah Barrow containing 320 acres has not been conveyed by either John, deceased or John Lancaster, Admr.

John Lancaster, admr., by his Attorney, Thomas Stuart, declares he has fully administered all the goods and chattels which were in his hands to be administered. case continued.
Jury: Joel Lewis, Joseph Woolfolk, John Graves, Griffith Rutherford,. James McMurry, Matthew Alexander, John Payton, Robert Shaw, Edmund Jennings, James Roberts, Alexander Kirkpatrick and Leonard Keeling. Jury finds for the pltf and assess the pltfs damages to eight hundred dollars and costs. [pp11/13]   Court Adjourned

Saturday May 14, 1803   Hon. David Campbell, Hugh L. White, Esqr., Judges

**Den, lessee of John Galloway vs Hugh Barr
    [In Ejectment]**
Den, by Howel Tatum his Attorney at Nov. Term 1801 filed his declaration: John Galloway on 1 Oct. 1801 in County of Sumner, let to Den a tract of land lying on what is called the dry forks of Bledsoes Creek, bounded as follows: point of beg. 80 poles NW of John Galloways Spring ... term of 10 years.

Notice to Hugh Barr - Advise you to appear at the next Superior Court of Law to be held for the District of Mero, Town of Nashville ..and it appearing by the affidavit of Edmund Crutcher, Dept. Shff of Sumner County, that Hugh Barr, Tenant in possession of the premises, has been served with a copy of the declaration. And Hugh Barr came into Court by Thomas Stuart his attorney, and says he is not guilty...continued until this Term
Jury: Joel Lewis, James Andrews, Joseph Hopkins, John Graves, Thomas Clynton, Griffith Rutherford, Hugh Crafford, William Gillaspie, George Gillaspie, Mark Richmond, George D. Blackamon & James Clendenon. returned and declared they could not agree ... Joel Lewis is withdrawn and the remainder are discharged. .. ordered that pltf give security for the costs of the suit on or before the next Term or the same to be dismissed. [ppp14-16]

Sarah Slaughter by her next friend James Hodge
    vs   [Petition for Divorce]
Robert Smith Slaughter]
On 17 Nov. 1801, Sarah Slaughter, by her next friend James Hodge, exhibited her petition to the Judges against Robert Smith Slaughter.
Petition - Sarah Slaughter of the County of Davidson, wife of Robert Smith Slaughter, late of the same County, by her next friend and brother, James Hodges, says: that on 19 March 1792, petitioner was lawfully married to the said Robert Smith Slaughter at the county aforesaid ... that two years since said Robert deserted your petitioner, that he departed unto places unknown to your petitioner without making any provision for the support to Sarah or her children and that he hath not since returned or contibuted in any way to the maintenance of his said family.
      Sarah (X) Slaughter
'personally appeared before me, John Nichols, one of the Justices of the Peace for the County of Davidson .... 16 Nov. 1801 John Nichols, J.P.
May Term 1802 - shff of Davidson County said Robert was not found. John Dickinson, appeared as attorney for Sarah Slaughter.

Decree   Shff has reported that Robert Smith Slaughter has not been found ... proclamation having been made for three days ... affidavit of Benjamin J. Bradford that notice has been given in *The Tennessee Gazette* for four weeks ...ordered that the bonds of matrimony be disolved and that said marriage be from henceforth null and void and further decreed that all the property both real and personal heretofore belonging to the said Robert Smith Slaughter in the State of Tennessee be transferred to and vested in in Sarah Slaughter, her heirs and that Sarah Slaughter pay the costs of this petition. 14 May 1803   David Campbell   H. L. White   [pp16-18]

Henry M. Truit, a Juryman is on his affidavit excused from further attendance this Term. [p18]

John Burrows who was bound by recognizance in the sum of $1,000 for his personal appearance here this day to answer the State on a charge of Murder, is together with Samuel Piper and Abram Piper his securities, discharged from their said recognizance. [p18]

The Grand Jury returned and presented an Indictment against Dempsey Kenneday, Turner, of the County of Smith, for Murder "a true bill" and having nothing further to present were discharged. [p18]

The following Jurymen proved their attendance at this Term and received their certificates:

	days	miles	ferriages
Sampson Williams	6	132	2
Thomas Edmiston	6	28	
William Montgomery	6	100	2
Peter Luma	6	44	2
Philip Parchment	6	50	2
Henry Rutherford	6	19 1/2	
James Neeley	6	48	
George Neville	6	80	2
Matthew Day	6	52	2
Micajah Barrow	6	6	2
Marvel Lowe	6	10	2
Joseph T. Williams	6	50	
Daniel McKinley	6	60	2

William Raines	6	6	
William T. Lewis	6	6	
Henry M. Truit	6	54	2
John L. Young, Constable	6		

[pp18/19]
Court adjourned until Monday morning nine o'clock - Monday May 16, 1803

The State vs Valentine Winfrey   [AB Appeal]
On 12 April 1803 an appeal from the County Court of Davidson was filed in the office of the Clerk of the Superior Court of Law for the District of Mero: Davidson County Jan. Sessions - the Grand Jury for the State of Tennessee, by William Black foreman, sworn to inquire for the county of Davidson say that Valentine Winfrey labourer, late of the county of Davidson on 21 Nov. 1802 did make an assault on Patrick Bigley. Jan. Sessions 1803 Winfrey appeared in Court, pleaded not guilty and thereon came a jury consisting of William Ewing, Stephen Bean, Thomas Cates, Charles Robertson, Nathaniel McCreary, John Bosley, Lewis Perkins, Robert C. Foster, Francis R. Nash, William Lytle, Absolom Hall and John B. Craighead. Winfred was found guilty as charged and by his attorney, Thomas Stuart, prayed and was granted an appeal to the Superior Court of Mero and at this term Winfred appeared in court and thereupon came a Jury - Isaac Roberts, Robert Shaw, Mathew Alexander, William Donnel, Alexander Kirkpatrick, James Roberts, Edmond Jennings, John Lancaster, John Hutcheson, James Crabtree, Chapman White and John Buchanan and find the defendant guilty as charged; fined $50 and costs.[pp19/20]

The State vs John Valentine etc.
[Indictment for horse Stealing]
At a Court held for the District of Mero at the Courthouse in Nashville on the 2nd Monday in November 1802, before the Judges of the Court by the oath of Griffith Rutherford, foreman, James Menees, Peter Turney, Allen Grace, John Alcorn, Caleb Williams, Isham F. Davis, Thomas Williamson, Samuel Buchanan, Thomas Strain, John Rains, Junr, Thomas Donnel, Matthew Day, Gersham Hunt & Joel Lewis, sworn as follows: The Grand Jurors for the District of Mero, present that John Valentine,

alias John Easton, alias John Easton Valentine, late of the County of Williamson, bricklayer and tayler, on 11 April 1802, in the county of Williamson, one Mare of the price of $100 of the goods of Charles Liggett, did steal. J. Whiteside, Atty General

John Valentine was led to the bar in custody of the sheriff of Davidson county, charged & pleaded not guilty; the trial was continued to the next Court and John Valentine was remanded to jail.

This Term John Valentine was tried by a jury of good & lawful men: Robert Kennedy, Thomas Hardeman, Henry Guttery, James Donnelly, Isaac Roberts, George Bell, Maclin Cross, Charles L. Carson, William Donnel, John Hutchinson, Robert Foster and Thomas Crutcher, and found guilty & remanded to jail. [pp20/21]

Matthew Williams, bound in the sum of $200, to appear this day, called but came not. The recognizance of the said Matthew Williams, together with Willie Barrow, Micajah Barrow & James Maxwell, his Securities, be forfeited. [p21]

Tuesday, May 17, 1803 - Court Met - Present the Hon. David Campbell & Hugh L. White, Judges [p22]

Daniel Young vs Leonard Keeling   [Cer.]
On the 2nd Monday of November 1801 a Writ of Certiorari issued from the Superior Court of Mero District, directed to the Davidson County Court, commanding the Justices of said Court to send and certify the record of the proceeding in the suit Daniel Young agst Leonard Keeling - - filed in Clerks office of the Superior Court on 13 April 1802 as follows 'summon Leonard Keeling to appear to answer Daniel Young in a plea of Debt of $14.50. signed Thomas Talbott

Summon Robert Heaton, Marvel Lowe, Braxton Lee & Russell Gower for the Pltf and Thomas Hickman & Thomas Dixon for the Deft, signed Thomas Talbott and on the back of said Warrant was marked 'summoned by' signed John L. Young Also on the back of the said warrant thus "Judgment for the Defendant for two dollars and costs of suit, as given under my hand this 8th day of Dec. 1800. Signed Thomas Hickman, J.P. The plaintiff appeals

and gives John Stump security as witness my hand this 8th day of Dec. 1800. Signed Daniel Young & John Stump
Jan. Sessions 1801 the plaintiff appeared in prosecution of his suit by Bennet Searcy, his attorney ...plaintiff did pay to Thomas Heaton the sum of fourteen dollars and twenty five cents and the request of the defendant ...Defendant represented by Howel Tatum, his Atty.
April Sessions 1801 jury called: Arthur Turner, George B. Curtis, Herbert Lenior, David Hood, John Shouse, Wm Gower, John Collins, Gidean Pillow, John Browder, George Ridley, Allen Brewer & William Cash who find in favor of the plaintiff & defendant obtained a new trial, continued and at Jan. Sessions 1802 came again into Court. Jury called: Lewis Demoss, John Fly, John Minees, Thomas Green, Acquila Carmick, James C. Maclin, James Hamilton, Hugh Liles, John Darr, Daniel Houser, John Cockrill & Beverly Ridley and find in favor of the plaintiff. Witness attendance: Marvel Lowe, Russel Gower, Philip Russell, James Stuart, Thomas Dickson. Costs & fees enumerated, signed Edley Ewing DS   Andrew Ewing
   Continued until this Term at which came the parties by their attornies and jury was called: Joel Lewis, James Roberts, Edmond Jennings, John Lancaster, John Hutchinson, James Crabtree, Chapman White, Marvel Lowe, Henry Hide, Robert Haton & Russell Gower and find for the defendant ... judgment for defendant for costs. [pp22-25]

Dempsey Kennedy of the County of Smith who stands indicted for Murder appeared in Court according to his recognizance dated 23 Dec. 1802, was charged and pleaded not guilty. [p25]

Joshua Balance, Admr vs **Caleb Cartwright**
      [In Debt Appeal]
13 April 1802 an appeal from the County Court of Davidson was filed:
Transcript: 18 Aug. 1800 To the Sheriff of Davidson County ... take the body of Arthur Turner if to be found in your County before the Justices of our Court of Pleas and Quarter Sessions, October next to answer Joshua Balance, Admr of Caleb Cartwright for debt & damages owed. signed Andrew

Ewing   Isaac Roberts, Pltfs security   Writ was returned to Oct. Sessions as executed, dated 21 Sept 1800 signed John Hutchings   DS
Oct. Sessions - Pltf appeared by his Atty, Nicholas Perkins and charged a note dated 3 Feb. 1798 and unpaid.   Deft appeared by John C. Hamilton and Joseph Herndon, his Attys ... Case has continued from Term to Term until Jan. Sessions 1802 and was appealed as 'not within the jurisdiction of the Court' and pltf appealed and obtained an appeal to the Superior Court ... Deft says he has paid the debt and cause continued until this date and jury called: Alexander Kirkpatrick, Joel Lewis, James Roberts, Edmond Jennings, John Lancaster, John Hutcheson, James Crabtree, Chapman White, Marvel Lowe, Henry Hide, Robert Heaton, Russell Gower and find for the plaintiff. Whereupon Deft by his attorney obtained a rule to shew cause and new trial to be had at next Court. [pp25-27]

Woolsey Warrington vs William L. Lovely
     [In Debt]
May Term 1801 a writ was issued at the suit of Woolsey Warrington vs William L. Lovely and William King and returned by the sheriff of Knox County 'executed on William L. Lovely and William King, not found' and at the term last mentioned a juda. atta. awarded against the estate of William King.and returned next term:'nothing found:' Whereupon Woolsey by his attorney John Hassell filed agst William L. Lovely who answered by his atty, George W. Campbell saying the debt had been paid ... cause continued from Term to Term until this Term and jury called: Alexander Kirkpatrick, Joel Lewis, James Roberts, Edmund Jennings, John Lancaster, John Hutcheson, James Crabtree, Chapman White, Marvel Lowe, Henry Hide, Robert Heaton & Russell Gower who find for the plaintiff for debt and damages.[pp27-29]

William Hargroves Guardian of Elizabeth Gardener
          vs   **[In Debt]**
William Hargroves, Admr of John Hargroves, Decd
William Hargroves, Adm of John Hargroves, dec'd was summoned to answer William Hargroves Guardian of Elizabeth Gardner in a plea of Debt, that he render the sum of $185 lbs 18 Shillings & 4 pence North

Carolina currency equal to $464.80 & damages of $300. Pltf by his attorney, Bennet Searcy at May Term filed the following declaration:
John Hargroves on 7 April 1791 bound himself to pay William Hargroves, Guardian for Elizabeth Gardener. John Hargroves departed this life intestate upon which at January Court 1799 William Hargroves administered on all rights and credits of said John Hargroves, dec'd but has refused to render the aforesaid amount.

William Hargrove, Adm. by Thomas Stuart, his attorney, saith he has fully administered all the goods and credits of John Hargroves, dec'd, in his hands. Continued from Term to Term until this Term - Jury called: John Buchanan, James Andrews, Isaac Roberts, Joseph Hopkins, John Graves, Thomas Clynton, Joseph Woolfolk, James McMurry, John Payton, Robert Shaw, Matthew Alexander & William Donnal. Jury finds for the pltf. Deft to pay debt together with damages and costs of the suit. [pp29-32]

Thomas Huey vs William V. Moorman   [In Debt]
William V. Moorman summoned to answer Thomas Huey of a plea of debt owed of $200. Plaintiff, by his attorney George W. Campbell, filed his declaration Nov. Term 1802 - Deft, by his attorney, Jesse Wharton, defended and said debt has been paid. Jury called: Alexander Kirkpatrick, James Roberts, Edmund Jennings, John Lancaster, John Hutcheson, James Crabtree, Chapman White, Marvel Lowe, Henry Hide, Robert Heaton, Russell Gower and James Hamilton. Verdict for pltf of $159.20 debt and $15.48 damages plus his costs. [pp32-34]

John Nolen vs Robert Johnston   {In Debt}
Nov. Term 1802 John Nolen by his attorney, Bennet Searcy, complains of Robert Johnston, in custody of the sheriff, of a plea of debt of $400. Robert signed a note for $400 on 23 Sept. 1799 to be paid at or before 1 Nov. 1800 and has not yet paid.

Robert Johnston, by his attorney, P. R. Booker, says he did pay the sum to the defendant and now at this term come the parties by their attorneys - Jury: Joel Lewis, Griffith Rutherford, John K. Wyne, Andrew Castleman, Thomas Edmiston, William Lytle, John Hanks, Christopher Stump, William

Donnelson, Edmund Baker, William Billings and Nathan Gatlin - find for pltf for debt of $400, damages of $61 and costs. [pp34/34]

John Williamson vs Edward Sanders, Anthony Winston & Thomas Watson   {In Debt}
John Williamson by his Attorney, Thomas Stuart, filed his declaration at Nov. Term 1802 against Edward Sanders, Anthony Winston & Thomas Watson on a charge of debt owed of $1876.06 and damage of $500.

Declaration - 5 June 1800 Edward Sanders, Anthony Winston & Thomas Watson signed a note to John Williamson to be paid on or before 1 Dec. 1800 and the debt or any part of it have been paid. Defendants alledge debt has been paid.

And now this Term came the parties and came also a Jury: James Roberts, Edmund Jennings, John Lancaster, John Hutcheson, James Crabtree, Chapman White, Marvel Lowe, Henry Hide, Robert Heaton, Russell Gower, James Hamilton & John Buchanan - jury finds for the plaintiff $794.31 & costs. [pp35/36]

Samuel Smithson, Adm of Isaac Etheridge, dec'd
    vs
William Sanders   [Case Appeal]
On 10 May 1803, an appeal from the Sumer County Court was filed -
Transcript - State of Tennessee Sumner County - To the sheriff of said county - you are commanded to the body of Williams Sanders if found to safely keep and have before the Justices of said County Court to be held at the house of James Trousdale in the Town of Gallatin on 1st Monday in January next to answer Samuel Smithson, Admr of Isaac Ethridge, deceased on a plea of Trespass. 5 Oct. 1802 David Shelby, Clerk

Writ was returned to Jan. Term 1803 "came to hand Oct. 6th   Executed the same day" signed Thomas Martin DS   Jan. Sessions 1803, the parties by their attornies; the Pltf by John C. Hamilton & Thomas Stuart and the Deft by Jesse Wharton & Samuel Donelson and a rule was made to plea at next Court.

Sumner County April Term 1803 Samuel Smithson, Admr of Isaac Etheridge deceased says William

Sanders was indebted to Isaac Etheridge for $244.47 and has refused to pay. Jury: Kasper Mansker, William Bowen, Henry Bun, John Weathers, Elmore Harris, Joseph Wallace, Robert Shaw, James Lauderdale, Senr, Thomas Howell, Seth Mabry, James Franklin & William Parr and found for the plaintiff for debt, damages & costs. whereupon the defendant by Jesse Wharton filed an appeal with the Superior Court . Reasons for appeal 1) verdict of the jury is contrary to the evidence, 2) because the verdict of the jury is contrary to law. Know also that we William Sanders, James Sanders, John G. Henderson are held and firmly bound unto Samuel Smithson in the sum of $500.
- And now at this Term of the Superior Court the appeal in this case not having been filed within the time proscribed by law on motion is considered that the judgment of the County Court be affirmed and the plaintiff recover agst the defendant. [pp36-40]

Thomas Farmer vs Martin Armstrong   [In Case]
Demurrer overruled

Zachariah Stull vs Willie Barrow
[Covenant Broken]
The plaintiff comes into Court and confesses he intends no further to prosecute; the defendant may depart and recover of the plaintiff his costs for defence. [p40]

Robert Cartwright vs James Hamilton   [In Debt]
James Hamilton was summoned to answer Robert Cartwright of plea of debt of $375 and damages of $200. Plaintiff by his Attorney, John Overton, filed Nov. Term 1802. On 5 Oct. 1799 James Hamilton and Daniel G. Brown signed a note to Robert Cartwright before 25 December next and said debt has not been paid. Defendant, by his Attorney, Thomas Stuart, says the debt has been paid.
Mero District November Term 1802 - Defendant comes into Court and confesses he cannot deny the plaintiff action for $405.15 and his costs. [pp40/41]

John Den lessee of Andrew Allison vs Bazzel Shaw   [In Ejectment]
On motion it is ordered that the plaintiff give security for costs of this suit on or before the 2nd day of next Term or same to be dismissed. [p42]

John Den lessee of Andrew Allison vs Frederich Earrick   [In Ejectment]
On motion it is ordered that the plaintiff give security for costs of this suit on or before the 2nd day of next Term or same to be dismissed. [p42]

John Den lessee of Andrew Allison vs David Vantress   [In Ejectment]
On motion it is ordered that the plaintiff give security for costs of this suit on or before the 2nd day of next Term or same to be dismissed. [p42]

John Den lessee of Andrew Allison vs John Stone & George Wilson   [In Ejectment]
On motion it is ordered the plaintiff give security for costs of this suit on or before the 2nd day of next Term or same to be dismissed. [p42]

John Den lessee of John Galloway vs Hugh Barr   [In Ejectment]
On motion it is ordered that the plaintiff give security for costs of this suit on or before the 2nd day of next Term or same to be dismissed. [p42]

John Weatherspon vs Andrew Jackson   [In Case]
Andrew Jackson was attached to answer John Weatherspon of a plea of Trespass upon the Case Damage five hundred dollars.
Plaintiff by his attorney, John Overton, at November Term 1803 filed his declaration: whereas the said Andrew of 10 August 1800 was indebted to the said John the sum of $300 for a certain grey horse and a note payable 15 Sept. 1796...
Defendant, Andrew Jackson, Esq'r, by his attorney, George W. Campbell, ... parties mutually submit all matters in this suit to the final determination of David McGavock and Randal McGavock and their award to be made the Judgment of the Court ...

The Arbitrators returned their award is these words "...First - we do award that the said Andrew Jackson shall pay to John Weatherspon the sum of one Hundred Dollars on the first day of October next and legal interest from the 14th Dec. 1795 ... 2nd also order said Andrew Jackson pay the sum of $150 , value of grey horse ... 3rd Weatherspoon shall upon payment execute unto Andrew Jackson a general release of the matter to us refered and lastly we order the said Andrew Jackson pay the costs of the suit. [pp43-45]

Andrew Jackson vs John Weatherspoon   [In Case]
Nov. Term 1801 Andrew Jackson, Esquire, by his Attorney, George W. Campbell, filed his declaration ... Jackson bought a certain grey gelding from Weatherspoon and in his deposition declares the horse was unsound, blind and otherwise diseased ... that his subsequent death was due to his blindness ...
May Term 1802 - parties mutually submit all matters in difference to the final determination of David McGavock & Randal McGavock and their award or the award of such person as they shall choose for an umpire
   Now know ye that I, Willie Blount, Umpire indifferently chosen by the said David & Randal McGavock to act having heard the allegations of both parties, do decree that John Weatherspoon shall pay to Andrew Jackson the sum of $150 and also that Weatherspoon pay the costs of the suit.
  Willie Bllount [pp45-48]
----   Court Adjourned till tomorrow morning 9 o'clock
Wednesday morning 18th May 1803 - Court met according to adjournment
Present the Hon David Campbell   Hugh L. White
   Esqr/Judges
---- Court Adjourned till tomorrow morning 9 o'clock
Thursday morning 19 May 1803   David Campbell/Hugh L. White   Esqr/Judges
----- Court Adjourned till tomorrow morning 9 o'clock
Friday morning 20 May 1803   David Campbell Hugh L. White   Esqr/Judges

---- Court Adjourned till tomorrow morning 9 o'clock
Saturday morning 21 May 1803   David Campbell
Hugh L. White   Esqr/Judges [p48]

Martin Armstrong vs Joseph T. Rhodes
[Attachment Case]
The defendant comes into Court and replevies the property attached and Joshua Hadley and Frederick Barfield enter themselves special Bail for Joseph T. Rhodes in the penal sum of two thousand dollars whereupon it is ordered that the Judgment by Default had in the case be set aside and the defendant has leave to plead to the said action any plea which he might have pleaded had there been no judgment. On motion of the plaintiff and by consent of the defendant leave is granted him to withdraw his declaration filed in this cause.[p49]

The following Jurymen proved their attendance & received their tickets:

	Days	Miles	Ferriages
James McMurry	13	70	2
Matthew Alexander	12	60	2
Robert Shaw	13	48	2
John Payton	12	44	2
Griffith Rutherford	13	56	2
Joseph Woolfolk	13	80	2
Thomas Clynton	13	150	4
Alexander Kirkpatrick	12	60	-
William Donnel	13	80	-
John Graves	12	20	-
Joseph Hopkins	13	10	-
Isaac Roberts	13	8	-
James Andrews	13	14	-
John Buchanan	12	8	-
Joel Lewis	12	5	-
John Lancaster	13	130	2
Edmund Jennings	12	110	2
James Roberts	13	132	2
John Hutcheson	12	50	2
James Crabtree	13	60	2
Chapman White	12	36	-
Robert Thomas, Constable - [p49]		15 days	

Sat., May 21, 1803

John Valentine alias John Easten alias John Easten Valentine late of the county of Williamson, Bricklayer & Taylor, convicted of Horse stealing was led to the bar & demanded of him if anything for himself he had to say; he said he had nothing except what had already been said; whereupon the Court ordered he be taken to the jail from whence he came and thence to the public Gallows of the County of Davidson and there be hanged by the neck until he be dead and that the execution be done by the sheriff on the 15th day of June next between the hours of 12:00 & four in the afternoon of that same day. [p50]

Court adjourned until Monday at 9:00 o'clock —
Court met Monday May 13, 1803 Present the Hon David Campbell & Hugh L. White - Esqr, Judges
Court adjourned till tomorrow Tuesday, May 24, 1803 - Present the Hon. David Campbell & Hugh L. White, Esqr. Judges

John McNairy vs Thomas Talbot   **[On Appeal]**
Arguments being heard, the Court will advise thereon till the next Term. [pp50]

Matthew Brooks vs David McGavock   **[On Appeal]**
An appeal was filed from the County Court of Davidson on 12 October 1802 as follows:
Present the worshipful James Robertson, James Mulheren, Joseph Philips, James Byrnes, John Witherspon, Daniel Young, James Dickson, Thomas Dillahunty, Thomas Hickman, James M. Lewis, William Nash, John Anderson, Joseph Coleman, Abraham Boyd, George M. McWhirter, Josiah Horton, Joel Lewis, Robert Thompson, Nicholas T. Perkins, Willie Barrow, Edmond Gamble, Sampson Harris, Robert Hewit, Thomas Tolbot, Robert Edmiston, William Donelson, John Davis, Samuel Bell, John Hope, Robert Weakley & John Nichols, Esquires when the following Petition of Matthew Brooks, Senr & Sundry others the Inhabitants of this county was heard and decided on by the aforesaid Court
Transcript - July Sessions 1802 A transcript of the Records made relative to the Petition and granting the keeping of a public Ferry to Matthew Brooks - "The Petition of Matthew Brooks & others the Citizens of said County sheweth to your

Worships that it would conduce much to the convenience of many citizens of said county & the citizens of Nashville if a public ferry was established over Cumberland river on the land of Matthew Brooks a little above the Town of Wainsborough at the mouth of Harrys branch, as the lands on both sides of said river at said place belong to the said Matthew Brooks and there is better landing on both sides than at any other ferry on said River, and that a nearer and better way can be got from Nashville to Christopher Stumps Mill on the direct road leading to Clarksville by passing at said Ferry than any other way. Your petitioner further state that the said road would also be a great convenience to said citizens. Your petitioner therefore pray your worships by an order of said Court to direct a public ferry to be kept by said Matthew Brooks over Cumberland river at the place aforesaid. Also that your worships would proceed according to law to order a public road to be established from Nashville to said Ferry and from thence to Christopher Stumps Mill ... The Court after deliberating thereon are of opinion that the keeping of a public ferry across Cumberland river at the first branch running into said river above Wainsborough be granted to Matthew Brooks Senr for the purpose of transporting travellers their horses & carriages across said river. Whereupon the said Matthew Brooks gave bond of five hundred dollars and Frederick Stump and John Nichols for his Securities for his faithfully performing of the duties required of him as a ferry keeper. And the Court also order that Daniel Frazier and eleven others, or any five of them being first duly sworn for the purpose, view, mark & lay off a road, the nearest and best from the Town of Nashville to the said Brooks ferry and thence to Christopher Stumps Mill and report accordingly to our ensuing County Court. From which decision of the Court in granting the said Ferry, David McGavock by his attorney, prayed and obtained an appeal to the Superior Court for the District of Mero with regards "to so much of said road as is from Nashville to the said ferry being given bond and security as by law & filed for reasons of Appeal.

And at May Term 1803 the Superior Court came the petitioner, Matthew Brooks also the said David McGavock, by their attornies, and arguments being heard, it is considered by the Court here that the Judgment of the County Court be reversed, annulled, and set aside, that the said Petition be dismissed and that the Petitioner pay the costs. [pp51/52]

Wed., May 25, 1803 - Present the Honorable David Campbell & Hugh L. White, Esq/Judges

Frederick Stump vs William T. Lewis   **[In Case]**
The parties submit all matters of difference to the judgment of James Robertson & their award or the award of such person as they shall choose as the decision of the Court. [p52]

Charles Robertson, James Gordon & Jacob Brown, Extrs of Charles Robertson, dec'd vs Robert Espy

[In Error of Judgment rendered by the Justices of the County Court of Davidson County - July Sessions 1786 in behalf of Robert Espy against Charles Robertson, Deceased}
Transcript "we Robert Espy and James Shaw both of the County of Davidson are bound to Charles Robertson ... condition of the above obligation is that Robert Espy has obtained an attachment against the estate of Charles Robertson from Daniel Smith, a Justice of the Peace 27 Dec. 1785 ... April Sessions 1786 plaintiff appeared, likewise Alexander Greer appeared in behalf of defendant// James Bosley & David Shelby became surities //July Sessions 1786 came a Jury: William Gillaspie, Samuel Deason, Adam Hampton, Andrew Casselman, B. Wm Pollock, John Donelson, Thomas Hickman, Harrison Parsons, James Sanders, Robert Weakley, Robert Ewing & Henry Bradford & find the following recited specially - "I, Charles Robertson, do promise to pay or cause to be paid to Robert Espy or his assigns the sum of one hundred and thirty three pounds six shillings & eight pence on or before the first day of October next for value rec'd...31 Jan. 1784" Therefore it is considered by the Court that the pltf do recover against the defendant his debt and interest and also his costs of suit. Afterwhich

the plaintiff transferred the use of said Judgment to Nicholas Coonrod, signed Robert Espy 25 Aug. 1786; and on the execution of the above is written a receipt 'rec'd of David Hay Sheriff for Davidson County, the contents of the within judgment' Oct. 16, 1786 & signed Nicholas Coonrod. J. Whiteside, atty for pltf
After due deliberation and arguments it is the opinion of the Court that the previous judgment of the County Court was in Error and should be reversed and Robert Espy pay the costs of the suit. [pp53-57]

John Read vs Anthony Crutcher [In Error]
On motion it is advised to issue Certiorari to the Justices of the County Court of Montgomery for a more complete record. [p57]

John Den lessee of Andrew Allison vs William Roper [Ejectment]
On argument it is ordered that the same be discharged [p57]

John Overton vs John B. Evens [Case]
By consent the plea in abatement is withdrawn. [p57]

Andrew Morris vs Gabriel Able [In Covenant]
Demurrer overruled & Enquiry of damages awarded//to be inquired of by a jury next term. [p58]

Redmond D. Barry vs John Richmond [In Covenant]
Deft not appearing it is considered by the Court that the plaintiff recover his damages//to be inquired of by a Jury at the next Court. [p58]

William Russell & Co. vs Thomas Batchelor
[Case Attachment]
Defendant not appearing it is considered by the Court that the plaintiff recover his damages//to be inquired of by Jury at next Court. [p58]

Christopher Stump & Co.
    vs [In Debt]
John Duke, Adm of Richard Myrick, dec'd & John Duke

The death of the Defendant John Duke being suggested & Scire facias is awarded them against Josiah G. Duke & Philip Duke and Wife, Administrators of John Duke returnable here at the next Court. [p58]

At a Superior Court of Law and Equity held for the District at the Courthouse in Nashville on the second Monday being the fourteenth day of November in the year 1803.

Present the Hon. David Campbell, Andrew Jackson & Hugh L. White, Esqrs/Judges

Tuesday Nov. 15, 1803

Robert Nelson vs John Kethley {In Covenant}
And this day came the parties by their and a jury called: Dan Hill, Eli Hammond, Henry Rutherford, Matthew Day, James Lauderdale, James Sawyers, William Hall, Micajah Barrow, Nicholas Boyce, Robert Ellis, John L. Martin, & Willie Barrow. Find for the plaintiff and assess his damages to $407 & costs; whereupon a Rule by defendant for a new trial. On argument it is ordered the verdict be set aside & a new trial be had at the next Court. [p59]

Robert White, Gent. took oaths to support the Constitution of the United States; of the State of Tennessee and oath of an attorney at law and is therefore admitted to practice in this Court. [p59]

John Den lessee of John Galloway vs Hugh Barr
{In Ejectment}
The Plaintiff not having given security, on motion by Defts Atty it is ordered that this suit be dismissed & the Plaintiff pay the costs. [p59]

Thomas Farmer vs Martin Armstrong [In Case]
Nov. Term 1850 at the suit of Thomas Farmer vs Martin Armstrong on a plea of trespass writ was returned by sheriff 'came too late for attention'; whereupon the plaintiff by his attornies Overton & Dickenson filed his declaration May Term 1801...

Declaration ...whereas by an Act of the General Assembly of the State of North Carolina Martin was appointed surveyor of the lands thereby reserved for the Officers & Soldiers of the Continental Line of said State ...therefore within the jurisdiction of this Court, the said Martin received of Thomas Farmer four military land warrants for 640 acres of land each, to wit, John Crabtree's bounty warrant No. 878, Thomas Brookins's warrant No. 879, John Eckland's heir of Francis Eckland No. 673 and Mary Parrs and others, heirs of Caleb Fenton, No. 760 and afterwards, the same day and year and also within the jurisdiction of this Court, Martin received of the said Thomas four other military land warrants for 640 acres of land each and then and there undertake and upon himself assume to locate and survey and return to the office of the Secretary of the State of NC with the proper platts and certificates within a reasonable time.

And whereas afterward, the said Martin was indebted to the said Thomas in the sum of fifteen hundred dollars agreed to pay to the said Thomas the sum of fifteen hundred dollars whenever he should be requested. Martin declares himself injured to the value of fifteen hundred dollars and brings suit by his attorneys, Overton & Dickinson.

And the Defendant by his attorney, Bennet Searcy, says he did not agree to pay the plaintiff as he has alledged. Also says he was not obligated to survey the same until the Plaintiff located the said warrants.

And the cause was continued from Term to Term until this Term and a Jury of good and lawful men - Josiah Fort, John Lancaster, William Gillispie, James Hibbitts, John Payton, Edmond Landers, Absolam Hooper, Andrew Grier, Samuel Blythe, Andrew Blythe, Matthew Brooks, & Archibald Lytle and find the defendant hath not fully paid and they assess the plaintiffs damages to $1500 besides his costs and therefore the Defendant obtained a Rule to show cause argued by defendants attornies, Humphrey & Searcy. Overruled by the Court and Defendant ordered to pay $1500 & costs. [pp60-64]

John Den lessee of Andrew Allison vs Bazzel Shaw   [In Ejectment]

This day came the parties by their attornies and a Jury was called: Dan Hill, Eli Hammonds, Henry Rutherford, Matthew Day, James Lauderdale, James Sawyers, William Hall, Micajah Barrow, Nicholas Boyce, Ellice, William Barrow & William Betts; By consent of the parties and with the assent of the Court, Dan Hill one of the Jurors is withdrawn keeping the rest of the Jury from rendering their verdict are discharged. It is considered by the Court the Defendant may depart without delay and recover against the Plaintiff his costs. [p64]

John Den lessee of Andrew Allison vs Frederick Earrick   [In Ejectment]
The Plaintiff not further prosecuting his action, it is considered by the Court that the Defendant may depart and recover against the Plaintiff his costs. [p64]

John Den lessee of Andrew Allison vs David Vantress   [In Ejectment]
The Plaintiff, by his attorney, intends no further to prosecute & the Defendant assumes all costs except the attorney fee. [p65]

John Den lessee of Andrew Allison vs John Stone & George Wilson   [In Ejectment]
The Plaintiff, by his attorney, intends no further prosecute; Defendant may depart and recover against the Plaintiff his costs. [p65]

John Den lessee of Jesse Jernigan vs John Davidson   [In Ejectment]
Be it remembered that on the 2nd Monday in November 1801, came John Den, by his attorney, Howell Tatum ...
    Whereas Jesse Jernigan, on 1 Jan. 1801, in the County of Montgomery, let to the said John a tract of land & plantation, containing 640 acres, lying in the County of Montgomery [formerly the county of Tennessee] on both sides of the middle forks of Bartons Creek, near the head of it, for a term of ten years and Richard Fen, on 4 February of the year afterwards, entered into the land and ejected the said John. Pledges to prosecute John

Doe & Richard Roe. signed Howel Tatum, atty for Pltf

Notice: To John Davidson: I am informed you are in possession of a claim title to the premises mentioned in this declaration of Ejectment -- John Davidson was served notice by sheriff of Montgomery County - came into Court and plead not guilty and rely on the title only and is admitted as Defendant by his attorney, Thomas Stuart. Continued from Term to Term until this Term, at which day defendant by his attorney, Howel Tatum, came into court and intends no further to prosecute, therefore it is considered by the Court that the defendant may depart and collect from the plaintiff his costs. [pp65/66]

Willie Cherry vs John Mitchel   [Case Appeal]
On 29 October 1803 an appeal from the County Court of Wilson was filed in the office of the Clerk of the Superior Court of Law for the District of Mero: *Record of the County Court:* 4th Monday in December 1802 in the town of Lebanon & County of Wilson To the Sheriff of Wilson County: 'you are commanded to take the body of John Mitchell & him safely keep so that you have him before the Justices of the Court of Pleas & Quarter Session to be held in the Town of Lebanon on 4th Monday in March to answer Willie Cherry on a Plea of Trespass to the damage of $500.' Test: John Alcorn, Clerk W.C. The above writ returned March Term 1803 with 'came to hand 29 Dec. 1802 & Executed 30 Dec. 1802' Nathaniel Perry, Sheriff, W.C., and at the March Term a rule of Court was made to plead and try at 'next June Term' and June Term the Plaintiff by Thomas Stuart his atty filed his declaration: whereas the said John Mitchell on the 7th July 1802, at the County of Wilson, that the said Plaintiff had agreed to pay said Defendant $100 at Christmas, and another $100 at the 1st of June for said Defendants improvement on Spring Creek ... was agreed that two years should commence on Christmas day 1803 ...
Defendant, by his atty John C. Hamilton, puts himself upon the county ...continued until September Term 1803 and Jury called: Thomas Bradley, Hugh Morrison, Alexander Braden, Ezekiel Bass, Thomas Moss, John Laurance, Littleton Cassle, George Swingley, Joseph Cole, Henry Baily, John

Herrod & William Burnpass, upon hearing the evidence find for the Defendant and that defendant should recover against the Plaintiff his costs.
From this judgment the Plaintiff by his attorney prayed an appeal to the Superior Court of Mero and entered into bond of $500 with Nathaniel Perry and Daniel Cherry his securities. "I, John Alcorn, Clerk of said Court, certify the foregoing is a true transcript signed with my private seal (the seal of the County being not provided yet)"

And at this Term of the Superior Court the plaintiff by his attorney, Thomas Stuart, comes into court and confesses that he intends no further to prosecute. Therefore it is considered by the Court that the defendant depart and the plaintiff pay the costs. [pp66-69]

Isaac Simpson vs Samuel Shannon   [In Covenant]
Samuel Shannon was attached to answer Isaac Simpson of a plea of Covenant broken to the damage of Isaac Simpson to the use of William Bishop of $1,000. The plaintiff, by Thomas Stuart, his attorney, comes into Court and confesses that he intends no further to prosecute, therefore it is considered by the Court that the Plaintiff pay the costs. [p69]

John Den lessee of John Nichols   [In Ejectment]
            vs
William Walker, William Walker,
William Lancaster, Oliver Badgers & David Boatwright
Daniel Boatwright, one of the Defendants in this suit, comes into Court and disclaims all right or title to the premises mentioned in the plaintiffs declaration of Ejectment. [p69]

Wed., Nov. 16, 1803
John Den lessee of John Irvin vs John Overton
     [In Ejectment]
November Term 1800 came John Den, lessee of John Irwin by his attorney, Thomas Stuart, brought into Court certain bills against Richard Fen of a Plea of Trespass and Ejectment ... whereas John Irwin on 1 January 1801, let to John Den three hundred and twenty acres of land lying on the head branches of

Browns Creek, beginning at Andrew Boyd's SE corner ... for a term of 7 years.
John Overton admitted as defendant and says he is not guilty, by his attorney, Whiteside.

And the cause was continued from Term to Term until this Term, at which came the parties by their attornies and a Jury: Dan Hill, Henry Rutherford, Matthew Day, James Lauderdale, James Sawyers, John Lancaster, James Hibbile, Nicholas Boyce, Robert Ellice, John L. Martin, John Payton & Willie Barrow and say the Defendant is not guilty of the Trespass and Ejectment therefore it is considered the defendant may depart and recover against the Plaintiff his costs. [pp70/71]

**Alexander Patton vs William Maclin, admr
of Zackfield Maclin   [Debt Appeal]**
21 April 1802 an appeal from the County Court of Davidson was filed to the Superior Court for the District of Mero:
transcript - the suit in the Davidson County Court Alexander Patton plt. agst Sackfield Maclin & Robert Searcy filed April 1800 - debt of $140 - John Patton became pltfs security; plaintiff appeared in July Sessions by his atty Joseph Herndon & Robert Searcy came into Court and plead payment and the cause was continued until October Sessions at which time Sackfield Maclin, the other defendant, appeared by his atty, and likewise Robert Searcy in person and Bennet Searcy, Atty for Maclin & Searcy - Sackfield Maclin came later into Court and confesses he does owe to the plaintiff as charged and it is ruled that the pltf recover the amount of the principal and interest computed to $154.79 and costs and thereafter the said Sacfield Maclin obtained an appeal. signed Andrew Ewing
May Term 1802 - Superior Court - cause continued until Nov. Term at which day comes the plaintiff by his attorney and the Defendant Zackfield Maclin being dead --- on the motion of the pltf by his attorney a Sire facias is awarded him agst William Maclin, Administrator of Zackfield. ...all administration of all goods and chattels of Sackfield Maclin have been commited to William Maclin, the said Sackfield Maclin having died Intestate - signed Randal McGavock, Clk

And now at this Term, William Maclin by his attorney Jenkin Whiteside comes & Alexander by his attorney John Dickinson ... and a Jury called consisting of Josiah Fort,
Eli Hammond, Micajah Barrow, James W. Cocke, John Davidson, William Hall, William Gillispie, Thomas Murry, Thomas Smith, Philip Parchment, Nicholas Coonrod, Francis Hodge and find for pltf and pltf shall recover the debt and his costs. [pp71-75]

James Elliot vs Andrew Bowman
[Orig. Attachment Cov't & Inquiry]
On 25 May 1801 James Elliot obtained an attachment against the Estate of Andrew Bowman for four thousand two hundred & fifty dollars. 'To the sheriff of Sumner county: Whereas James Elliot hath complained on oath before me Reuben Searcy one of the Justices for the County of Sumner that Andrew Bowman is justly indebted to thim, that also the said Andrew Bowman is not an inhabitant of this government... you are therefore commanded to attach so much of the Estate of the said Andrew Bowman as shall be of sufficient value to satisfy the debt and costs' signed Reuben Searcy
Sheriffs return 'levied on three 640 acre tracts of land lying on the long branch of Red River adjoining the land of Reuben Searcy one on Cooke branch of Red River' Edmund Crutcher, D.S.
At the last Term the proceeding were ordered to be stayed six months; and at May Term 1802, the plaintiff by his attorney Bennet Searcy filed his declaration. Whereas on 2 May 1798 Andrew Bowman signed his Covenant to one of his tracts of land lying on Red River and after viewing Elliot chose a tract near to where Andrew Sharp lived but Andrew did not nor hath not made the promised Deed; and the Defendant not appearing it is considered by the Court that the Plaintiff recover against the Defendant his damages to be enquired of by a Jury at the next Court At which Court towit November 1802 came the plaintiff and the inquiry was continued in May Sessions and Jury called: Dan Hill, Henry Rutherford, Matthew Day, James Lauderdale, James Sawyers, John Lancaster, James Hibbits, Nicholas Boyce, Robert Ellis, John L. Martin, John Payton & Willie Barrow who say the Plaintiff hath sustained damages to $640 besides

his costs and it is ordered that the sheriff make sale of the lands by him attached and out of the money pay and satisfy this judgment. [pp75-77]

Jesse Beasley vs Martin Armstrong   [In Covenant]
May Term 1802 the plaintiff by his attorney Redmund D. Barry filed his declaration of a plea of Covenant broken to his damage of $2000. Defendant on 1 September 1799 agreed to warrant title to a tract of land containing 220 acres lying in the county of Sumner on the waters of Dicksons lick branch adjoing the tract of land Tilman Dixon lives on - on his North boundary including the improvement Frederick Debow now lives - said title to be made within twelve months. Defendant by Bennet Searcy his attorney - continued and this day a Jury of Josiah Fort, Eli Hammond, Micajah Barraw, James W. Cocke, John Davidson, William Hall, William Gillespie, Thomas Murry, Thomas Smith, Philip Parchment, Francis Hodges and Lemuel McNight and say the Defendant hath not performed the Covenant & do further say the Defendant hath broken his said Covenant in manner and assess the plaintiffs damages to four hundred and ninety five dollars besides his costs. [pp77-79]

Micajah Barrow vs Arthur K. Turner & John Macon
    [In Debt]
Arthur K. Turner and John Macon were summoned to answer Micajah Barrow of a plea of debt . Whereupon the said Micajah by Jesse Wharton his attorney at May Term 1803 filed his declaration: Arthur K. Turner & John Macob on 13 September 1802 bound themselves to pay the sum of $375 and they say that they have paid. B. Searcy Atty
Plaintiff say they have not paid. Thos Stuart for Pltf
And at this term came the Defendants and confess they cannot deny the plaintiffs action for $375 and interest from 25 December 1802 and the Court rules they pay and his costs of suit and Plaintiff agrees to stay the Execution of this judgment four months. [pp79/80]

Martin Armstrong vs Joseph T. Rhodes
[Original Atta. Case]

On 26 Oct. 1801 Martin Armstrong obtained an attachment against the Estate of Joseph T. Rhodes for $960, returnable to November Term 1801, which attachment is in these words "Martin Armstrong hath complained on oath before me, James Mulherin, one of the Justices for the County of Davidson, that Captain Joseph T. Rhodes is indebted to him ....that Joseph T. Rhodes does not reside within the state ... you are therefore commanded that you attach the estate of the same Joseph T. Rhodes (if to be found in your county) that will be of value sufficient to satisfy the said debt. Which attachment was returned by the sheriff of Davidson County Oct. 27, 1801 'this day levied the within attachment on three thousand eight hundred and forty acres of land lying on the West fork of Stones River, adjoining the last lines run for the Continental Officers and Soldiers to include the land on both sides.' J. Boyd, Shff Whereupon the plaintiff by Bennet Searcy his attorney at May Term 1803 filed his declaration upon the same. that whereas on the day of December 1784 in the County of Davidson the said Joseph did contract with and employ the said Martin to locate and survey a Military land warrant granted to the said Joseph as a Captain in the Continental line of the State of North Carolina for three thousand eight hundred & forty acres ...and agreed to give the said Martin one fifth part of the said tract when his patent should be obtained from the state of North Carolina. In consideration of the said agreement said Martin made a Location in the Military land office for the said Joseph on the 7th day of December 1784 by virtue of the said Warrant No 607 on the West fork of Stones River ... B. Searcy Atty for pltf
And the said Joseph T. Rhodes by Thomas Stuart his attorney comes and puts himself upon the county ... And at this Term the plaintiff was solemnly called but came not neither is his suit further prosecuted therefore it is considered by the Court that he be nonsuited and pay to the defendant his costs. [pp80-83]

Pleas at the Courthouse in Nashville - November 17, 1803

William Marchbanks vs Philip Parchment
[In Detinue]
Philip Parchment was attached to answer William Marchbanks of a Plea of Detinue for two negroes: Sal, a negro woman slave of value of five hundred dollars and a child of Sal, named Charlotte, value of two hundred dollars; damage one thousand dollars.
Plaintiff by John Overton his attorney filed his declaration May Term 1802; Sal, about twenty three years of age and her child, Charlotte, being detained by the defendant ...
Defendant, by George W. Campbell, his attorney, ... case has been continued from Term to Term and this day comes a lawful jury: Dan Hill, Matthew Day, James Lauderdale, James Sawyers, John Lancaster, Nicholas Boyce, Robert Ellis, John L. Martin, John Payton, Willie Barrow, Josiah Fort & Eli Hammond. By consent of the parties and with the assent of the Court, Dan Hill, one of the jurors, was withdrawn and the case continued until the next Court. [pp83-84]

Francis Nusum vs William Betts   [In Covenant]
William Betts was attached to answer Francis Nusum of a plea of covenant broken - damage five hundred dollars. Plaintiff by his attorney, Thomas Stuart, at May Term filed his Declaration -- that on 15 August 1800 Francis Nusum did agree to build a grist mill to run one pair of stones with the place for another pair on Little Harpeth near the place the said Betts then lived, and likewise a good Dam and compleat all the works necessary to make a good mill and deliver her to the said William Betts as soon as it could conveniently be done and said Betts did agree by said writing to furnish seven hands including a pair of Sawyers and Nusum did agree to furnish three hands including a pair of Sawyers ...Betts did agree to pay Nusum the sum of four hundred dollars when the same should be completed ...Betts to furnish one pair of oxen. Said mill was delivered to Betts on the 25th December 1801 and plaintiff says that Betts did not furnish seven hands and Betts has not paid and thus he brings suit. Defendant William Betts by Jesse Wharton, his attorney, says he has not broken his covenant ...

Continued from Term to Term until this Term, at which came the parties by their attornies and a Jury was called: Dan Hill, Matthew Day, James Lauderdale, James Sawyers, John Lancaster, Nicholas Boyce, Robert Ellis, John L. Martin, John Payton, Willie Barrow, Josiah Fort & Eli Hammonds - find for plaintiff and assess the plaintiffs damages to $270.00 besides his costs. [pp84-86]

James Martin vs Winney Martin
[Petition for a Divorce]
On 11 May 1802 James Martin exhibited his petition of the Hon. Andrew Jackson, one of the Judges of the Superior Courts of Law & Equity for the State of Tennessee, against Winney Martin: ...that sometime in 1792 he was lawfully married to Winney Price, now Winney Martin, by whom he has had two children; that from time to time she has deserted his bed & board and continued away for a considerable time and that she is now gone away with a certain Dennis Cannaday to the State of North Carolina, and lives with the said Cannaday in a state of adultery... pays your Honor to take his petition into consideration and grant him a divorce.
Affidavit of Andrew Jackson dated May 11, 1802. Sheriff of Davidson made report at November 1802 Term that the process of subpoena had been issued and returned 'not found in this County' and on May Term 1803, that the said Winney was not to be found within his District.
   Now at this Term, the plaintiff comes into Court and confesses that he intends no further to prosecute his said Petition. Therefore it is considered that the said Petition be dismissed and the petitioner to pay the costs. [pp86-87]

Friday, November 18, 1803

John Den lessee of Thomas Blount & Jackey his wife & Thomas Edward Summer
          vs
William Lytle, John Smith, Joseph Dean, William Nance, Bird Nance, Bradley Gambrell, John Gambrell & James Morton [Ejectment]

Declaration filed for John Den by Jenkin Whiteside, his attorney, May Term 1802 - John Den by his attorney complains of Richard Fen in custody of the sheriff ...that whereas Thomas Blount and Jackey, alias Jacentha, his wife, on the first day of May 1801, at Franklin in the County of Williamson, devised and let to the said John Den seven cottages and a certain tract of land containing twelve thousand acres lying in what was Davidson, now Williamson County, on the waters of Big Harpeth river, Arrington Creek, Stuarts Creek & Mill Creek, for a period of ten years; and afterward Thomas Edward Summer at Franklin in said County of Williamson did devise and let to John Den the seven cottages and twelve thousand acres of land ... and said Richard Fen did injuries to Den ...
Defendants, William Lytle, John Smith, Joseph Dean, William Nance, Bird Nance, Bradley Gambrel, John Gambrel and James Morton by their attorney, George W. Campbell, came into Court and plead Not Guilty - Jury called: Hill, Matthew Day, James Lauderdale, James Sawyers, John Lancaster, Nicholas Boyce, John L. Martin, John Payton, Willie Barrow, Josiah Fort, Eli Hammon & Henry Rutherford find the defendants not guilty of the trespass and ejectment.

On motion of the plaintiff by his attorney, it is ordered that the verdict be set aside and a new trial be had at the next Court. [pp87-89]

Rezin Davidge, Gent - took the oath to support the constitution of the U.S. - State of Tennessee and oath for an attorney at law - therefore admitted to practice as an attorney in this Court. [p89]

Washington L. Hannum, Gent - took the oath to support the constitution of the U.S. - State of Tennessee and oath for an attorney at law/ admitted to practice as an attorney in this Court. [p89]

Saturday, Nov. 19, 1803

John Cummins vs James Hamilton   [Case Appeal]
On 16 Oct. 1802 an appeal was filed from the County Court of Davidson on the following case - James Hamilton charged with trespass. John Nichols became Plaintiffs security; writ issued by Joseph Johnston, sheriff; April 1801 Sessions plaintiff

represented by Jesse Wharton; defendant represented by Thomas Stuart. John sold to James a certain negro fellow on credit and James has not paid. Case continued until July Sessions 1802 when jury called; Andrew Casselman, Matthew Talbot, William Pettway, James Marshall, Joseph Love, John Casselman, John Motheral, Thomas Wilson, Samuel Weakley, Joseph Garrett, Samuel Buchanan & William Caldwell. Jury found for plaintiff $160 and costs. Defendant filed an appeal and the cause was continued from Term to Term until this term and a jury called: Robert Ellis, James Hibbits, Micajah Barrow, Edmund Gamble, James W. Cocke, John Davidson, William Hall, William Gillespie, Dan Hill, Matthew Day, James Sayers and John Lancaster and find for the plaintiff and he shall recover from the defendant and John Duffell, Senr, his security in the appeal his damages and interest. [pp90-92]

James Taylor vs James Blackburn   [Case Appeal]
On 22 Oct. 1802 an appeal was filed from the County Court of Smith County. John Blackburn to appear before the Justices of the Court of Pleas and Quarter Sessions to be held at the house of Tilman Dixon on the 3rd Monday in September 1802 in a plea of Trespass. Sampson Williams, Clerk - Issued June 17, 1801. Writ executed by John L. Martin and returned Bail Bond signed by Thomas Draper and James Armstrong as his security. James Taylor complains of James Blackburn - whereas the plaintiff at the special instance of the defendant entered into an obligation or article of agreement jointly to a certain Samuel Wilson of Kentucky a certain tract of land containing four hundred acres ...Wilson was to pay two hundred dollars in horses and did actually pay a horse worth eighty five dollars... Case continued from term to term until June Term 1802 when the following jury was called: Majer Pinkston, Edward Cage, Zaddock B. Thackson, Isham Beasley, William Haynie, Wilson Cage, Adam Sanders, Edward Farris, James Ballow, Benjamin Merrit, Obediah Sanders and Edmund Jennings. Jury finds for the plaintiff and assess his damages to eighty five dollars and costs, whereupon the defendant by his attorney requested and was granted an appeal. Sampson Williams, Clerk of Wilson

County. 8 Oct. 1802. This cause continued from term to term until this term and the following jury called: Nicholas Boyce, John Payton, Willie Barrow, Josiah Fort, Eli Hammond, Henry Rutherford, Joseph Collins, Ezekiel Douglas, James Cummins, Luke Anderson, Joseph Cooke & Samuel B. Harris. The jury found for the plaintiff whereupon the defendant by his attorney Whitesides moved for a writ of Judgment. [pp92-94]

Grand Jurors attendance at this Term:

	days	miles	ferriages
John Baldridge	6	36	0
Samuel Gray	6	40	0
Richard Strother	6	52	2
Jordan Bass	6	96	2
Joseph Taylor	6	96	2
Asa Woodworth	6	52	2
James McMurry	6	70	2
John Hutchison	6	60	2
Christopher Stump	6	8	2
William Murry	6	8	2
John H. Hide	6	90	2
James Menees	6	7	0
William Yandle	6	90	2
Stephen Childress	6	32	0
Thomas Dillahunty	6	14	2
David Trimble Constable	6	6	2

[p95]
Saturday Nov. 19, 1803

Andrew Morris vs Ezekiel Able   [In Covenant]

May Term 1801 a capias ad respondendum at the suit of Andrew Morris against Robert Lane, William Macky and Ezekiel Able of a plea of Covenant broken - damage $500 was returned by the sheriff of Davidson "executed on Ezekiel Able and the others not found." plaintiff by his attorney, Bennet Searcy filed and said 'whereas on 19 Sept. 1798 in the County of Davidson Robert Lane, William Macky and Ezekiel Able bound themselves to convey to the plaintiff two hundred ages of land within six miles of Logan Courthouse 18 months after date ... Ezekiel by his attorney, John Overton defends ... at this

Term, May 1803, comes a jury - Robert Ellis, James Hibbits, Micajah Barrow, Edmund Gamble, James A Cocke, John Davidson, William Hall, William Gillespie, Dan Hall, Matthew Day, James Sayers and John Lancaster find for the plaintiff. [pp95-97]

Monday - November 21, 1803   Pleas at the Courthouse in Nashville

John Den lessee of Joseph Lemonds vs Henry Alexander   [In Ejectment]
John Den, by his attorney Thomas Stuart, filed his Declaration May Term 1802.
Richard Fen was attached to answer John Den on a plea of trespass in Ejectment - filed in Davidson County 1 Jan. 1802 re 150 acres of land near the ridge between Mill Creek and Stones River at the North edge of the big Hurricane ... part of larger tract granted to Miner Cannon by patent dated 26 Nov. 1789. Henry Alexander, by Bennet Searcy, his attorney, saith he is not guilty and this term comes the following jury: Josiah Fort, Willie Barrow, Dan Hill, Micajah Barrow, Matthew Day, James W. Cocke, James Sawyers, John Davidson, William Hall, John Lancaster, William Gillespie and Nicholas Boyce and they find the defendant not guilty. And on the motion of the plaintiff by his attorney, a rule is granted him to shew cause why the verdict should be set aside and a new trial had - continued to next court for argument [see 250, 288][pp98-99]

Monday, November 21, 1803

William Russell & Co. vs Thomas Batchelor
[Case Judicial Attachment]
At November Term 1802 at the suit of William Russell and Company vs Thos. Batchelor of a plea in Trespass, was returned by the sheriff of Davidson county "not found" and at the Term last mentioned on the motion of the plaintiff by their attorney a judicial attachment is awarded against the estate of Thomas Batchelor, at which Term the sheriff of Sumner county made return on the writ "levied on an old wagon & gears and two horses." signed Thomas Martin, DS.

State of Tennessee - Sumner County - We, David Wilson, William Cage and James Cryer, Justices of the Peace for said county, do hereby order the sale of one wagon & gear & two horses being the property attached this 15th day of January 1803.

Mero District - May Term 1803 - Thomas Batchelor late of the county of Davidson in the District aforesaid was attached by his property, to answer unto William Russell and Company Merchants, in a plea of trespass --- Thomas, in November 1801 at Charleston delivered a promissary note to Russell ---Jury: Eli Hammond, Henry Rutherford, Edward Gamble, James Hibbits, Robert Ellis, John Payton, William Caldwell, William Wilson, Daniel Young, Stephen Bean, John Davis & Thomas Taylor; assess damages to $1190.62 & costs. [pp 100-102]

Nathaniel A. McNairy, Gentleman Licenced to practice law in the several courts in this state, took the oath to support the Constitution of the United States, Constitution of the State of Tennessee and the oath of an attorney - admitted to practice in this court. [p102]

Redmond D. Barry vs John Richmond [In Covenant]
John Richmond was attached to answer Redmond D. Barry on a Plea of Covenant broken - whereupon Redmond by Jenkin Whiteside, his attorney at May Term 1803 filed his declaration ... 'said John on 28 Sept. 1801, in the county of Smith ... description of John Richmond late of South Carolina and then of Smith county in the state of Tennessee ...'covenanted with Redmond Dillon Barry of Sumner County and state of Tennessee... and the defendant not appearing, it is therefore considered by the court that the plaintiff recover against the defendant to be inquired of by a jury at the next court ---Jury: Josiah Fort, Willie Barrow, Dan Hill, Micajah Barrow, Matthew Day, James W. Cocke, James Sayers, William Hall, John Lancaster, William Gillispie, John Motheral & Joshua Taylor find for the plaintiff and assess his damages to $759.25 and costs. [pp102-103]

The State vs Matthew Williams [Ind't AB Appeal]
On 12 April 1803 an appeal from the County Court of Davidson was filed --

Transcript - January Sessions 1803 - The Grand Jurors for the State of Tennessee, upon their oath, say that Matthew Williams, labourer, late of the county of Davidson, on 21st November 1802 did assault Patrick Bigley - prosecutor, Jesse Wharton, County Solicitor - Which Bill of Indictment the Grand Jury by William Black, their foreman, endorsed a true bill - Matthew Williams appeared in Court at January Sessions 1803 and pleaded not guilty - thereafter came a Jury: George B. Curtis, John Kirkpatrick, William Lintz, Acquilla Carmick, Deliverance Gray, George Burnett, Benjamin Philips, Foster Sayers, Thomas Greene, James Garrett, John McConnel and Charles Hays - find him guilty and assess against the defendant the sum of one hundred dollars.; Defendant obtained an appeal to the Superior Court.

May Term 1803 - came a Jury - Eli Hammond, Henry Rutherford, Edmund Gamble, James Hibbits, Robert Ellis, John Payton, William Caldwell, .William Wilson, Daniel Young, Stephen Bean, John Davis & Thomas Taylor - find defendant guilty and assess his fine to $75 - motion by the Defendant - continued till the next Court. [pp104-105]

Evans Moore vs Oliver Johnston   [In Case]
Oliver Johnston was attached to answer Evans Moore on a Plea of Trespass, whereupon the said Evans by Jesse Wharton, his Attorney, at Nov. Term filed his declaration --- put into possession of said Oliver ninety and a piece barrels of salt to cover debt of $1800 ...Thomas Struart, atty for defendant ... cause continued until this Term; came a Jury - Josiah Fort, Willie Barrow, Dan Hill, Micajah Barrow, Matthew Day, James W. Cocke, James Sayers, William Hall, John Lancaster, William Gillispie, Nicholas Boyce, & Gideon Pillow. Find for the Defendant and he to recover against the plaintiff his costs. [pp105-107]

Tuesday, November 22, 1803

The State vs Dempsey Kenneday
      [Indth for Murder]
May Term 1803 - Jurors for the State charge that Dempsey Kennedy late of the County of Smith did on the 17 Nov. 1802, with force and arms, at the said

County of Smith, upon one Griffin West, make an assault, and that he, Dempsey Kennedy, with a certain oak plank about five feet long, five inches broad and one inch thick, which he the said Dempsey Kennedy in both his hands, upon the said Griffin West, upon the left side of the head, above the left ear, did strike & hit and giving to said West one mortal bruise and West did linger from the 17th November 1802 until the 14th day of January 1803 when West died in the County of Smith ... Plea not guilty --- Continued until this term when came a Jury: Isaac Roberts, Jonathan Magness, Jones Henning, Willie Barrow, Nicholas Boyce, Joseph Walker, William Gillispie, Benjamin J. Bradford, Gideon Pillow, Nicholas Coonrod, David Cloyd, & Samuel B. Harris...and say that Dempsey Kennedy is not guilty as charged in the Indictment and nothing further appearing or being alledged it is considered by the Court that the said Dempsey be acquitted and discharged of the murder aforesaid.[pp107-109]

David Trimble, Gent. produced a license to practice as an attorney//took the oaths and hereby admitted to practice as an attorney in this court. [p109]

John Gorden vs John Cummins   [In Case Trover &   ] John Cummins was attached to answer John Gordon of a plea of Trespass damage $300. John Gordon, by his attorney, Bennet Searcy, filed his declaration Nov. Term 1802 ...John Gordon was possessed of a horse ... horse was lost and came into possession of Cummins ... Plea Not Guilty ... Defendant by Jesse Wharton ... Jury: Matthew Day, James W. Cocke, Dan Hill, John Lancaster, John Davidson, Henry Rutherford, Eli Hammonds, Josiah Fort, James Sayers, John S. Martin, Robert Ellis, & Edmund Gamble - find defendant guilty and assess damages to $00 and judgment for costs. [pp109-110]

Valentine Winfrey - On the petition of sundry inhabitants of the County of Davidson and Williamson, praying for a remission of the fine imposed upon Valentine Winfrey at the last Court for an assault and battery. It is ordered that forty dollars of said file be remitted. [see 19] [pp110]

Wednesday, November 23, 1803

John Den lessee of Nicholas Coonrod vs James Vincent [In Ejectment]
John Den by Thomas Stuart his attorney at November Term 1801 -- complaining of Richard Fen in custody of sheriff of Wilson county that whereas Nicholas Coonrod on 1 Jan. 1796 at Sumner County demised to John Den a certain tract of land lying and being in the then county of Sumner (now the County of Wilson) containing 640 acres being a preemption entered the 13 August 1784 and granted to the said Nicholas by the State of North Carolina by Grant dated 10 July 1788 ... leased the 640 acres to John Den for 10 years from December last ... Thos Stuart for Pltf
Notice - Mssrs John Claxton & Arthur Hankins, gentlemen. I am informed that you are in possession of the premisses mentioned in this declaration of Ejectment ....Richard Roe Feb. 16, 1802
Nov. Term 1802 James Vincent, Landlord to aforesaid John Claxton & Arthur Hankins
prays to be admitted Defendant, agrees to rely on the title only ... admitted defendant and puts himself upon the country. Continued until this Term - Jury called: John Payton, William Hall, Micajah Barrow, James Hibbits, Willie Barrow, Nicholas Boyce, William Gillispie, Andrew Greer, Joshua Taylor, Robert Nelson, John Robertson & Charles M. Hall ... find the defendant guilty of Trespass and Ejectment ... assess plaintiffs damages to one cent and costs. [pp111-113]

Lewis Demoss - Ordered that Lewis Demoss be fined Ten Dollars for his Contempt of this Court, and that he be in custody until the said fine and costs be paid. [see 134] [p113]

Thursday, Nov. 24, 1803

The State vs John McConnel, Junr
        [Indictment AB]
On Sat., 19 Nov. in this present term, before the Hon. David Campbell, Andrew Jackson and Hugh S.

White, Judges of the Superior Court of Law & Equity, by the oath of James Menes, foreman, Samuel Gray, James Taylor, Stephen Childress, John H. Hide, Richard Strother, John Baldridge, Wilson Yandle, Jordan Bass, John Hutcheson, Christopher Stump, Thomas Dillahunty, Asa Woodworth, William Murry and James McMurry, on Grand Jury present that John McConnel Junior, late of the county of Davidson, Hatter, on the 16th day of November 1803 and during the November Term of the Superior Court, 'did make an assault on John Shouse so that his life was despaired of'. J. Whitesides

John McConnel appeared in Court according to his recognizance entered into yesterday and being charged says that he cannot deny but that he is guilty of the assault and puts himself upon the mercy of the Court; considered by the Court that he be fined ten dollars and pay the costs of the prosecution. [pp113-114]

Nov. 25th 1805 Petit Jury

The following Jurors proved their attendance and received their tickets:

	Days	Miles	ferrages
John Davidson	9	100	
James Hibbits	12	100	2
John Payton	12	44	2
John L. Martin	12	100	2
Robert Ellis	12	60	2
Nicholas Boyce	12	48	2
William Gillispie	12	40	2
John Lancaster	12	130	
William Hall	12	16	
James Sawyers	12	60	2
James W. Cocke	12	90	2
Matthew Day	12	54	2
Edmund Gamble	12	6	2
Micajah Barrow	12	5	2
Henry Rutherford	12	19 1/2	
Eli Hammond	12	22	
Dan Hill	12	36	
Willie Barrow	12		
Josiah Fort	12	70	2
James Lauderdale	5	40	2
William Germain	Const. 12		

Tuesday November 22, 1803

The State   [On a Scifa]
    vs
**Matthew Williams, Willie Barrow,
Micajah Barrow & James Maxwell**
Matthew Williams, Willie Barrow, Micajah Barrow and James Maxwell were bound by recognizance in the penalty of two hundred dollars for the personal appearance of Matthew Williams at a Superior Court on the second Monday in May 1803 to answer an Indictment against the said Matthew and the said Matthew was called and came not - but made default - and the said Willie Barrow, Micajah Barrow and James Maxwell being likewise called to bring in the body of Matthew Williams, came not but made default and they are called to appear before the Superior Court in November next ... and now on the day above mentioned came the defendants and on their motion it is ordered that the forfeiture be set aside and that they pay the costs of the Scifa. [p115]

Tuesday, November 29, 1803

**Stothart & Bell vs Archibald McReynolds
[Debt   Attachment]**
On 26 Sept. 1803, Robert Stothart & George Bell obtained an attachment against the Estate of Archibald McReynolds for the sum of $439.29 ... Whereas Robert Stothart, a partner of the firm of Stothart & Bell, merchants & copartners in trade, complained on oath to me, John Anderson, a Justice of the Peace of the County of Davidson, that Archibald McReynolds is justly indebted to the said Stothart & Bell ... also that Archibald McReynolds is a inhabitant of the State of Kentucky ... order that you attach the estate of the said McReynolds ... which was returned by the sheriff 'no property found' and now at this Term the plaintiffs confess they intend no further to prosecute; therefore it is considered by the Court that the defendant by his attorney, J. Wharton, assumes the payment of all costs except the attorneys fee. [p116]

Joseph T. Elliston vs William Germain & James Caldwell   [In Debt]
William Germain & James Caldwell were summoned to answer Joseph T. Elliston (assignee of Benjamin Gains) in a plea of Debt. Whereupon the said Joseph by Perry W. Humphreys, his attorney, filed his declaration Nov. Term 1803. Defendant by his attorney, Bennet Searcy, Plaintiff by his attorney confesses he intends no further prosecution ...considered by the Court that the Defendants may depart and recover against the Plaintiff their costs. [pp117-118]

Wednesday, November 30th, 1803

Christopher Stump vs Josiah G. Duke & Philip Duke   [Debt Sci facias]
 Admr's of John Duke, deceased
Whereas at a suit before the Judges at May Term 1803, of Christopher Stump & Co. against John Duke, Administrator of Richard Myrick, Dec'd, and John Duke of a plea of debt for $404.76, wsas returned by the sheriff of Montgomery County that all the goods and chattles of the said John Duke hath been committed to Josiah G. Duke, Philip Duke and
      his wife, the said John Duke having died intestate ... witness Randall McGavock the second Monday in May in the year 1803. And now at this Term it appears from the return of the sheriff that the defendants have been duly warned and not appearing though solemnly called. Therefore on the motion of the plaintiff it is the judgement of the Court that pltfs may have execution foir $504.76. B. Searcy, Att'y for plaintiff .... and the said John Duke being dead, Scifa is granted against Josiah G. Duke and Philip Duke, Administrators of the said decedent.[pp118-120]

Robert Stothart & Co.   [Certiorari]
     vs
John Caffrey & Archibald McRenolds
In May 1802 a writ of Certiorari was issued from the Superior Court for the District of Mero to the Justices of the Court of Pleas and Quarter Sessions for the County of Davidson commanding the said Justices to certify the record and proceedings in

a certain action between Robert Stothart & Co. and John Caffrey and Archibald McReynolds. Whereas Robert Stothart & Co. in our Court of Davidson April Sessions 1800 obtained judgment against James Dougherty for the sum of $88.37 with costs of suit .. after which on the last day of July Sessions 1800 Abraham Stanly who had been one of the said Doughertys Bail surrendered him into Court in discharge of himself, whereupon the said Dougherty brought into Court John Caffrey who had been his former Bail ...Caffrey and McReynolds who became the said Doughertys bail. Plaintiffs appeared in prosecution of their suit by Bennet Searcy and John Dickinson their attorneys --- likewise the defendants by Thomas Stewart & Jesse Wharton, their attorneys. And this cause was continued from Term to Term until this Term and argued by their attorneys and it seems to the Court that it is not sufficient and plaintiffs be barred from having their action and plaintiffs to pay the costs of this suit. [pp120-126]

William Lytle   **[In Case]**
    vs
John Overton, Andrew Ewing & James Mulherin Executors of Thomas Molloy, deceased
William Lytle complains of Andrew Ewing, James Mulherin and John Overton, executors of Thomas Molloy, deceased. Whereas, Thomas Molloy and William Tyrrell on 22 May 1796 at the County of Davidson did sign a promissory note to purchase military land warrants of the State of North Carolina at a price not exceeding sixty dollars for 640 - the whole quanity not to exceed 12,000 acres... Molloy agreed to locate such warrants and to superintend the surveying thereof ... 1797 Molloy acknowledged to have received the full 12,000 acres of Military land warrants excepting two, one of 640 acres and one of 350 acres, which were entered in the name of William Tyrrel was justly entitled to one half of all such surveys ...and the cause was continued until this Term ... at which time the plaintiff by his attorney confesses that he intends no longer to prosecute - therefore it is considered the defendants may depart and recover his costs. [pp126-128]

John Morris vs William Sanders   [In Case Appeal]
On 27 October 1803 an appeal from the County Court of Smith was filed and signed Sampson Williams. On the back of Writ was marked 'issued 15 Feb. 1802' came to hand the same day executed John L. Martin And at March Term 1802 the Plaintiff by his attorney Redmund D. Berry filed his Declaration. Morris did employ Sanders to work and labor at a Mill of the defendant ... has refused and still refuses to pay the plaintiff. Defendant came into Court by Thomas Stewart, his attorney ... Morris says work was accomplished so unskillfully that Mill & Dam were lost John Overton filed Demurrer....case continued from Term to Term until June term when it came before a jury: John Litton, James Cochran, Thomas Sutton, George McWhirter, William Litton, Francis Findley Archibald Sloan, Hugh Stephenson, Robert Smith, John Briward, Daniel Hitton, Jeffrey Litton. Find for Plaintiff ~ plaintiff to recover his damages whereun the defendant filed appeal. [pp129-1320]

Wednesday, November 30th 1803

Robert Stothart & Co.   [Upon a Certiorari]
   vs
John Caffrey & Archibald McReynold
In May 1802 a Writ of Certiorari was issued for a rehearing of the case of Stothart & Co. vs Caffrey & McReynold.
Record of the County Court - July Sessions 1800 - Davidson County Court - Judgment against James Dougherty for $38.31 and on 19 July 1800 Abraham Stanley, who had been one of Doughertys bail, surrendered him into Court in discharge of himself whereupon Dougherty brought into Court John Caffrey who had been his former bail ... on the first of which writs of Scifa as above recited Joseph Johnson Sheriff made return Jan. Sessions 1801 ... plaintiffs attorneys Bennett Searcy & John Dickinson - defendants att'ys Thomas Stewart and Jesse Wharton ... considered by the Court that the plaintiffs be barred from having their action aforesaid ... plaintifs pay the costs of this suit. [pp120-126]

William Lytle   [In Case]

vs
John Overton, Andrew Ewing & James Mulherin
Executors of Thomas Molley, deceased
John Overton, Andrew Ewing & James Mulherin, executors of Thomas Molloy, deceased, are attached to answer William Lytle, assignee of William Tyrell in a plea of trespass, damage fifteen thousand dollars; whereupon William Lytle by Thomas Stuart, his attorney at Nov. Term 1802 filed his declaration ... whereas the said Thomas Molloy and William Tyrell on 25 May 1796 made an agreement whereby William Tyrrel did agree to purchase as many Military land warrants of the State of North Carolina as he could at a price not exceeding sixty dollars for 640 acres, the whole quantity not to exceed 12,000 acres and the warrants were to be assigned to the said Thomas Molloy and himself and to transmit the warrants to Molloy within six months from the date of said writing obligatory and Molloy by the same writing obligatory did agree to locate all such warrants within the lands reserved by law for the same and to superintend the surveying at his own expense ... on 8 Sept 1797 said Thomas acknowledged to have received of said William Tyrell the full quantity of 12,000 acres, by said note he acknowledged, except for two, one of 640 acres and one of 357 acres which were entered in the name of William Tyrrel and Tyrrell transferred the said agreement to William Lytle and did authorize Lytle to settle with Molloy ... has failed to convey his half of the profits .... cause continued until this Term at which time the plaintiff by his attorney confesses that he intends no further action ... considered by the Court that the defendants may depart and recover against the plaintiff their costs. [pp126-128]

Den, lessee of Michael C. Sweetman
vs   [Ejectment]
Daniel Wilburn & James Wormack
On motion, it is ordered that unless the costs of this suit be paid into the Clerks Office within two months from this day, an execution issue against the said Wilburn & Wormack for the same.[p128]

Den lessee of Peter D. Robert
vs   [Ejectment]

Robert Nelson
Ordered that unless the costs of this suit be paid within two months from this day, executions issue against lessee of the plaintiff for the same. [p128]

Wednesday, Nov. 30, 1803

John Morris
    vs   [In Case]
William Sanders
On 27 October 1803 an appeal from the County Court of Smith was filed in the Office of the Superior Court of Law for the District of Mero as follows: On 15 Feb. 1802 an order was issued to the sheriff of said county to have William Sanders appear on a charge of trespass, witness Sampson Williams, signed John Morris & T. Dixon and at March Term 1802 the plaintiff by his attorney, Redmund D. Barry com plained of William Sanders: said Defendant had employed the Plaintiff to work at a Mill as a millright in a workman like manner...says he has performed the work in a workman like manner and the defendant refuses to pay him. Defendant represented by Thomas Stewart said that it was due to lack of skill that said mill was entirely swept away; plaintiff by his attorney John Overton filed Demurrer and the cause continued until June Term 1803 when the following jury was called: John Litton, James Cochran, Thomas Sutton, George M. McWhirter, William Litton, Francis Findley, Archibald Sloane, Hugh Stephenson, Robert Smith, John Briarce, Daniel Hitton, Jeffrey Litton and consider the plaintiff should recover against the defendant his damages of one hundred dollars and costs -- whereupon the defendant did appeal to the Superior Court and now at this term of the Superior Court it is ordered that the aforesaid appeal be dismissed and that the appellant pay the costs. [pp129-132]

John McNairy
    vs   [Upon a petition appeal]
Thomas Talbor & Co.
By an Act of the General Assembly of the State of North Carolina entitled an Act for the relief of

the Officers and Soldiers of the Continental line and for other purposes therein mentioned, it was declared that 640 acres of land should be reserved adjoining each Salt Lick or Salt Spring within the Tract of country reserved for said officers and soldiers. By another Act of the General Assembly in 1784 and entitled an act for establishing a Town on Cumberland River at a place called the Bluff near the French Lick certain directors or Trustees were directed to lay off two hundred acres of land situate on the South side of Cumberland River at a place called the French Lick into a Town by the name of Nashville, accordingly a Town was soon after laid off within the Tract of six hundred and forty acres reserved including the French Lick ... afterward by an act of the said General Assembly passed in 1785 entitled an act for the promotion of learning in the county of Davidson, it was enacted that two hundred and forty acres of the Land reserved for the use of the State being that part of said land which is most remote from the Salt Lick should be vested in the Trustees of Davidson Academy for the use of that Seminary. By another act of the said Assembly passed in the year 1789 entitled an act directing the sale of the Salt Licks and Springs with the adjoining land within the District of Mero certain Commissioners therein mentioned were authorized to expose to sale the French and other Licks ... to sell them separately to the highest bidder ... The overplus lands remaining unappropriated within the tract of six hundred and forty acres reserved for public use adjacent to the French Lick and by this petitioner supposed to amount to two hundred acres were exposed to sale at the Courthouse in the Town of Nashville and sold to this petitioner as highest bidder... afterwards a survey was directed intended to include the whole of the lan purchased and accordingly on the 14th of December 1790 by Anthony Foster then being a Deputy of Martin Armstrong entry taker and Surveyor of the land reserved for the Officers and Soldiers of the Continental line ... and a Grant was issued to this petitioner bearing date December 20, 1791 ... mistake was made and he included in the said plat a part of the land surveyed and laid off for the use of Davidson Academy so this petitioner is deprived of his just right and greatly damaged. This petition presented to the County Court of Davidson at July Sessions 1801 ... continued and heard October 1801 and granted ... opposed by Thomas Talbott and sundry others and continued to be postponed until this term when petitioner came by his attorney and on his motion leave is granted him to withdraw his petitioned and it is ordered that the petitioner pay the costs. [pp132-134]

Lewis Demos [petition]
On the petition of Lewis Demos who was fined ten dollars on 23rd day of this month, it is ordered that eight dollars be remitted. [p134]

John Boyd, Senior [In Covenant]
    vs
Joseph Barnes
At May Term 1803 a capias was returned by the sheriff of Davidson county not found, And on the motion of the plaintiff by his attorney an alias capias against the defendant returnable here at the next Court, at which Court the sheriff made return 'not found' - the plaintiff not further prosecuting his action ordered that the same be discontinued and that he pay the costs of the suit. [pp134-135]

William T. Lewis
    vs [In Covenant]
James Ore
James Ore was attached to answer William T. Lewis of a plea of covenant broken damage one thousand dollars and the said William not further prosecuting his said action ordered that the same be dismissed and that he pay the costs. [p135]

George Mansell [In Case]
    vs
William Howard
William Howard was attached to answer George Mansell of a plea of Trespass upon the case, damage three thousand dollars and the said George not prosecuting his said action any further, it is ordered that the same be dismissed and he pay the costs of the suit. [p135]

14 May 1804   Superior Court of Law for the District of Mero - the Honorable David Campbell, Hugh L. White, Judges

The following persons were elected and sworn a Grand Jury of Inquest for the body of this District: Joseph Philips, foreman, Obediah Bounds, Joel Dyer, George Rasee, Matthew Figures, Thomas H. Perkins, Nathaniel Jeffers, Willie Cherry, Jonas Manifee, William Hope, Joseph S. Williams, Richard Bradley, James Mulherrin, Aaron Fletcher and Zachias Wilson

Tuesday, May 15, 1804

Robert Nelson   [In Covenant]
     vs
John Kethly
This day came the parties by their attorneys and a jury: Micajah Woodward, Cary Fells, Lovick Vantress, Patrick Barr, William Kerr, Thomas Mitchell, Benjamin Totton, Wilson Gibson, Andrew Grerr, Aaron Rawlings, Henry Bradford and James Keeling - find the Defendant hath broken his covenant and they assess the plaintiffs damages to two hundred seventeen dollars besides his costs. [p136]   [See Book A, p519; B, p59]

Joshua Balance, Administrator of the Estate of Caleb Cartright, deceased
     vs
Arthur Turner   [In Debt   Appeal]
This day came the parties by their attorneys and a Jury: John Lancastor, Leonard Fite, Beal Bosley, David Cloyd, Ezekiel Douglass, Joseph Collins, John L. Martin, Peter Looney, Micajah Barrow, Sommerset Moore, Robert Tait and John Fite; find the defendant hath not paid the debt and assess the plaintiffs damages to eleven dollars and forty cents and costs.

The State   [Delinquent Juror]
     vs
William R. Bell
To the Sheriff of Montgomery County - Whereas William R. Bell was summoned to attend a Superior

Court of Law in November 1803 as a Juror and came not -- a conditional judgment was entered against him for the penalty -- you are commanded to make known to him that he be before the Judges of our said Court at the next Court to shew cause ... and now at this term came the said William R. Bell and on his affidavit it is ordered that the forfiture be set aside and the Defendant pay the costs. [pp137/138]

John Den, lessee of Joseph & Richard Caveat
    vs   [In Ejectment]
Daniel Thompson, Geo Birdwell, Wm Birdwell
John Den, by John Overton, his attorney filed his Declaration Nov. Term 1801:
Whereas Joseph & Richard Caveatt, sons of Richard Caveatt on 1 Oct 1800 devised to John Den a tenement and 640 acres of land situate in Davidson County, being a preemption right - Grant #407, beginning one mile above Heaton Station ... to hold the same for ten years and whereas Daniel Thompson, George Birdwell and William Birdwell ejected the said John Den and therefore he brings suit ... and the suit was continued from Term to Term until this Term and thereupon came a Jury: William Hall, Frederick Stump, Anderson Tait, Thomas Wilcox, John Stump, John Harvey, Andrew Castleman, Daniel Hitton, William Jackson, Edmond Jennings, Enoch Enochs and John Lancaster and the plaintiff not furthur prosecuting his said action; on the motion of the Defendant the jurors to be discharged and the plaintiff be nonsuited and pay to the Defendants their costs. [pp138/139]

John Nichols   [In Debt]
    vs
John Caffery
The plaintiff not prosecuting his said action any further, ordered therefore the same be dismissed and that he pay the costs of this suit. [p139]

Adam Young   [In Covenant]
    vs
Edmund Jennins
Edmund Jennins was attached to answer Adam Young of a plea of Covenant broken and the plaintiff not

further prosecuting his action it is therefore ordered the same be dismissed and he pay the costs of the suit. [p139]

James Robertson [In Debt]
vs
John Jones
On the second Monday in May 1802 a writ was issued from the Superior Court for the District of Mero directed to the Justices of the Court of Pleas and Quarter Sessions for the County of Robertson commanding the said Justices to send and certify the record and proceedings on a certain action between James Robertson Plaintiff and John Jones, Defendant --to have a rehearing ... record and proceedings were filed on 8 Nov. 1802 ... 'James Robertson hath complained on oath that John Jones is indebted to the amount of $250.00 and that John Jones has removed himself out of the county ... we therefore command you that you attach the Estate of John Jones if to be found in your county or so much as to satisfy the said debt and costs ... witness Hardy S. Bryan, Esqr, Justice of said Court of Robertson County, 18 Feb. 1802. To which at April Term 1802 the Sheriff .made the following return: Levied on the fourth part of the following Articles: all the pigmetal scraps ... open land, wares, six horses, 4 waggons, gears, etc, stock of cattle and hogs belonging to Adam Shepherd & Co., blacksmith tools and farming tools. James Meness February 25, 1802 ..... ordered that the property be sold of Thos. Johnson ... cause continued from Term to Term until this Term at which time came the parties by their attorneys and by their mutual consent it is ordered to be dismissed and that each party pay his own costs. [pp140-141]

John Kethly [In Covenant]
vs
Robert Nelson
Robert Nelson was attached to answer John Kethly of a broken covenant and the plaintiff confesses he intends no further to prosecute, there the defendant may depart and recover against the plaintiff his costs. [p142]

Mark & Nathan Rickman [In Case]

vs
Marshall Stroud
Marshall Stroud was attached to answer Mark Rickman and Nathan Rickman of a plea of Trespass - damage two thousand dollars; whereupon May Term 1802, plaintiff by John Overton his attorney filed his Declaration.. land lying on West Goose Creek in the County of Sumner being part of a tract of 640 acres granted to Levi Colter by the State of North Carolina, being a military right ... said land cannot be of any use to plaintiff because defendant does not have complete title. Defendant, by Samuel Donalson, his attorney, puts himself upon the county ... Jury: Micajah Woodward, Cary Felts, Lovick Vantress, Patrick Barr, William Karr, Thomas Mitchel, Benjamin Totten, Wilson Gibson, Andrew Greer, Aaron Rawlings, Henry Bradford and James Heeting... The plaintiff not further prosecuting the matter, therefore on motion of the defendant by his attorney is is declared by the Court that the plaintiff be nonsuited and that the jury be discharged and plaintiff to pay the costs of the suit. [pp142-144]

John Lyon [In Case]
vs
Marshal Stroud
John Lyon, by John Overton his Attorney, at May Term 1802 filed his Declaration - complains of Marshal Stroud ... defendant would buy of him one hundred acres of land lying on West Goose Creek in the County of Sumner, being part of a tract of 640 acres ... part of a military right ... has not a good and complete title to said land. Defendant, by Samuel Donalson his attorney ... cause continued from Term to Term until this Term at which time came the Defendant, by his Attorney, and the plaintiff not further prosecuting it is considered by the Court the plaintiff be nonsuited and the plaintiff to pay costs. [pp144/145]

David Henry [In Case]
vs
Marshall Stroud
Marshall Stroud was attached to answer David Henry of a plea of trespass; whereupon David Henry by his

attorney, John Overton, at a May Term 1802 filed his Declaration ... said plaintiff would buy of him one hundred acres of land on West Goose Creek in the County of Sumner being part of a Tract of 640 acres granted to Levi Colter, being a military right ... had not a good sufficient and complete title to the land -- Defendant by his attorney, Samuel Donalson - issue was continued from Term to Term until the last above at which time came the defendant by his attorney and the plaintiff not furthur prosecuting, it is considered by the Court that the plaintiff to pay the costs. [pp146/147]

Joseph Mallard   [In Case]
    vs
Marshall Stroud
Marshall Stroud was attached to answer Joseph Mallard of a plea of Trespass, damage one thousand dollars. Joseph Mallard, by John Overton, his attorney, at May Term 1802, filed his Declaration .Plaintiff was to buy from the defendant 100 acres of land on West Goose Creek in the County of Sumner, being part of 640 acres of land granted Levi Colter by the State of North Carolina, being a military right. Defendant did not have a good Title. Defendant, by Samuel Donelson, his Attorney ... and the case was continued from Term to Term until this Term at which time came the Defendant by his attorney and the Plaintiff not further prosecuting, it is considered by the Court that the Plaintiff be nonsuited and the defendant may recover from the plaintiff his costs. [pp147-149]

Meeker, Denman & Co.   [Attachment]
    vs
George Wilson & John Eastin
On 17 Jan. 1804 Meeker, Denman & Co. obtained an attachment against the Estate of George Wilson and John Easton for the sum of $1,090.58. Whereas Edward Thursby, agent for William Meeker, Samuel Denman and William P. Meeker, Merchants and copartners in trade, have complained on oath to Thomas Hickman, one of the Justices of the Peace for the County, that George Wilson and James Eastin, copartners in trade under the firm of Wilson & Eastin are justly indebted to the amount of $1090.58. Said George is an inhabitant of the

State of Kentucky and the said John of the City of New Orleans, ... therefore command that you attach the estate of the said George & John ...Whereupon the Sheriff of Davidson County made return that he has summoned William Eastin, as Garnashee, in writing and no property found. And now at this Term, by the direction of the plaintiff, it is ordered that this suit be dismissed and the plaintiff pay the costs. [pp149-150]

Meeker, Cochran & Co
[Attachment]
     vs
George Wilson & John Eastin
On 17 Jan. 1804 Meeker, Cochran & Co. obtained an attachment against the Estate of George Wilson and John Eastin for the sum of $446.09. Edward Thursby, agent for Samuel Meeker, William Cochran and Alexander Cochran, late Merchants and copartners in the name of Meeker, Cochran & Co., hath complained on oath to Thomas Hickman, one of the Justices of the Peace for the County, that George Wilson & John Eastin, copartners in trade under the firm of Wilson & Eastin are indebted to the said Samuel, William and Alexander for the sum of $446.09...said George is an inhabitant of the State of Kentucky and said John of the City of New Orleans... At this Term, by the directions of plaintiffs attorney it is ordered that this suit be dismissed and it is further ordered that the plaintiff pay the costs of suit. [pp150-151]

The State   [Upon a Scifa}]
    vs
George Neville, an absent Juror
To the Sheriff of Montgomery County: Whereas George W. Neville was summoned at attend a Superior Court of Law for the District of Mero on the second Monday in November 1803 as a Juror and having been called, came not .... execution of this Judgment still remains. signed Randal McGavock, Clerk Nov. 1803 Upon which Scifa the Sheriff of Montgomery County made return that he had made the same known to the said George. At this Term said defendant came and on his affidavit it is ordered that the forfeiture aforesaid be set aside and the defendant to pay the costs. [pp151-152]

The State [Upon a Scifa]
  vs
Daniel Bridgment
State of Tennessee to the Sheriff of Smith County: Whereas Daniel Bridgement was bound by recognizance for his personal appearance at the Superior Court on the 2nd Monday in November 1803 to give testimony on behalf of us against Dempsey Kennedy who stood indicted for murder and the said Daniel Bridgement having been called but came not, it was therefore considered by the Court that the recognizance was forfeited ..command you to make known to said Daniel that he be before the Judges of our Court at next Court ... And now at this Term came the Defendant and on his affidavit it is ordered that the forfeiture be set aside and further ordered he pay the costs. [pp152-153]

John Den, Lessee of Thomas Blount & others
         vs
[Ejectment]
William Lytle & others
This day came the parties by their attorneys and came also a jury: Micajah Woodward, Cary Felts, Lovick Ventriss, Patrick Barr, William Kerr, Benjamin Totton, William Gibson, Andrew Greer, Aaron Rawlings, Beal Bosley, Joseph Collins and William Hall - find the defendant not guilty and defendant to recover against the plaintiff their costs.[p153]

John Den, Lessee of Thomas Hickman
      vs   [Ejectment]
John Ward
On 21 June 1802 an appeal from the County Court of Davidson was filed in the Clerks Office of the Superior Court: Whereas Thomas Hickman, on 16 January 1801, let to John Den two thousand five hundred and sixty acres of land lying in Davidson on the Waters of White Creek and on the North side of Cumberland River; NE corner of David Shannons preemption ...N boundary of Joseph Kincades tract thence E to John Walkers SW corner, N to a point on Daniel Johnsons SW boundary, S to a Sycamore on John Marshalls line, E to James Marrs line ... being a tract originally granted by North Carolina

to Martin Armstrong and Anthony Crutcher. Thomas Stewart for the Pltf.. Sheriff made return to April Sessions 1801, the said John Ward was not found in said County but during the said Sessions Howell Tatum, attorney for the said Ward acknowledged said writ and moved that said John Ward should be named Defendant. Case continued until April Sessions 1802 and thereon comes a Jury: Bennet Blackman, Charles M. Hall, Beal Bosley, John Coots, James Maxwell, Jesse Maxwell, Thomas Shute, Jonathan F. Robertson, Samuel Buckhannon, Moses Atkins, Sackfield McClain & William Redich and the Jury do say John Ward is guilty of the trespass whereupon the said John obtained an appeal to the Superior Court -- Cause continued from Term to Term until Term & came also a Jury: Joseph Collins, Micajah Woodward, Wilson Gibson, Cary Felts, Lovick Ventress, Patrick Barr, Thomas Mitchell, Benjamin Totton, Aaron Rawlings, William Kerr, Andrew Greer and Francis Sanders... reported they could not agree thereupon with consent of the court Joseph Collins, one of the Jurors, is withdrawn and the rest of the jurors are discharged and the cause is continued. [pp153-157] {see 302}

The State
    vs   [Upon a Scifa]
James Page
Whereas James Page was bound by recognizance in the penalty of one thousand dollars to appear Nov. 1803 in behalf of us against Abram Nowlin who stood admitted for horse stealing and the said Page called but came not -- writ issued and thereupon came the defendant and on his affidavit it ordered the forfeiture be set aside and defendant to pay costs. [pp157/158]

John Den, lessee of Robert Hays
            vs   [In Ejectment]
James Byrnes & James Byrnes, Junr
Robert, by Jenkin Whitesides, his attorney, filed his Declaration November Term 1802: Whereas Robert on 10 June 1801 at Franklin in the County of Williamson, devised and to farm let a tract of land containing two thousand five hundred & sixty acres, lying in what was then Davidson and is now Williamson County, on West Harpeth River & bounded

as follows: Beg at NW corner of Col. William Polks survey ... term of ten years and James Brynes Senior and Junior, did evict said John Den and said Byrns by their attornies, John Overton & Thomas Stewart and say they are not guilty. Jury: Thomas Mitchell, Micajah Woodward, John Fite, John Lancaster, Leonard Fite, John Davis, George Titus, Slyvanius Castleman, Abram Kennedy, John Stump, Barnabas Boyes and Heydon Wells and find for the plaintiff and assess plaintiffs damages to one cent besides his costs. [pp158-159]

Friday May 18, 1804
Pleas at the Courthouse in Nashville May Term 1804

Stephen Robertson
    vs   [In Debt]
John Lancaster, Administrator
John Lancaster, Administrator of John Lancaster, dec'd to answer Stephen Robertson of a plea of Debt for fifteen hundred dollars. May Term 1802, Stephen by John Overton, his Attorney, filed his declaration; to wit - Whereas John Lancaster on 30 Auigust 1798 in the District of Mero by his writing, sealed with the seal of the said John, Dec'd, obliged himself, his heirs, etc. to pay the said fifteen hundred dollars. John, Administrator hitherto have refused and still refuses to pay -
   John Lancaster, Administrator, by his Attorney Thomas Stuart answers: the above obligatory is such that of the above bound John Lancaster shall convey a Deed in fee simple for 320 acres of land lying in the County of Sumner on Smiths Fork, a fork of Caney Fork River, being one mority of a 640 acres entered in the name of Shearrod Barrow, the South side of the Creek, beginning ... etc. for the compliment of 320 acres as aforesaid then the above obligatory to be void. Lancaster saith he has fully administered the goods and chattels of John Lancaster, deceased.....Continued from Term to Term until this date when came a Jury: John Stump, Harris Droling, Edmund Jennings, Absalom Hooper, Arthur K. Turner, Neel Thompson, William Jackson, Robert Tait, Beal Bosley, Thomas Taylor, John L. Martin and Barnard Herrod and they find for the Plaintiff eight hundred and eighty dollars with interest from this day until paid. [pp160/161]

John Coffee complains of Elisha Prewit
[Trespass]
Plaintiff gave his note to the said defendant for the payment of $110 - promised to make a boat for the plaintiff but the said plaintiff did not deliver a good boat of the dimensions, but a bad boat, incapable of answering the purposes of navigation and lost   bushels of lime and bushels of corn by the sinking of said boat owing to its being badly built ... Defendant by Jesse Wharton, his Attorney   answers - continued until this Term when comes the plaintiff by his Attorney and confesses that he intends no further to prosecute. Considered by the Court that the defendant may recover against the plaintiff his costs.

The Grand Jury returned into Court and presented an Indictment against Michael Murphy for murder "a true bill" and having nothing further to present were discharged. {See 181}

Friday 18 May 1804
The Grand Jury proved their attendance and received their Tickets:

	days	**miles**	**ferriages**
Joseph Philips, Foreman	5	14	2
Obediah Bounds	5	50	2
Joel Dyer	5	110	2
George Keisee	5	90	2
Matthew Figures	5	72	0
Thomas H. Perkins	5		
Nathaniel Jeffers	5	120	2
Willie Cherry	5	66	
Jonas Mannifee	5	10	
William Hope	5	40	
Joseph T. Williams	5	50	
Richard Bradley	5	50	2
James Mulherrin	5	13	2
Aaron Fletcher	5	180	2
Zachias Wilson	5	56	2
David Ramsey Constable	5		
Leveck Vantress Juror	11	36	2

[p163]

Saturday May 19, 1804

William Betts
    vs   [Case Appeal]
Bennet Searcy

On 18 April 1803 an appeal from the County Court of Davidson was filed in the office of the Superior Court for the District of Mero. Writ dated second Monday in October 1799, issued Dec. 28, 1799 Searcy to answer Betts on charge of Trespass. Plaintiff appeared at Jan. Sessions 1800 by his Attorney, Seth Lewis. Betts has been, since 13 December 1792 an Ordinary Keeper, duly licensed to keep an Ordinary in the Town of Nashville and between the dates of 13 December 1792 and 13 August 1799 did receive the said Bennet into his Inn and furnish him with boarding and lodging and did deliver to him divers quantities of Rum, Wine, Whiskey & Brandy and allow him to use his house and billiard Table and did keep entertain and maintain divers servants and horses amounting to a value of $135.50 ... defended by Samuel Donelson and continued from Term to Term.

Plaintiff now represented by Thomas Stuart. April Sessions 1802 came a Jury - a juror was withdrawn by consent of the parties and the Jury dismissed. October Sessions 1802 came a Jury - John Topp, Robert Kennedy, Lewis Perkins, Robert Heaton, Robert C. Reaves, William Corbett, William Scott, William Billings, Charles M. Hall, Edward Sanders, Zachariah Stull and George Ury. Andrew Henry and Joseph Herndon witnesses in the cause and the jury find his damages to four hundred dollars and fifty cents. After which the defendent in person filed a bill of exceptions which bill is signed by Redmund D. Barry and William Smith, attorneys who appeared and spoke in the defence of the defendant - Davidson County Court and the Court then setting consisting of John Anderson, Edmond Gamble, Abraham Boyd and Thomas Talbott refused to sign the same. From which judgment of the Court the said Bennet Searcy prayed for and obtained an appeal and the cause was continued from Term to Term in the Superior Court until this Term when the defendant comes and confesses he cannot deny the plaintiffs action for $400.50, the amount of the judgment in the County Court with interest ... therefore with the assent of the plaintiff it is considered that he recover against the said Defendant the amount of $400.50 and his costs. [pp164-170]

Monday, May 21, 1804

The State
    vs   [for Horse Stealing]
Samuel Inman

At a Court held for the District of Mero at the Courthouse in Nashville on the second Monday in November 1803 before the Judges the said Court by the oath of James Menees, foreman, Samuel Gray, James Taylor, Stephen Childress, John H. Hyde, Richard Strother, John Baldridge, Wilson Yandle, Jordan Bass, John Hutcheson, Christopher Stump, Thomas Dillahunty, Asa Woodworth, William Murry and James McMurry, lawful men of the State and District, sworn and charged to inquire for the body of this District presented - 'that Samuel Inman late of the County of Davidson, laborer, on 10 May 1803, with force and arms, one mare of black colour, value of one hundred dollars of one Nancy Cortney, did steal ... and the said Samuel Inman was led to the bar in custody of the sheriff of Davidson County was charged and pleaded 'not guilty' and was continued to the next Court.

And now at this Term, Samuel Inman appeared in Court according to his recognizance, and thereupon came a jury: Lovick Vantress, Peter Pinkston, Thomas Taylor, Benjamin Totton, Andrew Hays, Thomas Johnston, Aaron Rawlings, James Wills, William Lytle, Henry Hide, John Stump and Wilson Gibson, and find the said Samuel Inman is guilty as charged and to be taken to the Jail from whence he came, there to remain until 2 June
next and there to be hanged by the neck until he be dead, between the hours of twelve in the forenoon and four in the afternoon. [pp170/171]

Aquila Jones assee of Zebedie Hicks
          vs   [Covenant]
Peter Johnston & Abner Johnston

Peter and Abner Johnston were attached to answer Azuila Jones, Assee of Zebedee Hicks of a plea of Covenant broken - damage fifteen hundred dollars. The plaintiff by Bennet Searcy, his attorney, filed his declaration May Term 1803: ...whereas on 17

August 1799 in County of Davidson Peter and Abner Johnston signed a covenant that they would made a general warranty deed to one hundred acres of land, being the same surveyed to said Peter and Abner and adjoining John Motheral on the East, lying up the creek above said Motheral and David Raulson on or before 25 December 1800; Zebedee Hicks by his endorsement on the back of the same assigned the within Bond or Covenant to Aquila Jones for value received and the said Aquila Jones further declares that Peter and Abner have not made a deed of conveyance for the said one hundred acres of land. Defendants, by Thomas Stuart their attorney, say they did tender to Aquila Jones a sufficient general warrantee deed which Jones refused to accept....cause continued until this Term, at which day came the plaintiff by his attorney and confesses that he intends no further to prosecute, the defendants by their attorney assume the payment of costs. [pp172-174]

James Sanders
    vs   **[Debt Appeal]**
Josiah Watson

On 16 July 1803, James Sanders, assignee of Robert Burton, obtained an attachment against the estate of Josiah Watson for $904.52 with interest from the first day of December 1800. "State of Tennessee To the Sheriff of Robertson County ...James Sanders has complained on oath to me Andrew Jackson Esquire, one of the Judges of the Superior Courts of Law and Equity for the State of Tennessee, that Josiah Watson is justly indebted to him in the sum of $904.52 ...being the balance on bond given by said Josiah Watson to Robert Burton, dated 29 May 1798, oath having been made that the said Josiah Watson is an inhabitant of Virginia ... therefore command you that you attach the estate of the said Josiah Watson, if to be found in your county ..." Which attachment was returned by the sheriff of Robertson County "levied August 10, 1803, on the undivided moiety of six tracts of land of 640 acres each lying on the waters of the Sulpher Fork of Red River"
On Motion, it was ordered that the proceedings be stayed six months.

Plaintiff, by his attorney John Dickinson, files his declaration. 'Josiah Watson, of the town of Alexandria and State of Virginia, granted himself to be held and bound unto the said Robert Burton Esqr, of Granville County and State of North Carolina ...

And the Defendant not appearing, tho solemnly called, it is considered by the Court that the plaintiff recover against the defendant the debt, together with his costs, and it is ordered that the sheriff make sale of the lands by him attached and satisfy this judgment and return the surplus, if any, to the defendant, And also that he return an account to the next Court. [pp174-176]

John Den lessee of Thomas Hickman
    vs   [In Ejectment Appeal]
David Hodges

On 11 October 1802 an appeal from the County Court of Davidson County was filed in the Superior Court of the District of Mero; John Den complains of a Richard Fen ... whereas Thomas Hickman on 16 Jan 1801 had let to John Den, for a period of ten years, two thousand five hundred and sixty acres lf land in the County of Davidson on the waters of Whites Creek on the north side of Cumberland river, beginning at the NE corner of David Shannons preemption ... N boundary of Joseph Kincaid ... N boundary of Philip Walker, then E to John Walker ... point on Danial Johnstons S boundary, then W with his and Ebenezer Titus' line... S to John Marshals line ... John Mears' line crossing the creek at Mears' NE corner ... it being a track originally granted to Martin Armstrong and Anthony Crutcher by Patent #7255 bearing date the tenth day of December 1790. John Den says he is injured and has damages of $100, Thomas Stuart attorney for the plaintiff.

"Notice to Mr. David Hodges: that you are in possession of or claim title to the premises mentioned in the declaration of ejectment ...ask that a rule be made to cause you defendant in my stead. signed your loving friend Richard Fen"

Joseph Johnston, Esq., Sheriff, made return to April Sessions 1801 that he had delivered the same to David Hodges on 6 March 1801; Agreeable to such notice David Hodges appeared at April Sessions 1801 by his attorney, Howell Tatum, and moved that he might be made defendant in the stead of Richard Fen. "John as is included in the following ... boulder on David Shannons N boundary .. containing 128 acres, part of the premises aforesaid ...beginning at James McAllisters corner on David Shannons N boundary, running thence W to Samuel Shannon (now the said Hodges) corner ... then N with Samuel Shannons (now David Hodges) line to his NE corner, thence W to Robert Davis (now Joshua James) corner on Shannon which include the land ranged to Howel Tatum; E with the patent line to its NE corner on Adam Homes line, he the said David Hodges in nowise guilty of the trespass; puts himself on the county by Howel Tatum, his attorney and the plaintiff the same by Thomas Stuart, his attorney.

The Court then appointed Thomas Harney to survey, and return into the County Court plats of the disputed premises, which was done, continued until July Sessions 1802, at which time came the parties by their attorneys and comes a Jury: Benjamin Joslin, Jeremiah Hinton, William Douglass, Philip Pipkin, John Williams, John Mitchel, David Buchanan, George Taylor, John McMorn, Hugh Robertson, George Buchanan and John Johns and find the defendant not guilty - therefore it is considered the defendant may recover of the plaintiff his costs, from which judgment the plaintiff obtained an appeal to the Superior Court.

Cause continued from Term to Term until this Term, come the parties by their attornies and a Jury: John Stump, Andrew Hays, Timothy Oneal, James Dupree, John Top, Joseph McKean, James Jackson, George Burnett, William Tait, James Mcfersin, Thomas Stubblefield and Jonathan Magnees and find the defendant is not guilty of the trespass therefore the defendant may depart and recover his costs from the plaintiff. [pp177-180]

The State
    vs   **[Indictment for Murder]**
Michael Murphy
Be it remembered that on Friday, 18 May, this present Term, in the State of Tennessee and District of Mero before the Judges, by the oath of Joseph Phillips, foreman, Obediah Bounds, Joel

Dyer, George Keesee, Matthew Figures, Thomas H. Perkins, Nathaniel Jeffers, Willie Cherry, Jonas Manifee, William Hope, Joseph J. Williams, Richard Bradley, James Mulherrin, Aaron Fletcher and Zacheus Wilson, upon their oath present, that Michael Murphy, late of the County of Smith, in the District aforesaid, on the 19th of April 1804, at Paytons Creek in the said County of Smith, in and upon a certain male negro slave named Ben, then and for a long time before, there being the property of the said Michael Murphy, did make an assault and that the said Michael Murphy, with a certain piece of oak timber, about six feet long and three inches thick, in and upon the left side of the neck and left jawbone, below the left ear of him the said slave named Ben, did strike and hit, one mortal bruise of the length of six inches and the said male negro slave instantly died. And so the Jurors do say that the said Michael Murphy did kill and murder against the peace and dignity of the State. J. Whiteside, Attorney General
And the said Michael Murphy pled 'not guilty' whereupon came a Jury - Thomas Overton, George Titus, Aaron Rawlings, Nathaniel McCreary, Frederick Stump, Patrick Barr, James Dupree, James Wills, Joseph McKean, Andrew Greer, Thomas Hickman and Enock Enocks and having tried the evidence, upon their oath do say that the said Michael Murphy is not guilty as charged and that the said Michael Murphy be acquitted and discharged. [see 163] [pp181-182]

John Den lessee of Thomas Hickman
    vs   [In Ejectment Appeal]
David Cloyd
On 13 April 1803 an appeal from the County Court of Davidson was filed in the Superior Court for the District of Mero. Jan. Term 1801 John Den complains of Richard Fen of a plea of Trespass in Ejectment. Whereas Thomas Hickman on 16 Jan 1801 did to farm let to the said John Den 2560 acres of land, lying in Davidson County on the Waters of Whites Creek and on the North side of Cumberland River; NE corner of David Shannons preemption [see description **Den vs Hodges**] Thomas Stuart for the Plaintiff

Notice to David Cloyd - I am informed that you are in possession of a claim title to the premise mentioned ...appear to cause yourself to be defendant ...
On which declaration of Ejectment Joseph Johnston, Esq, Sheriff made return at April Sessions 1801, that he had delivered a copy of the same to David Cloyd on 5 March 1801. The said Cloyd appeared by his attorney, Bennet Searcy. July Sessions 1801 defendant says he is not guilty of the trespass charged against 225 acres of land ...beginning corner of the original tract granted to Alexander Caveat...thence E ... being all the land the said David Cloyd has title to and said David hereby disclaim having any right to all the residue of the said tract except the said 225 acres and is not guilty of any trespass. Bennet Searcy for the defendant - Thomas Stuart for the plaintiff ... by assent of the Court this and the plaintiffs cause against Joel Beavers is consolidated and no survey is required by either party, continued until October Sessions 1802 and a Jury: John P. Wiggins, John Top, Robert Sample, Robert C. Reaves, George Ury, Benjamin Phillips, William Murry, Robert Heaton, Joseph Boyers, Thomas Watson, William Billings, Zachariah Stull similar issue between plaintiff and Joel Beavers, cause consolidated, likewise Alexander Caveat the original grantee through whom the defendant derived his title ... Jury return and find the defendants are not guilty .. considered by the Court the defendants do recover against the plaintiff their costs of suit - From which judgment the plaintiff obtained an appeal to the Superior Court ... Cause continued until this Term and comes the plaintiff by his attorney and confesses that he intends no further to prosecute. Considered by the Court the defendants may depart and recover their costs against the plaintiff. [pp182-185]

John Den lessee of Thomas Hickman
        vs   **[In Ejectment Appeal]**
Joel Bowers and Richard Caveat
On 13 April 1803 an appeal from the County Court of Davidson was filed in the Superior Court for the District of Mero - John Den complains of Richard Fen ... whereas Thomas Hickman on 16 January 1801

demised and to farm let to John Den 2560 acres of land [see description in **Den vs Hodges**] for ten years which has not yet expired ...
Notice to Joel Beavers - I am informed that you are in possession or claim title to the premises mentioned in this Declaration of Ejectment and I being sued in this action, do advise you to appear and be made a defendant in my stead...Richard Fen 2 Feb 1802
Joseph Johnston, Sheriff, made return to April Sessions 1801 that he had delivered same to Joel Beavers on 5 March 1801...Joel Beavers appeared at the aforesaid sessions by Bennet Searcy, his attorney ... Likewise on the prayer of Richard Caveat, he also is admitted defendant with the said Joel Beavers ...July Sessions 1801 Beavers and Caveat by their attorney said they are not guilty on 255 acres being the balance of the tract of land originally granted Alexander Caveat for 580 acres. Bennet Searcy for the defendants and Thomas Stuart for the Plaintiff

By consent of the parties and assent of the Court this and the plaintiffs cause against David Cloyd is consolidated ... October Sessions 1802 came a Jury - John P. Wiggins, John Topp, Robert Sample, Robert C. Reaves, George Ury, Benjamin Phillips, William Murry, Robert Eaton, Joseph Boyers, Thomas Watson, William Billings & Zachariah Stull who find the defendants not guilty of the trespass and ejectment - defendants to recover against the plaintiff their costs. Plaintiff obtained an appeal - Cause continued from Term to Term until this Term ... plaintiff by his attorney confesses that he intends to no further prosecute - defendants may depart and recover their costs against the plaintiff. [pp185-189]

Barnebas Herrod
    vs   **[In Trover]**
James Wills
James Wills was attacked to answer Barnebas Herrod of a plea of Trespass, whereas Barnabas, by Thomas Stuart his attorney, at May Term 1803 filed his declaration - the plaintiff was possessed of a certain yellow bay mare of the value of $150 and said defendant came into possession of said mare by finding ... plaintiff by Thomas Stuart

defendant says 'not guilty' represented by Jenkin Whiteside. Cause continued until this term and came a Jury - Joseph Collins, Beal Bosley, Micajah Woodward, Wilson Gibson, Cary Felts, Lovick Vantress, Andrew Grier, Patrick Barr, John Stump, William Karr, Frederick Stump and William Nash. Find the defendant guilty and access damages to sixty five dollars and costs.. [See 251] [pp189-190]

John Den lessee of John Carter & McAnutty
                 vs   [In Eject]
Benjamin Totton
Benjamin Totton to answer John Den, lessee of John Carter and John McAnutty, of a plea of trespass. John Den lessee by Thomas Stuart his attorney filed his declaration Nov. Term 1802 - Whereas John Carter & John McAnutty on 20 Sept. 1802 devised to John Den one tenement and three thousand acres of land formerly in the County of Smith but at the time of devise in the County of Jackson, lying in the middle district on Eagle Creek, the waters of Obed's river, including an improvement made by Alexander Sute ... granted by the patent of the State of North Carolina 20 August 1800 to the said John Carter and John McAnutty. Benjamin Totton, by his Attorney Jenkin Whitesides, says he is not guilty ... Cause continued until this Term at which day comes the plaintiff by his attorney and confesses that he intends no further to prosecute. Defendant to recover his costs against the plaintiff. [pp190-191]

Fanning Jones
       vs   [In Debt Cer.]
Redmond D. Barry
A writ of certiorari was issued on the second Monday of May 1803 from the Superior Court of Mero, directed to the Justices of the Court of Pleas and Quarter Sessions for the County of Sumner, commanding the said Justices to send and certify the record and proceedings in an action between Fanning Jones and Redmond D. Berry. Record was filed in the Clerks office of the Superior Court on 10 Oct. 1803.
Record of the County Court - Pleas before the Court of Pleas and Quarter Sessions of Sumner at the town

of Gallatin on the first Monday in April 1803 To the Sheriff of said County ... take the body of Redmond D. Berry if he be found in your county ...so you have him before the Justices to be held for said county at the Courthouse in the town of Cairo ...to answer Fanning Jones assignee of Moses Harding in a plea that he render unto him the sum of $216.75 which to him he owes ... Issued 17 May 1802   David Shelby

Sheriff made return to July term 1802 'came to hand 22 May and executed the 2nd June, E. Crutcher. Term last mentioned, the plaintiff by Jesse Wharton filed his declaration

July Term 1802   Fanning Jones assignee of Moses Harding, complains of Redmond D. Barry ...whereas Redmond D. Barry on 19 Nov. 1797 at the County of Sumner made and executed his writing obligatory ... aforesaid Moses Hardin by his indorsement on the back of said writing obligatory dated 4 Dec. 1798 ordered and directed the contents thereof to be paid to the said Fanning Jones ... said Redmond then and there had notice ... yet the said Jones says that though often asked he hath not paid the aforesaid sum ...October Sessions 1802 a Jury came: William Trigg, Joseph Seawell, John B. Craighead, James Desha, Henry Lyon, John Hutchings, John Burrow, John McConnell, John Jones, Anthony Sydner, Michael Mitchell and Jack Reeves who find in favor of the plaintiff for $153.75 debt and $7.74 damages. Whereupon a rule to shew cause for a new trial was ordered and awarded. April Sessions 1803 came the parties by their attornies and a Jury: Kasper Mansker, William Bowen, Henry Bunn, John Weathers, Elmore Harris, Robert Shaw, William Brigance, John Mills, James Lauderdale, Seth Mabry, Thomas Howell and William Parr and say that the defendant has paid the sum mentioned in the declaration except $146.75 which he has not paid ... assess the plaintiffs damages to $46.75 appealed - continued ...

This Term came the parties by their attornies and a Jury: John L. Martin, David Beaty, Willie Cherry, Vinson Ridley, William Nash, James Boyd, Charles F. Mabius, William Turner, John Payton, Thomas Brittain, Nathan Ewing and James Frazeir who find for the plaintiff for $183.24, the residue of the debt and costs. [pp191-194]

Hadley & Rawlings
    vs   [In Case]
William P. Anderson
May Term 1803 - William P. Anderson was attached to answer Hadley and Rawlings, merchants trading under the firm of Hadley and Rawlings of a plea of trespass, damages one thousand dollars. The defendant, by Thomas Stuart his attorney, saith he did not assume as declared and cause has been continued until this Term at which day cam The plaintiff by Jesse Wharton, his attorney, at May Term 1803 filled their declaration: Joshua Hadley and Benjamin Rawlings, merchants trading under the name of Hadley and Rawlings complain of William P. Anderson - that the said William on 5 February 1803, made his note in writing ... promised to pay the sum of four hundred and twenty dollars in merchantable bailed cotton to be delivered in the month of February in Nashville at the price of $14.00 per hundred weight for value received ... defendant hath not delivered any part thereof in February or any time since. e the parties by their attornies and the Defendant relinquishes his plea and confesses for $420.00 with interest from 1 March 1803. Therefore with the assent of the plaintiff and considered by the Court they recover the same together with costs of the suit. [pp195-196]

Friday, May 25, 1804

Marvel Lowe
    vs   [Scifa Cert]
John Caffery & Abram Stanley bail for James Dohertie
On the 2nd Monday of May 1803, a Writ of Certiorari issued from the Superior Caourt for the District of Mero directed to the Justices of the Court of Pleas and Quarter Sessions of the County of Davidson ... demanding the said Justices to send and certify the record in a certain action between Marvel Lowe plaintiff and John Caffere bail for James Dohertie Defendant, which records were filed in the clerks office of the Superior Court on 11 October 1803... Whereas Marvel Low heretofore in our Court July Sessions 1801, recovered against James Dougherty

the sum of twenty four dollars and sixty seven cents ... for which there was issued a writ of fieri facias against the goods and chattels lands and tenements of the sd Doughertie wherein the sheriff made return to October Sessions 1801 that he found no property of the said Dougherty in his county ... Sheriff made return to January Sessions 1802 that he found not the body of the said in his county ... that after serving the writ on the said Dougherty, John Cummins became his bail, John Caffery and Abraham Standly became the said Doughertys bail. Issued April 29, 1802 Andrew Ewing
On the first of which writs Edley Ewing DS made return to April Sessions 1802 that he had made the same known to said Caffery on 27 Feb. 1802 in presence of John Johnston, and that Standley was not found in his county, and on the latter he made return to July Sessions 1802 . July 1802 plaintiff appeared by his attorney, Bennet Searcy; Caffery appeared by Samuel Donelson, his attorney. Cause continued until April Sessions 1803 when Caffery by his attorney waives his plea and offers no further defense and the said Abraham Standley failed to do either in person or by an attorney - therefore it is considered by the Court that the plaintiff do recover the sum of twenty four dollars and sixty cents.
Cause continued in the Superior Court until this Term at which day came the parties aforesaid; defendants by Jesse Wharton their attorney, and say they did deliver up the said James Doherty in discharge of themselves to Joseph Johnston, the then sheriff of Davidson County. Came a Jury - David Beaty, Willie Cherry, Patrick Barr, Vinson Ridley, James Boyd, Charles F. Mabius, William Turner, John Payton, Thomas Brittain, Nathan Ewing, James Frazier and Merril Philips who say that the Defendants did not surrender James Doherty in discharge of themselves. Plaintiff may have execution for $24.67 and defendants to pay the costs. [pp196-198]

James Elder & Co.
    vs   **[Scifa Appeal]**
Joseph Porter & William Brown bail for Daniel Brown

On 11 October 1803 an appeal from the County Court of Davidson was filed with the Clerk of the Superior Court for the District of Mero - 'To the Sheriff of Davidson County: whereas James Elder & Co. heretofore in our Court of Pleas & Quarter Sessions April Sessions 1801 obtained Judgment against Daniel G. Brown for the sum of $29 with the endorsed fees for which a writ was issued - sheriff made return to July Sessions 1801 that he found not the body of the said Daniel G. Brown in his county and that at the time for serving the writ on the said Brown, Joseph Porter & William Brown became his bail, as appears by their obligation filed dated Oct. 15, 1799. John Childress Jun. D.S. made return to October Sessions 1801 "Porter not found" . Plaintiff appeared by Howell Tatum their attorney and the defendant Porter by Joseph Herndon ... January Sessions 1803 plaintiff appeared by John Dickinson, their attorney in the room of Howel Tatum, their former attorney and the said William Brown to whom it does not appear Scifa was made known was then solemnly called upon to come into Court ... after which came a Jury: John Walker, Marlin Cross, William Caldwell, Deliverance Gray, Stephen Bean, Henry Hyde, William Ewing, William Corbitt, John Donelson, William Ward, Micajah McQuerry and Thomas Cates and say 'they find that the defendant did not surrender up the principal in discharge of himself' Therefore it is considered by the Court that the plaintiff do recover of the said Joseph Porter according the sum of $29 and costs of suit. Porter obtained an appeal to the Superior Court but afterward during the same session the defendant withdrew his appeal and said that since the commencement of the original suit against defendant Daniel G. Brown and before the swearing out the Scifa said Brown deceased and this he is ready to verify. P.W. Humphreys for the Deft.

Plaintiff by John Dickinson, their atty, said the said Brown did not die before the swearing out of said writ ..cause continued until April Sessions 1803 at which time came a Jury: John Shute, Thomas Hudson, Stephen Bean, John Duncan, Francis Nusam, Thomas Shute, John Buchanan, John Costileo, Francis Carper, William Douglas, Frederick Stump & Micajah Barrow and say they find that the said Daniel G. Brown did not die before the swearing out of the

Scifa, neither has the defendant surrendered him in discharge of himself - Therefore it is considered by the Court that the plaintiff do recover of the defendant the sum of $29.00 and cost of the suit. Whereupon the Defendant prayed and obtained an appeal to the Superior Court. Andrew Ewing, County Court Clerk May 30, 1803

Cause continued until this Term at which day came the parties by their attorneys and the defendant Joseph Porter relinquishes his pleas by him before pleaded ; therefore with the assent of the plaintiffs it is considered by the Court the plaintiff may has execution for $29.00 and costs. [pp199-201]

James Ore
    vs   **[Debt]**
Stephen Bean
Stephen Bean was summoned to answer James Ore on a plea that he render unto him the sum of $196.28 which he owes and damage one hundred dollars. James Ore, by Jesse Wharton, his attorney filed his declaration: Mero District May Term 1803 James Hamilton of Hamilton District and State of Tennessee, by his attorney complains of Stephen Bean ... whereas Bean made and executed his certain writing obligatory at Nashville in the District of Mero, dated 13 Nov. 1802 and promised to pay to the said James $196.98 yet has not paid ... And the said Stephen by Jinken Whiteside his attorney, says he has paid and is ready to verify ... Cause continued until this Term when came the parties by their attorneys and a Jury: Joseph Collins, Beal Bosley, Micajah Woodward, Wilson Gibson, Cary Felts, Andrew Grier, John Stump, Thomas Mitchel, Benjamin Totton, Aaron Rawlings, William Karr, and Arthur Hogan. Jury say the defendant hath not paid the debt and assess the plaintiffs damage to $17.64 & costs. [pp202-203]

Robert Tait, assignee
    vs   **[In Covenant]**
George Parks
George Parks was attached to answer Robert Tait, assignee of John Buchahan in a plea of Covenant broken, damage one thousand dollars. Tait, by Bennet Searcy his attorney, filed his declaration:

May Term 1803 - Whereas George Parks made his covenant, wherein he bound himself in the sum of $2000 that he would make unto John Buchanan a lawful deed by the first day of December next (meaning 1796) being his second choice of a two thousand acre tract lying on Big Harpeth 250 acres to be run off in a square or an oblong so as to get good water... whereas on 8 Aug. 1796 the aforesaid John Buchanan by his assignment on the back of the said Covenant to Robert Tait ... and the said Robert doth aver that the said George had notice of the said assignment, doth further aver that on and before the first day of December 1796 the said John Buchannon made his choice of the aforesaid 250 acres of land which being the second choice out of the two thousand acre tract and notified the said George of the same when it was so laid off but that the said George failed to make a good and lawful deed to the same, and the said Robert doth further aver that after the 8 August 1796 that he made choice of 250 acres of land which being the second, out of the two thousand acre tract which being the same that John Buchanan made, and the said George being notified of the same and required to make the deed to him according to the writing obligatory, stated aforesaid ... neither did not since conveyed ...but hath broken. the said covenant George Parks, by Thomas Stuart his attorney, saith he hath performed all the covenant ...cause continued until this Term and this day came the parties by their attornies and a Jury - David Beaty, Willie Cherry, Patrick Barr, Vinson Ridley, James Boyd, Charles F. Mabius, William Turner, John Payton, Thomas Britain, Nathan Ewing, James Frazier, and Merril Phillips and say the defendant hath not performed the covenant and assess the plaintiffs damages to $375 and costs. [pp203-205]

Friday May 25, 1804

John Den lessee of Randal McGavock
    vs   **[In Ejectment]**
Matthew Brooks & Nicholas Coonrod
At a Court held for the said District on the second Monday in November 1802 came John Den by Jenkin Whiteside his attorney and brought a bill against

Richard Fen of a plea of Trespass & Ejectment ... whereas Randal McGavock on 1 November 1802 to farm let to John Den a parcel of land containing 34 acres lying in Davidson County bounded as follows ... on the bank of the river at Ables old ferry landing thence west ... for a term of ten years ... said Richard did trespass ... to damage of five hundred dollars and brings suit.
Notice - Mr. Matthew Brooks. I am informed you are in possession of or claim title to the premises in the above Declaration of Ejectment, do advise you to appear at the Superior Court May next ... signed Richard Fen December 25, 1802
And the said Matthew Brooks, Tenant in possession and Nicholas Coonrod, landlord of the said Matthew who is admitted by the court to defend for and with said Matthew come & pray to be admitted defendants -- plea not guilty and on the trial to confess lease entry and ouster and insist on title only... Now come the parties by their attorneys and a Jury - Joseph Collins, Beal Bosley, Micajah Woodward, Wilson Gibson, Cary Felts, Andrew Grier, Thomas Mitchel, Benjamin Totten, Aaron Rawlings, William Karr, Robert Weakley and Sampson Williams ...ordered that the plaintiff be nonsuited and jury be discharged and Richard Fen being called but came not but made default; plaintiff to recover against the defendant his term. And on the motion of the plaintiff by his attorney writ of possession is awarded him returnable here at the next court. [See 250] [pp206/207]

Nicholas T. Perkins
    vs   [In Debt]
Francis Mabury
Francis Mabury was summoned to answer Nicholas Tait Perkins surviving obligee of Nicholas Perkins of a plea that he render to him $766 which he owes as surviving joint obligee. Nicholas T. Perkins by John Overton & John Dickinson, his attornies, filed declaration ...whereas on the second day of January 1797 at the county of Davidson Francis Maybury made his writing obligatory to pay to Nicholas Tait Perkins and a certain Nicholas Perkins now deceased by the first day of November 1799, yet Maybury, although often requested, hath not paid.

Francis Maybury by Jenkin Whitesides comes and says he has paid ... continued until this Term at which time came the parties by their attornies and a Jury - Joseph Collins, Beal Bosley, Micajah Woodward, Wilson Gibson, Cary Felts, Andrew Greer, Thomas Mitchel, Benjamin Totton, Aaron Rawlings, William Karr, Sampson Williams & John L. Martin who say the defendant hath paid the debt except $301.5 and award damages of $150.96 and costs. [pp208-210]

Elisha Nicholson
    vs   [In Covenant]
William Mullin
William Mullin was attached to answer Elisha Nicholson of a plea of Covenants broken, damage five hundred dollars. Elisha Nicholson, by John Dickinson his attorney, filed his declaration November Term 1803. Whereas on 8 March 1803 William Mullin made his certain writing obligatory to deliver to the said Elisha on or before the 25th of August next a likely negro girl, ten years old, sound and clear of any known bodily infirmity and well grown of that age and said William did not deliver and has not kept his covenant. The defendant, altho solemnly called, came not but made default. Considered by the Court that the said Elisha recover his damages to be inquired of by a Jury at the next Court. At which day the said Elisha, by his attorney comes and a Jury - David Beaty, Willie Cherry, Patrick Barr, Vinson Ridley, James Boyd, Charles F. Mabion, James Frazier & Merril Phillips who say the plaintiff hath sustained damages by occasion of the defendants nonperformance of $261.75 and costs. [pp210-211]

Patrick Joice & John Dunn
    vs   [Scifa app]
James Hamilton & Joseph Porter bail for Daniel G. Brown
On 11 October 1803 an appeal from the County Court of Davidson was filed in the Superior Court in the following words: To the Sheriff of Davidson County - Whereas Patrick Joyce & John Dunn in our Court of Pleas & Quarter Sessions April 1801 obtained judgment against Daniel G. Brown for the sum of $173.90 whereon the sheriff made report to July Sessions 1801 that he found not Daniel G. Brown in

his county ... appears that William Anderson and William Brown became his bail but the said bail being objected to. At October Sessions 1799 James Hamilton & Joseph Porter became the said Daniel G. Brown special bail, dated Oct. 16, 1799. Sheriff made return to October sessions 11801 that he say Hamilton but had not had opportunity of making the same known to him and Porter was not found. Nov. 9, 1801, John Boyd, sheriff, made known to James Hamilton in presence of William Madlock & Samuel Shannon, Senr and made known on 16 Nov. 1801 to Joseph Porter in presence of James Meness and Nicholas Scales. January Sessions last the plaintiffs appeared by Howel Tatum, their attorney and the defendants then appeared by Joseph Herndon, their attorney ... cause continued until January Sessions 1803 at which time the plaintiffs by their attorney John Dickinson in the stead of Howel Tatum their former attorney and thereon comes a Jury - John Walker, Maclin Cross, William Caldwell, Deliverance Gray, Stephen Bean, Henry Hyde, William Ewing, William Corbitt, John Donelson, William Ward, Micajah McQuerry & Thomas Cates and find the defendants did not surrender the principal in discharge of themselves. Therefore it is considered that the complaintants do recover of the defendants the sum of $173.90 and the costs of the suit. From which judgment the defendants prayed and received an appeal to the Superior Court of Mero District but afterwards during the same sessions the defendants withdrew their appeal and obtained of the Court a new trial, defendants assumed on themselves the payment of all costs and say that since the commencement of the original suit and before the swearing out of the Scifa ... said Brown died and they are ready to verify. P. W. Humphreys for Defts.

Plaintiffs by John Dickinson, their attorney, say that said Daniel G. Brown did not die before the suing ... cause continued to April Sessions 1803 and came a Jury - John Shute, Thomas Hudson, Stephen Bean, John Dunn, Francis Nusam, Thomas Shute, John Buchanan, John Castilio, Francis Campior, William Douglass, Frederick Stump & Micajah Barrow and they say that Brown did not die before the time of the suing , neither has the defendants surrendered him in discharge of themselves and it is considered by the Court that the plaintiffs do recover according to the Scifa and also the costs of suit.

From which judgment the defendants prayed and obtained appeal to the Superior Court for the District of Mero and the cause was continued until this Term at which time came the parties by their attorneys and the defendants relinquished their plea therefore it is ruled by the Court the plaintiffs may have execution for $123.90 as the writ aforesaid mentioned and also recover against defendants the cost of the suit. [pp212-215]

William Seawell
    vs   **[In Covenant]**
John Hackett & Charles McClung
John Hackett & Charles McClung were attached to answer William Seawell of the County of Sumner in the District of Mero in a plea of covenant broken to his damage of $1500. William Seawell by Jenkin Whiteside, his attorney filed his declaration Nov. Term 1803... Charles McClung and John Hackett, residents of Knox County in District of Hamilton, on 2 March 1798 at Nashville by their certain writing obligatory and signed with their seals that they or either of them would convey to said William Seawell two hundred acres of land lying in the County of Davidson to be well watered, timbered and fit for cultivation, within three months and said William says they have not kept their covenant. Defendants by Jesse Wharton, their attorney, say they have not broken their covenant ... cause continued until this Term and came the parties by their attorneys and a Jury - David Beaty, Willie Cherry, Patrick Barr, Vinson Ridley, James Boyd, Charles F. Mabius, William Turner, John Payton, Thomas Brittain, Nathan Ewing, James Frazier and Merrel Philips and say the defendants have not performed the covenant and assess the plaintiffs damages to four hundred dollars besides his costs. [pp215-216]

James Hennen & William Dickson
    vs   **[In Debt]**
Robert Searcy
Robert Searcy was summoned to answer James Hennen & William Dickson, merchants and copartners in

trade under the firm of *Hennen & Dickson* of a plea that he render to them $1,025.91 that he owes, damages of $500.00. James Hennen & William Dickson, by John Dickinson, their attorney, filed their decoration November Term 1803. On 2 April 1803, in County of Davidson, Robert Searcy made his certain writing obligatory to pay one day after date of writing for value received and has not yet paid altho often requested. Defendant, by Bennet Searcy his attorney, says that he paid and satisfied the debt and is ready to verify ... trial continued .... came the parties by their attorneys and a lawful Jury - Joseph Collins, Beal Bosley, Micajah Woodward, Wilson Gibson, Cary Felts, Andrew Greer, Benjamin Totton, Aaron Rawlings, William Karr, John L. Martin & John Stump and say the defendant hath paid the debt, except $795.10 ... plaintiff recover the remainder and the costs. [pp217-218]

John C. Hamilton
   vs   [In Covenant Appeal]
Stephen Boren
19 April 1804, an appeal from the County Court of Robertson was filed with the Clerk of the Superior Court for the District of Mero - "To the Sheriff of Robertson County ..take the body of Stephen Boren if to be found in your county ..to answer John C. Hamilton in a plea of covenant broken. Thomas Johnston, Clerk April 1803 Whereas Stephen Boren together with a certain Edward Cheatham, by their certain writing obligatory, made at the County of Robertson on 21 July 1802, obliged themselves to deliver to John C. Hamilton one likely well grown sound and sensible negro girl between the age of eleven & thirteen on or before the last day of March next and Cheathan & Boren did not deliver. The defendants appeared by P. R. Booker, his attorney... came a Jury - Matthew Day, Samuel Robbins, Jacob Fry, Amos Cohia, Jerlins Elm..., James Mays, James Henry, Willy Skinner, Jesse Martin, Abraham Pinkley, Samuel McMurry & George Browning and say they find for the plaintiff and assess damages to $310 from which verdict the defendant prayed & obtained an appeal to the Superior Court, gave bond in the sum of $650 with Bazel Boren & Isaac Doris, his securities.

Now, at this Term of the Superior Court came the parties by their attornies and a Jury - Joseph Collins, Beal Bosley, Micajah Woodward, Wilson Gibson, Cary Felts, Andrew Grier, Thomas Mitchel, Benjamin Totton, Aaron Rawlings, William Karr, John L. Martin & John Stump and say that the defendant hath broken his covenant and assess the plaintiffs damages to $320.50, therefore it is considered by the Court that the plaintiff recover his damages and his costs. [pp218-220]

Thomas Waller
    vs   [In Debt]
Neil Thompson
Neil Thompson was summoned to answer Thomas Waller on plea that he render to him $320 he owes. Waller, by Thomas Stuart his attorney, filed his declaration Nov. Term 1803. Whereas the said Niel Thompson by his certain writing obligatory made on 30 Jan. 1802, promised to pay Thomas Waller on or before the 25th day of December next...tho often requested debt has not been paid.

Defendant, by Jesse Wharton his attorney, says he has paid the debt ... trial continued until this Term defendant relinquishing his plea and confesses that he cannot deny the plaintiffs action therefore the assent of the plaintiff it is considered by the Court that the plaintiff recover against the defendant the $320 with interest and his costs of suit. [pp220-221]

The following jurors proved their attendance at this Term and received tickets:

	Days	Miles	Ferriages
Micajah Woodward	12	34	
Cary Felts	12	10	
Patrick Barr	12	65	2
John Stump	11	9	2
Beal Bosley	11	4	
Aaron Rawlings	12	200	4
Benjamin Totton	12	240	4
Wilson Gibson	12	84	2
Joseph Collins	12	100	2
Andrew Grier	12	90	2
William Karr	12	56	2
Thomas Mitchel	8	40	

[p222]

Friday May 25, 1804   May Term 1804

James Wall
    vs   [Sci. fa]
Simpson Harris, bail for Samuel Hill
To the Sheriff of Davidson County: Whereas James Wall, late in our Superior Court for District of Mero recovered against Samuel Hill $17.15 for his costs for his defense; execution thereof still remains to be made, and whereas Simpson Harris, prosecution bail for the said Samuel Hill, that he should pay all such costs as should be adjudged to the said James Wall, or that he the said Simpson Harris would do it for him as appears also of record. Samuel Hill hath not paid, therefore we command you to make known to Simpson Harris that he be before the Judges at the next court ... Randal McGavock, Clerk of Court, 2nd Monday in Nov. 1803. John Boyd, sheriff of Davidson County, returned he had made known to the said Simpson March 16, 1804. Now comes the plaintiff by Howel Tatum, his attorney, and the said Simpson Harris not appearing, it is considered by the Court that the said James Wall may have execution against Simpson Harris for $17.50, the costs of the Scifa and said Defendant pay the costs. [pp222/223]

William Pillow
    vs   [Sci fa]
Peter Johnston, bail for Wilson Curle
To the Sheriff of Davidson County - Whereas William Pillow late in our Superior Court recovered against Wilson Curle $5.39 for his costs about his defense ... execution still remains to be made and Peter Johnston prosecution bail for the said Wilson Curle, therefore we command you to make known to Peter Johnston that he be before the Judges of our Superior Court at the next Court ...Randal McGavock, Clerk Nov. 1803. On which writ John Boyd, sheriff of Davidson, returned to May Term 1804 that he had made the same known to Johnston March 23, 1804. And now, the plaintiff, by Jessee Wharton his attorney, comes and the said Peter Johnston not appearing it is considered by the Court that the plaintiff recover against Johnston for $5.39 and the costs of the Scifa. [p223]

David Vaughn & Wife
    vs   [Scifa]
Jonathan Darden, bail for Joseph Barnes
To the Sheriff of Robertson County - Whereas David Vaughn and Susanah, his wife, late in the Superior Court for the District of Mero, recovered against Joseph Barnes $25 for debt, also $115.78 for costs of suit; nevertheless execution thereof still remains and whereas Jonathan Darden undertook that if the said Joseph Barnes should be convicted in the action, that he should pay the condemnation or render his body to prison in execution... therefore we command you to make known to said Jonathan Darden ...Randal McGavock Clerk Nov 1803 On which writ B. Menees, Jr., Sheriff of Robertson County made return 'Executed April 17, 1804'
   And Jonathan Darden, by Thomas Stuart his attorney, comes and defends ...saith that at May Term of the Superior Court on 12 May 1801 he surrendered the body of said Joseph Barnes in open Court in discharge of himself and he is ready to verify by said record. Said plaintiffs were solemnly called but came not, neither is their suit further prosecuted, therefore it is considered by the Court the plaintiffs be nonsuited and pay the costs of the Scifa. [pp224/225]

John Payton
    vs   [Scifa]
Samuel Donelson, bail for William Morgan
To the Sheriff of Sumner County - Whereas John Payton, late in the Superior Court of the District of Mero, recovered against William Morgan $67.47 for his costs about his defense, nevertheless execution thereof still remains to be made and the said Samuel Donelson was his bail, therefore we command you to make known to the said Donelson that he be before the Judges of our Superior Court on the second Monday, May next ... On which writ E. Crutcher, sheriff of Sumner County, made return 'made know Jan. 26, 1804'
   And now on the day comes the plaintiff by his attornies, John C. Hamilton & Thomas Stuart, and the said Donelson not appearing tho solemnly called, it is considered by the Court that the plaintiff may have execution against Samuel

Donelson for $67.47 and that Donelson pay the costs of the Scifa. [pp225/226]

John & Ephraim Payton
   vs   [Scifa]
Joel Dyer, bail for James Morgan
To the Sheriff of Smith County - Whereas John Payton & Ephraim Payton, late in the Superior Court of the District of Mero recovered against James Morgan $103.67 for costs, return remains to be made and whereas Joel Dyer undedtook that if the said Morgan should be convicted he, Morgan, should pay all costs & damages - therefore you are commanded to make known to Joel Dyer that he be before the Superior Court on the second Monday in May next ...Randal McGavock, Clerk, Nov. 1803 - on which writ John Douglass, Sheriff of Smith County, made return 'Executed March 5th, 1804.' Now comes the plaintiff by Thomas Stuart their attorney, and say they intend no further to prosecute and the said Joel Dyer, in proper person, assumes the payment of the costs. [p226]

Isaac Herbert & James Bulgin
   vs   [Scifa]
Martin Duncan, bail for Beverly A. Allen
To the Sheriff of Robertson County - Whereas Isaac Herbert & James Bulgin, late in out Superior Court of the District of Mero, recovered against Beverly A. Allen $15.72 for their costs about their defense, nevertheless execution thereof still remains to be made, and Martin Duncan undertook in the penalty of $600 that if the said Allen be convicted he should pay all costs as adjudged ... therefore we command you to make known to said Duncan that he be before the Judges of Superior Court of the District of Mero at May Term next ... signed Randal McGavock, Clerk Nov. 1803. On which writ B. Menees, sheriff of Robertson County made return 'Executed April 25th.'

And now come the plaintiffs by Howel Tatum, their attorney and said Martin Duncan not appearing tho solemnly called it is ruled by the Court that the plaintiff may have execution against Duncan for $15.72 and costs of the Scifa. [p227]

John Davidson
    vs   [Scifa}]
John Overton & William Dickson, bail for Jesse Jernigans lessee

Whereas John Davidson late in our Superior Court of the District of Mero, recovered against John Den lessee of Jesse Jernigan $16.04 for his costs, nevertheless execution thereof still remains to be made and whereas John Overton and William Dickson prosecution bail would do it for him ... we therefore command you to make known to them ... on which writ E. Ewing, Deputy Sheriff of Davidson County made return 'made known.'

And now the plaintiff by Thomas Stuart, his attorney, comes and the said Overton & Dickson not appearing, therefore it is considered by the Court that the plaintiff may have execution against Overton & Dickson for $16.03 and costs of the Scifa. [p228]

William Smith, Gentleman produced a licence to practice as Attorney in the several Courts within this state and having taken the oath to support the Constitution of the United States, the Constitution of the State of Tennessee and the oath of an attorney at law, he is therefore admitted to practice as an attorney in this Court. [p229]

John Overton
    vs   [Case]
John B. Evens

On 16 April 1800 John Overton obtained an attachment against the Estate of John B. Evins for the sum of twenty five hundred dollars with interest ... due to endorsements made on the back of two promissory notes given by David Allison to Charles R. Arthur, bearing date Oct. 31, 1794, one for the sum of one thousand dollars, the other for fifteen hundred and oath being made that the said John B. Evins is not an inhabitant of this state ... James Mulherrin. On which attachment the sheriff of Davidson

County made return to May Term 1800 that he had "levied the within on the title and interest of John B. Evins to the following tracts of land on the Waters of Overalls Creek of Stones River; 320 acres, half of 640 granted to Howel Tatum & Henry Wiggins as assignee of Breton Jones Grant #3286, also 640 acres granted to the same persons as assignee of John Grayhams heirs & Grant #3287, also 320 acres of land, half of 640 acres granted to the same persons as assignee of Levi Branton Grant #13281, the 15th day of April 1800."

Whereupon the said John Overton by Jessee Wharton his attorney, at May Term 1800 filed his declaration ... complains of John B. Evins ... John B. Evans & Co. directed the contents of said notes to be paid to John Overton & Allison & Arthur had notice ... John B. Evins had notice at Philadelphia... On 2 January 1795 at Philadelphia, Overton presented said note to David Allison for payment who refused to pay whereupon said note was taken to Peter Lochia, a Notary Public who protested against said note for nonpayment ... continued from Term to Term - May Term 1802 came the plaintiff by his attorney and the Defendant replevies the property attached and Jinkin Whitesides & John Irwin come and undertake for the Defendant ... continued until this date ... considered by the Court that the plaintiff take nothing by his bill and that the defendant depart this Court & recover against the plaintiff his costs. [pp 229-237]

Saturday, May 26, 1804

John Den, lessee of William Edwards
    vs   **[In Ejectment]**
James Brigance & John Gordon
Be it remembered that at a Court held for the District on the second Monday in May 1799 came John Doe by Benjamin Seawell his attorney and brings his bill against James Brigance and John Gordon of a plea of trespass and ejectment ...

James Brigance and John Gordon of the County of Sumner to answer to John Doe ... he entered a tract of land lying in the county of Sumner on Station Camp Creek containing 640 acres and bounded as follows: Beginning on Michael Shavers East boundary ... to the Creek ... which said tract William Edwards demised to the said John Doe for a term which is not yet expired and ejected him from his tract. Term commencing from 1 January 1797 for the term of fifteen years, and the said Brigance and Gordon on 1 February 1797 with force and arms ...entered into the said tract ... Brigance and Gordon say they are not guilty and the cause was continued from Term to Term until this Term at which day comes the defendant by his attorney and the plaintiff was called but came not, therefore it is considered by the Court that the plaintiff be nonsuited and pay the costs. [pp237-239]

The State
    vs   [Scifa]
Jeremiah Brown an absent Juror
To the Sheriff of Wilson County - Whereas Jeremiah Brown was summoned to attend a Superior Court of the District of Mero at the Courthouse in Nashville on the second Monday 1803 as a Juror and having been solemnly called, came not...whereupon a conditional judgement was entered for the penalty prescribed by law & costs ... Nevertheless execution of this judgment still remains., We therefore command you to make known to the said Jeremiah Brown that he before the Judges of our said Court at the next Court to be held.
  And now at this Term, on the affidavit of the said Jeremiah, it is ordered that the forfiture aforesaid be set aside and that the said Jeremiah pay the costs of the Scifa. [p239]

John Read   **[In Error of Judgment rendered by the Justices of the County Court for the County of Montgomery at April Sessions 1798]**
    vs

Anthony Crutcher

To the Justices of the County Court of Pleas and Quarter Sessions for the County of Montgomery -

Whereas in rendering judgment in a certain action between Anthony Crutcher and John Read and also in issuing execution on said Judgment, manifest error hath intervened...and we being willing that the error be corrected, do command you to that the record be sent to the Judges of the Superior Court for the District of Mero ....signed Andrew McNairy, Clerk, May 1801

'the record I send to the Judges of the Superior Court. signed William Caldwell Jamison, Clerk at office in the Town of Clarksville this 10th day of May

transcript - '4th Monday in July 1797 Present Robert Prince, Robert Nelson & William Mitcheson, Esquires. It appears from the appearance Docket that there was an original attachment returned and the return of the Sheriff was 'nothing found' but it is missing from the other papers. Rules of Court, Judicial Attachment to issue. At October Term 1797 Present George Neville, Robert Nelson & Haydon Wells. "attachment was returned in the following words, 'Whereas Anthony Crutcher sued out 'an original attachment from under hand and seal of Robert Dunning, one of the Justices of the Peace for the county of Montgomery against the property of John Read an Inhabitant of the State of North Carolina returnable to our July Term 1797 for the sum of $150 on which Joseph Burgel Nevell, Sheriff of said County at our July Court made return 'nothing was found,' you are therefore commanded to attach the goods and chattels, lands and tenements of the said John Read if to be found in your county. Singed Barkley William Pollock, Clerk July 1797. Issued 11 Sept 1797. Endorsed Levied on 730 acres of land. G. Neville. Jan. Term 1798 Present Hayden Wells, Robert Nelson, Robert Dunning, Timothy Anderson & William Mitcheson, Esquires... continued

Issued 1 Dec 1797. To Jan 1798 Endorsed came to hand December 16th levied on seven hundred and thirty acres of land on Wells Creek. G. Neville The complaint of Anthony Crutcher for the sum of $150 due and owing on an instrument of writing in the words following, "Nashville April 4, 1785 Received of A. Crutcher Sixty pounds specie Certificates on aut. of Major John Read" signed by Edmond Jennings, which said certificates were paid and delivered at the request of the said John by him the said Anthony to the said Edmond. The said sum of sixty pounds specie certificates equal in value to one hundred and fifty dollars ..." Jo Herndon, Atty

Nashville   April 4, 1785   Received of A. Crutcher sixty pounds specie Certificates on acct of Major John Read   Edmond [his mark] Jennins   Test. John Nichols

April Term 1798 the following present: George Nevill, Amos Bird, William Connell & Robert Prince Esquires - Jury came: John Dodd, Samuel Campbell, Joseph Robertson, Lewis Elliott, Josiah Watson, Isaac Peterson, James Taylor White, Esau Capshaw, Hugh Bell, John Nevil, Thomas Clinton & Valentine Sevear, who find for the plaintiff $267 & property to be sold or so much as will be sufficient to satisfy the debt and costs.

Sold the ninth of June for ninety one dollars seven hundred and thirty acres of land. J. B. Nevill, after which time execution issued again in the following words: To the sheriff of Sumner County ' you are hereby commanded that of the goods, chattels, land and tenements of John Read you cause to be made the sum of $267 dollars to satisfy a judgement obtained against him at our April Court 1798   ...'   B. William Pollock, Clerk

'Issued 17 August to October 1798   Endorsed Levied on 365 acres of land on Dixons Creek and 640 on Stones River and after giving legal notice was sold on 10 October for $101 dollars. J. Cage'

May Term 1801 comes the said John Read, by Thomas Stuart his attorney...bill of errors listed; continued Term by Term until May Term 1804 comes said Read & Crutcher by their attornies and the opinion of the Court that the judgment be reversed and that Anthony Crutcher pay the costs. [pp240-246]

Wed., May 30 1804

John Sevier Governor of the State of Tennessee
vs
Nathaniel Perry Collector of the County of Wilson & John Hays, William Crabtree & Joseph Crabtree, his Surities
On the motion of Robert Searcy, late Treasurer for the District of Mero, it appearing that Nathaniel Perry, collector of Wilson County for the year 1802, has failed to pay the sum of three hundred and seventy four dollars and seventy three and one fourth cents part of the state tax for the year aforesaid to the Treasurer, considered by the Court that recover against Perry and John Hays, William & Joseph Crabtree, his Securities the sum plus costs. [p246]

John Sevier Governor of the State of Tennessee
vs
James Menees Collector of the County of Robertson
John James, Joseph Robertson and Anderson Cheatham, his Surities
On motion of Robert Searcy, late Treasurer for the District of Mero ... it appearing that James Menees collector of the County of Robertson for the year 1801, has failed to pay the sum of two hundred and sixty nine dollars and eighty eight cents - part of the State Tax for the year 1801 ... recover against Menees, James, Robertson & Cheatham the amount plus costs. [246/247]

John Sevier Governor of the State of Tennessee

vs
James Menees Collector of the County of Robertson
and Benjamin Menees & George Briscoe his Surities
On the motion of Robert Searcy, late Treasurer for the District of Mero, and it appearing that James Menees collector of the County of Robertson for the year 1802 has failed to pay the sum of five hundred and three dollars and seventy seven cents, the State Tax for the year aforesaid .. recovered against James Menees and Benjamin Menees and George Briscoe the said sum and costs. [p247]

John Sevier Governor of the State of Tennessee
vs
John Sanders Sheriff and collector of the County of Montgomery
Thomas Clynton, James Stuart, Hugh F. Bell, James Ford, William R. Bell, Isaac Peterson & Reuben Pollard, his Surities
On the motion of Robert Searcy, late Treasurer for Mero District, and it appearing to the satisfaction of the Court that the Sheriff and Collector has failed to pay the Treasurer the sum of three hundred and fifty six dollars and eighty four and three fourth cents ... Tax due for the years 1799 and 1800. Ruled that it be recovered against John Sanders, Sheriff and his Securities together with costs. [pp247/248]

Allen Corbett a Constable proved fifteen days attendance on Court at this Term. [p248]

William Tait
vs [Debt Appeal]
John Childress & Sarah Robertson
On 15 May 1804 an appeal from the County Court of Davidson was filed -
transcript - to the Sheriff of Davidson County to have John Childress and Sarah Robertson before the Court of Davidson to answer William

Tait on a plea of Debt for $325.12 - returned 'executed on Sarah Robertson third day of January, 1803 and executed on John Childress 4th of Jan. 1803' signed John Boyd, Shff
Jan Sessions appeared the plaintiff by Bennet Searcy his attorney - Whereas on 25 Nov. 1799 in County of Davidson John & Sarah made their certain writing obligatory and their promise to pay to the said William Tait thirteen months after date the sum of $325.12 and debt has not been paid. The defense by Jesse Wharton, their attorney, entered for plea 'payment, issue joined' and so remained by sundry continuances until January Term 1804 when the attorney for the defendants withdraws their plea and makes no further defense; therefore it is considered by the Court that the plaintiff recover (after all credits) the sum of $236.53 being the amount of the principal and interest and the defendants prayed and were granted an appeal to the Superior Court.

And now, at this Term comes the plaintiff by his attorney, and the appeal not having been brought up within the time prescribed, and on the motion of the plaintiff it is ordered that the judgment of the County Court be affirmed. [pp248-250]

Wed, May 30, 1804

John Den lessee of Randal McGavock
    vs   [In Eject.]
Richard Fen & Matthew Brooks & Nicholas Coonrod
On the motion of the plaintiff, by his attorney, Matthew Brooks & Nicholas Coonrod pay costs of the suit. [See 206} [p250]

James Taylor
    vs   [Case Appeal]
James Blackburn
It seems to the Court that the verdict aforesaid is insufficient and erronious ...judgment arrested ... defendant may recover his costs from the plaintiff. [See 92] [p250]

John Den lessee of Joseph Lemonds
    vs   [In Eject]
Henry Alexander
It is ordered that the verdict aforesaid be set aside and that a new trial be had at the next court. {See Page 98,288} [p250]

Barnabas Herrod
    vs   [Trover]
James Wills
Ordered that the plaintiff pay the cost of all witnesses summoned by him, up to May 1803. [See 189] [p251]

John Den lessee of John Gallaway
    vs   [In Ejectment]
Hugh Barr
It is ordered that Execution issue against John Galloway for the costs of this suit. [See 14,42,59] [p251]

Pierce Butler
    vs   [In Attachment]
David Allison
Be it remembered that on the sixth day of October 1798 Pierce Butler obtained an attachment against the estate of David Allison for the sum of ten thousand four hundred and fifty nine dollars and ninety two cents with interest. John Sommerville, Attorney in fact of Pierce Butler, hath complained on oath to David Campbell, one of the Judges of the Superior Court, that David Allison is indebted to Pierce Butler.... signed David Campbell, Justice of the Superior Court at Knoxville, 6 Oct. 1798. On which attachment the Sheriff of Davidson County made return ..'came to hand 11 Oct. 1798 it appears that the defendant David Allison owned eighty five thousand acres of land on the three forks of Duck river within the bounds reserved to the Indians, grants bearing date 27 June 1793, commencing with No. 216 and ending with

No. 225, and some more commencing with No. 229 and ending with No. 235, which said land was mortgaged to Norton Pryor. Now if it be lawful I, N. P. Hardiman, do levy the within attachment upon the 85,000 acres of land..'

Nov. Term 1798 came the plaintiff by Thomas Stuart his attorney, and it is ordered the proceedings be stayed six months, and at May Term 1799 came the plaintiff by his attorney, and the defendant being dead, it is ordered that a Scire facias be issued against William Blount, Executor of the said David Allison. On which Sci fa the Sheriff made return that he had made the same known to William Blount in presence of James Woods Leachey and John Dickinson the 3rd July 1799. Nov. Term 1799 William Blount, by George W. Campbell his attorney ...and the cause was continued from Term to Term until this Term, and the plaintiff not further prosecuting the same is discontinued, therefore it is ordered that the plaintiff pay the costs. [pp251-254]

Christopher Stump
    vs   **[In Debt]**
Josiah G. Duke, Adm. of Thomas Hargroves, dec'd
Be it remembered that May Term 1803 a Capias was rendered at the suit of Christopher Stump & Co. against William Hargrove & Josiah G. Duke, administrator of Thomas Hargrove, dec'd in a plea of Debt that they render to them the sum of five hundred and forty eight dollars thirty two cents which they owe, was returned by the Sheriff of Montgomery County 'Executed on Josiah G. Duke administrator - William Hargrove not found.' Nov. 1803 the Sheriff of Davidson County made return that the said William Hargrove was not found, whereupon the plaintiffs by Bennet Searcy their attorney, filed their declaration. ...'on 22 Feb. 1802 in the County of Davidson a certain William Hargrove and Thomas Hargrove made their certain writing obligatory ...' And the defendant Josiah G. Duke not appearing tho solemnly called it is considered by the Court that the plaintiff recover against the defendant

the debt with legal interest to be levied of the goods and chattels of the said decedent if sufficient shall come to the hands of the said Josiah, if not then of the proper goods of the said Josiah G. Duke. [pp254-256]

Samuel Meeker & William Cochram
vs   [Debt]
Samuel Jackson

Be it remembered that on 28 May 1804 an appeal from the County Court of Williamson was filed. Original order signed by Nicholas P. Hardiman, Clerk Williamson County, Bennet Searcy became the plaintiffs security. May Term 1803 Samuel Meeker and William Cocohran obtained a judicial attachment against Samuel Jackson. Sheriff made return on the right title and interest that Samuel Jackson has to 5657 acres of land being a part of General Moors big survey adjoining Pinktham Eaton on Harpeth waters ... August Term 1803 Whereas to Samuel Meekor and William Cochran, Jackson owes debt of $240.14 ...'whereas at the Supreme Court of the Commonwealth of Pennsylvania held at Philadelphia the eight day of December 1802 recovered against Samuel Jackson the sum of $240.15 and six cents cost which was adjudged to the said Meeker and Cochran in the said Court for their damages sustained for his nonpayment of an accepted bill of exchange. August Sessions 1803 Thomas Masterson & John Dickinson came into open court and entered themselves special bail for the defendant and replevied the property attached, says he is an inhabitant of the County of Grainger in this state and should be sued in that court...Nov Sessions 1803 ruled the defendant to recover against the plaintiffs his costs about his defense and the defendants being dissatisfied obtained an appeal to the Superior Court .. And now at this Term comes the plaintiffs by his attorney and the appeal not having been brought up within the time prescribed by law it is ordered that the judgement of the County Court be affirmed.

Defendant depart and recover his costs from the plaintiff. [pp256-261]

John Sevier, Governor
    vs   [In Debt]
Robert Searcy, Andrew Jackson & William Dickson
Robert Searcy, Andrew Jackson & William Dickson were summoned to answer John Sevier, Governor of the State of Tennessee in Office, to Archibald Roane, late Governor of the State, $20,000 debt and the said plaintiff not further prosecuting said action is discontinued, plaintiff to pay the cost of this suit. [p261]

Joseph Williams
    vs   [In Debt]
Yancy Thornton
Yancy Thornton was summoned to answer a plea that he render to Joseph Williams $282.25 debt & $100 damages. Plaintiff called, but came not neither is his suit further prosecuted. Plaintiff be nonsuited and pay to the defendant his costs. [p261]

James Knox
    vs   [In Covenant]
Lemuel Suggs
At Suit of James Knox vs Lemuel Suggs, plea of Covenant Broken and plaintiff not further prosecuting the same is discontinued and ruled by the Court that the plaintiff pay the costs. [p261]

John Doe lessee of James Armstrong
    vs   [In Ejectment]
Joseph Williams
Joseph Williams was attached to answer James Armstrong of a plea of Trespass in ejectment. James by P. W. Humphreys his attorney, at May Term 1804 filed his declaration ... 'James Armstrong on 20 May 1803 at the parish of Tennessee, County of Jackson, had demised to the said John Doe five thousand acres of land on

North side of Obeds river at the mouth of Spring Creek, for term of 15 years and Joseph Williams on 20 July 1803 entered into the said 5000 acres of land and ejected the said John Doe ...Plaintiff confesses that he intends no further prosecution ... defendant to recover his costs from plaintiff. [p262]

State of Tennessee - Mero District   At a Superior Court of law held for the District aforesaid at the Courthouse in Nashville on the second Monday, being the twelfth day of November of the year 1804 ..Present the Hon. David Campbell, Hugh L. White & John Overton, Esquires, Judges

The following persons were elected and Sworn a Grand Jury of Inquest for the body of this District, Viz, Robert Edmiston, foreman, William Hazzard, Peter Looney, H. James Vinson, William Alexander, Buckner Killebro, Zacheus Wilson, Thomas Strain, William Tease, Grant Allin, James Yates, Robert Searcy, Alexander Patton, Absalam Hooper & Josiah Fort, - and having received their charge withdrew to consider of presentments.

John Houston
   vs   [In Covenant]
William Brown
Be it remembered that on 19 Nov 1798 John Houston obtained an attachment against the Estate of William Brown for $699.50, with interest. Daniel G. Brown, agent for John Huston, hath complained on oath to David Campbell, Justice of the Superior Court for the State, that William Brown is indebted to said John Huston, and said Brown hath removed himself out of the County of Davidson and out of the state... command you to attach the estate of the said William Brown, if to be found ... on which attachment the Sheriff of Davidson made return ' levied the within on William Browns right to

100 acres of land lying on the north side of Cumberland River near to Thomas's Ferry on 10 March 1799'. Whereupon John Houston, by Thomas Stuart his attorney, at May Term 1799 filed his declaration.... whereas the said William by his certain writing obligatory made at the county aforesaid on 10 Nov. 1789 ...or his order one likely sound sensible field negro country born between the age of fourteen and twenty to be delivered at the house of Mr. John Waddel in Nolechucky ...defendant did not pay or deliver. Defendant not appearing tho solemnly called it is considered by the Court that the plaintiff recover ...enquiry of damages was continued from Term to Term and came a Jury - Thomas Williamson, William Lancaster, Theophilus Bass, James Boyd, Joseph Hopkins, Charles Hudspath, James S. Wilson, John McDonald, David Jones, Richard Puckett, William Griffin and George Purtle- find for plaintiff $549.75 and costs. [pp263-265]

William Burton, Bennett H. Henderson & Nathaniel Washington Williams took the oath to support the Constitution of the United States, State of Tennessee and the oath of an attorney at law, therefore are admitted to practice as attornies or counsellors. [p265]

The State
    vs   [Scifa]
John Walthall
To the Sheriff of Williamson County --- John Walthall was summoned to attend a Superior Court for the District of Mero May 1804 as a Juror and came not, but made default whereupon a conditional judgment was entered against him ...judgment still remains to be made. Randal McGavock, Clerk On which writ, S. Childress, Sheriff of Williamson County made return. 'Executed July 11, 1804' - and now came the defendant and on his affidavit it is ordered the forfiture be set aside and defendant pay the costs. [pp265/266]

The State
   vs   [Scifa]
James Neely a delinquent Juror
To the Sheriff of Williamson County - Whereas James Neely was summoned to attend a Superior Court for the District of Mero May 1804, as a Juror, and having been called, came not, whereupon a conditional judgment was rendered ... nevertheless execution still remains to be made -- On which Sci fa S. Childress, Sheriff of Williamson made return ' Executed July 10, 1804.' And now comes the defendant and on his affidavit it is ordered that the forfiture be set aside and defendant pay the costs. [p266]

The State
   vs   [Scifa]
Henry Gardner a delinquent Juror
To the Sheriff of Robertson County - Henry Gardner was summoned to attend a Superior Court of the District of Mero May 1804 as a Juror, and having been solemnly called, came not, whereupon a conditional judgment was entered against him - this Judgment still remainst to be made .. On which writ John Cheatham, Sheriff of Robertson County made return 'Served on Gardner 21st of September 1804' - And now comes the defendant and on his affidavit it is ordered the forfeiture be set aside and defendant pay the costs. [pp266/267]

The State
   vs   [Scifa]
Thomas Watson a delinquent Juror
To the Sheriff of Montgomery County - Whereas Thomas Watson was summoned to attend a Superior Court for the District of Mero, and having been solemnly called, came not, whereupon a conditional Judgment was entered and remainst to be made .. on which Scifa John Cocke, Sheriff of Montgomery County made return 'made known 10 Oct. 19-4'' - And now comes the defendant and

on his affidavit, it is ordered that the forfiture be set aside and defendant pay the costs. [pp267/268]

John Den, Lessee of John Howell
           vs   **[Eject]**
Richard Fen & Ezekiel Bass
Ezekiel Bass was attacked to answer John Den Lessee of John Howell of a plea of trespass. John by John Dickinson his attorney, made his Declaration Nov. Term 1803, John Den, by his attorney, complains of Richard Fen...Whereas John Howell on 17 August 1803 at the County of Wilson did demise to John Den 640 acres of land on South side of Cumberland River and Round Lick Creek, granted to John Howell by Patent #1440 bearing date 20 December 1792 - to the said John Den from 1 July last past for 15 years ... Overton & Dickinson for the plaintiffs
Notice - Ezekiel Bass, Sir, I am informed that you claim title to the premises or to some part thereof ... And it appearing by the affidavit of George Hallam, Sheriff of Wilson County that Ezekiel Bass Tenant in Possession hath been duly served with a copy of the above ... And now came the plaintiff by his attorney and the said Richard Fen being solemnly called but came not, considered by the Court that the plaintiff recover against the defendant and on the motion of the plaintiff by his attorney a writ of possession is awarded him returnable here at the next Court. [pp268/269]

John Den lessee of John McNairy
           vs   **[In Ejectment]**
Richard Fen & William Hankins
Whereas John McNairy on 16 October 1803, at the County of Smith, demised to John Den 2560 acres of land, lying and being in the County of Smith, on Wolf Creek, the waters of Cany Fork ... to said John Den from 10 Sept last past for the term of 15 years ... signed Dickinson atty for plaintiff

Notice - Mr. William Hankins. I am informed that you are in possession of or claim title to the premises mentioned in the within declaration ... And it appearing by the affidavit of Lee Sullivan, Sheriff of the District aforesaid that William Hankins tenant in possession of the premises hath been duly served .. And now came the plaintiff by his attorney and the said Richard Fen being solemnly called came not, therefore it is considered that the plaintiff recover against the defendant and on the motion of the plaintiff by his attorney a writ of possession is awarded him returnable to the next Court. [pp269-271]

John Den lessee of John McNairy
    vs   [In Eject]
Richard Fen & William Smith
John Den, by John Dickinson his attorney, filed his declaration charging William Smith with trespass ... Whereas John McNairy on 16 October 1803, at the County of Smith, demised to John Den three cottages and 2560 acres of land, in county aforesaid on the waters of Wolf Creek, the waters of Cany Fork, for the term of fifteen years ... on affidavit of Lee Sullivan, Sheriff of Smith County that William Smith, Tenant in possession, hath been duly served. Now came the plaintiff by his attorney and the said Richard Fen being solemnly called came not but made default. It is therefore considered by the Court the plaintiff recover against the defendant and a writ of possession is awarded him returnable here at the next Court. [pp271/272]

James Taylor
    vs   [Scire facia]
Charles Hedgepeth
To the Sheriff of Jackson County - Whereas Charles Hedgepeth was summoned under the penalty of one hundred and twenty five dollars to appear at a Superior Court of the District of Mero Nov. 1803 and give testimony on behalf of James

Taylor against James Blackbourn and the said Charles Hedgepeth having been solemnly called but made default ... coinsidered by the Court Hedgepeth be fined the said $125 for the use of said James Taylor unless he show sufficient cause. Randal McGavock Clerk B. Totton, Sheriff of Jackson County returned he had made the same known and the plaintiff by his attorney comes into court and confesses that he intends no further prosecution ...Court orders plaintiff pay the costs. [p272/273]

John Den lessee of William Goodloe, John M. Goodloe, Henry Goodloe, David S. Goodloe & Samuel Jones and Elizabeth Jones his wife
     vs   **[Eject]**
Richard Fen & Thomas Lockhart
John Den, by Bennet Searcy his attorney, filed his Declaration - Whereas William Goodloe, John M. Goodloe, Henry Goodloe, David S. Goodloe and Samuel Jones & Elizabeth Jones, all heirs of Robert Goodloe, dec'd, on 10 May 1803, at the County of Davidson, had demised to John Den 640 acres of land lying in the county of Davidson on the North waters of Little Harpeth on the right hand trace leading from Johnsons Lick to said Little Harpeth, James Robertsons SW corner, Samuel McCutchens line, being originally granted to Robert Goodloe in his lifetime by North Carolina by Grant #1382 bearing date the 20 Dec. 1791. Den demised the 640 acres from 10 Dec. 1803 for term of fifteen years --Richard Fen afterwards, on 20 May 1803, drove out and ejected the said John Den.
Notice: Mr. Thomas Lockhart ...informed you are in possession of or claim title to the premises mention in this declaration or some part thereof ... E. Ewing Deputy Sheriff of Davidson made return 'I have read and delivedred a copy of the within declaration of Ejectment to Thomas Lockhart. Now comes the plaintiff by his attorney and confesses that he intends no further to prosecute ... plaintiff to pay costs

of this suit, except a fee to the defendants attorney. [pp274-277]

William Marchbanks
vs [Detinue]
Philip Parchment

And the cause was continued until this Term, at which came the parties by their attornies and a Jury - William Lancaster, James Boyd, Joseph Hopkins, Charles Hudspeth, James S. Wilson, John McDonald, David Jones, Richard Puckett, Matthew Brooks, Richard Brittain, John Anderson & Thomas Williamson who say that the defendant doth detain the negro slaves, Sal & Charlotte as the plaintiff hath alledged that the said Sal is of the value of $325 and Charlotte is of the price of $125 ... plaintiff to recover his negroes if they be had, but if not, then the price aforesaid and damages of $89.00. [See 83} [p277]

Frederick Stump
vs [In Case]
William T. Lewis

William T. Lewis attached to answer of a plea of Trespass - Whereupon the said Stump, by Bennet Searcy his attorney, filed his declaration .. whereas William T. Lewis the 27 December 1795 in the county of Davidson was indebted to Stump $773.49 for goods & merchandise ... William Tyrrell Lewis by Thomas Stuart, his attorney, says plaintiff was indebted to him for same sum ... trial continued until May 1803, at which time came the parties by their attornies and mutually submit all matters in dispute to the final determination of James Robertson and Robert Weakley and the same is ordered
May 1804 came the parties by their attornies and the arbitrators who say they have chosen Willie Blount as umpire ...
We are of opinion that the Grant in the name of Frederick Stump for 274 acres as assignee of Martin Armstrong bearing date Sept. 26, 1795 is a better title than the grant of William Tyrrell Lewis on entries one of 228 acres bearing date

Nov. 29, 1792 one of 185 acres bearing date Dec. 6, 1792, all of which are on the waters of Whites Creek in Davidson County adjoining the lands of Stump whereon he now lives and we do award that Lewis pay unto Stump the value of three hundred and ninety five acres being the above named and described lands which valuation is to be made by Hayden Wells of Montgomery County ...Lewis conveying to said Stump lands lying either in Montgomery County or Stuart County, costs to be equally paid by Stump and Lewis. May 17 1804

R. Weakley, Jas. Robertson, Willie Blount
And now come the parties by their attorneys and Heydon Wells ... ordered by the Court, with the assent of the parties that the award and valuation be confirmed and each party to pay half the costs of said suit. [See 52] [pp277-282]

John Lancaster administrator of John Lancaster, dec'd
          vs   [In Cov't]
Micajah Barrow

John Lancaster, administrator of John Lancaster, dec'd, by Thomas Stuart his attorney, filed his Declaration Nov. Term 1802 ...complains of Micajah Barrow in custody of the Sheriff of Davidson County of a plea of Covenant broken .. Barrow, by his certain writing obligatory, on 19 March 1798, for the sum of $5,000... that he would execute a good and sufficient deed to John Lancaster deceased, to two tracts of land containing 640 acres each, lying as follows; one adjoining a claim of Cummins warrant No. 2384 Granted to Sharrod Barrow, assignee of heirs of Freeman Joiner, No. 2739. The other tract being also granted to Sherrod Barrow assignee of the heirs of Barnet Parvis, No. 2754, adjoining the claim of Barrow, No. 2739, within twelve months from the date. John Lancaster, administrator, saith that the said Barrow did not execute a deed for both nor either of the above altho often requested ... Defendant, by Bennet Searcy his attorney, says he did do so ... cause continued from Term to Term at which time came the parties by their attornies and a Jury - Duncan Stuart, Griswold Latimer, John L. Martin, Theophilus Bass, William Griffin, James McCruston, Samuel Weakley, Thomas James, John Smith, Joel Rice, David Davis and William Thomas and say that the defendant hath not performed his covenant and assess plaintiffs damages to $1280 plus costs. [See 340] [pp282-284]

The State
    vs   [Scire facias]
William Sanders
To the Sheriff of Sumner County - William Sanders was summoned to attend a Superior Court for the District of Mero in May 1804, as a Juror and being called, came not ...conditional judgment was entered against him and remains to be made. Randal McGavock May 1804 ... Thomas Maston, Sheriff of Sumner made reply 'Executed this 15th October,' And now came the defendant, and on his affadit is is ordered the forfiture be set aside and defendant pay the costs of the scifa. [p285]

Parry W. Humphrey
    vs   [Original Attachment proceedings
John Verrell   stayed 6 months]
Richard Brittain, who was summoned as garnishee in this case being sworn, says that he has in his possession a stud horse, the property of the said Verrell, on which this attachment is levied - and that he owes the said Verrell nothing, nor does he know of any other person indebted to the defendant. [p285]

The State
    vs   [Scire facias]
John Vantree
To the Sheriff of Smith County - John Vantree was summoned Superior Court of District of Mero May 1804 as a Juror, and having been called,

came not ... conditional judgment was entered and execution remains to be made. Lee Sullivan, Sheriff of Smith County made return to November Term, 'Executed.' Now came the defendant, and on his affidavit it is ordered that forfiture be made and defendant pay costs. [p286]

John Overton, Andrew Ewing & James Mulherrin,
Executors of Thomas Molloy, deceased
    vs   [Detinue]
Roger McDaniel
Roger McDanial attached to answer Andrew Ewing, James Mulherrin and John Overton, Executors of the Last Will of Thomas Molloy, deceased, in a plea that he render to them one female negro, Fanny, of the price of four hundred dollars, and her mulatto child, commonly called Paddy, about five months old, of the price of two hundred dollars. Plaintiffs by J. Whiteside their attorney, made their declaration Nov. Term 1802
Roger, by Thomas Stuart his attorney says he does not detain the two. Cause continued from Term to Term until this Term when come the parties by their attornies and a Jury -Thomas Williamson, William Lancaster, Theophilus Bass, James Boyd, Charles Hudspeth, John L. Martin, John McDonald, Joseph Hopkins, David Jones, Richard Puckett, Griswold Latimer and Duncan Stuart - who say the defendant doth detain the negroes, Fanny and Paddy - considered by the court that the plaintiff recover their negroes if they may be had, if not, then the price of them, together with their damages and costs. [pp286-288]

Andrew Johnston
    vs
Samuel Caldwell and Elizabeth McRaynolds,
  Administrators of Robert McRaynolds, deceased
James C. Wilson who was summoned as garnishee in this cause, being sworn, says that he has in his hands only one dollar and fifty cents belonging to the estate of Robert McRaynolds, deceased,

and that he knows of nothing in the hands of any other person. [p288]

The Grand Jury returned into Court and presented an indictment against John Anderson, Laborer, for an assault with an intent to murder "a true bill" and retired to consider of further presentiments. Wed. Nov. 14, 1804   [p288]

John Den, lessee of Joseph Lemmonds
    vs   An   Ejectment]
Henry Alexander
This day came the parties by their attornies, and a Jury - William Griffin, Vinson Ridley, William Caldwell, Joshua Rickman, William Billings, James Hamilton, William Philips, Charles Caveness, Edmond Jennings, Matthew Brooks, James S. Wilson & Zachariah Betts - say the defendant is guilty of the trespass and ejectment and assess the plaintiffs damage to one cent, besides his costs. [See 98, 250] [pp288/289]

George Finley
    vs   [In detinue]
John Top
John Top attached to answer George Finley of plea of detinue, that he render to him a negro woman slave named Doll, about nineteen years of age, value four hundred dollars, negro boy slave named Tom, about four years old, value of two hundred dollars, and one other negro boy slave named Jim, about two years, value of one hundred and eighty dollars. [Tom & Jim being children and offspring the the said negro woman slave] George, by W. Campbell, his attorney filed his declaration Nov. Term 1802.
John Top, by Jenkin Whitesides his attorney, says he does not detain as charged ... cause continued from Term to Term until this Term at which time came the parties by their attornies and a Jury - William Lancaster, James Boyd, Joseph Hopkins, Charles Hudspeth, James Wilson,

Richard Puckett, Duncan Stuart, Griswold Latimer, Thomas Williamson, Theophilus Bass, William Griffin and John McDonald - jury finds for the defendant and recover against the plaintiff his costs. [pp289-291]

John Mills
    vs   [In Case - Cer]
Robert Trousdall & David Orr
November 1802 a writ of Certiorari was issued from the Superior Court of Mero District directed to the Justices of Court of Pleas & Quarter Sessions for the county of Sumner to send and certify the record and proceedings in an action between John Mills and Robert Trousdall and David Orr.
transcript - Pleas before the Court of Pleas and Quarter Sessions for the County of Sumner in the Town of Cairo Jan. 1803: Robert Trousdall, James Trousdall and David Orr to answer a charge of trespass - damage $500.00 - issued 25 Jan. 1802 signed David Shelby CSC
Sheriff made return 'came to hand 25 January and executed 26 February on Robert Trousdale and David Orr, James Trousdall not found' signed E. Crutcher, D.S. Writ reissued against James Trousdall and returned 4 September, 'Not found' ...October Term plaintiff by Thomas Stuart, his attorney, filed his declaration: Robert Trousdale, David Orr and James Trousdale covenanted and agreed that James Trousdale would bring and deliver to John Mills a sensible, well grown and well featured american born negro girl, above 13 and not exceeding 20 years of age before 1 July 1801 and in case of failure they became liable to the payment of $320 at the time of delivery and whereas the said John Mills at the county of Sumner by his certain writing obligatory made 1 February 1801 was bound to William Lauderdale to deliver on demand to Lauderdale a well grown, sensible, hearty and sound American born negro girl above twelve and under twenty and Mills & Lauderdale agreed that if James Trousdale would deliver to said William

Lauderdale to satisfy the bond of John Mills ... in October 1801 the said James Trousdale delivered a certain negro woman to William Lauderdale and affirmed the said negro was sound and sensible whereupon Lauderdale directed a certain James Henry (with whom John Mills had deposited his bond on said James Robert & David for the purpose ... said negro was not sound but laboured under divers diseases, to wit, palsy - was not sensible, but a fool wanting common sense ... Defendants, by John C. Hamilton & John B. Johnson, their attornies, appeared at October Term 1802 - rule made to plead & try at next court - came a jury - Edward Bradley, George Stubblefield, Patrick Barr, John Gillespie, George McGuire, Israel Moore, William Trigg, James Desha, Joseph Seawell, William Bradshaw, Robert Bratney, & Henry Bradford and find the defendants are guilty and assess damages to $348.80 and costs. Writ was issued to the Sheriff to have those monies before the Justices at the next sessions to be held for said county at the house of James Cryer in the Town of Gallatin on April next. signed David Shelby C.S.C. 10 Jan. 1803

And the cause was continued from term to term until this term at which time came the parties by their attornies and a Jury - John L. Martin, David Jones, William Betts, John Payton, James Menees, James Merrit, Robert Page, Henry Rutherford, Josiah Payne, William Douglass, John McCuen and David Allen - and the plaintiff was solemnly called but came not neither is his suit further prosecuted, therefore it is considered that the plaintiff be unsuited and pay to the defendants their costs. [pp291-296]

Thomas Masterson & Co.
    vs   [In Case]
James A. Tabb
James A. Tabb was attached to answer Thomas Masterson, Robert Stothart and George Bell, Merchants and copartners in trade under the firm of Thomas Masterson & Company - trespass, damage

$1500. Masterson & Co. by John Dickinson, their attorney, filed their declaration November Term 1803 - Whereas Samuel Sugars Hill, on 1 February 1803, at Franklin, in the County of Williamson, made a certain bill of Exchange, directed to said defendant by the name of Col. James Tabb. Defendant, by Jesse Wharton his attorney ... And the cause was continued until this Term at which day came the plaintiffs by their attornney, and the defendant in this cause being dead, it is ordered the same be abated and plaintiffs pay the costs of this suit. [pp296-299]

John Den, lessee of Thomas Dillon
        vs   [In Eject]
Elijah Chism & Sampson Williams
Elijah Chism & Sampson Williams were attached to answer John Den, lessee of Thomas Dillon of a plea of trespass in the County of Jackson. John, by Perry W. Humphrey, his attorney filed his declaration Nov. Term 1803 - Whereas Thomas Dillon on 1 March 1803 demised to John Doe 1633 acres of land, situate in the county of Jackson, bounded, Beg. W of where one Hyser lives ... for a term of 15 years ... says Elijah Chism & Sampson Williams on 20 March 1803 did eject said John Doe ... Defendants by their attorney, Jesse Wharton say they are not guilty ... Cause continued until this term at which day comes the plaintiff and confesses that he intends no further to prosecute. It is therefore considered that the defendants may depart and plaintiff to pay their costs. [pp299-300]

The Grand Jury again returned into Court and presented an indictment against John H. Jones, Joseph Jones and John Blanton for Larceny - 'a true bill as to John H. Jones' and 'not a true bill as to Joseph Jones and John Blanton' and again retired to consider of further presentments. [p300]

George W. L. Marr, Gentleman, took the oath to support the constitution of the United States, the Constitution of the State, the oath of an attorney at law, he is therefore admitted to practice in this Court.[p300]

The Grand Jury returned into Court and presented an indictment against Samuel Forrester for murder "a true bill" and again returned to consider of further presentments. [p300]

John Den lessee of Thomas Hamilton
    vs   [In Eject]
Charles Mundine
John Den, by Thomas Stuart his attorney, filed his declaration May Term 1803 - Whereas Thomas Hamilton on 1 May 1803, in the county of Smith, demised to John Den 640 acres of land, situate in the county of Smith, formerly in the county of Davidson, lying on the north side of Cumberland River on the waters of the first creek above the Cany Fork; Lieutenant Anthony Hart's SE corner; being a tract of land granted by the state of North Carolina to the said Thomas Hamilton by Patent bearing date of Sept. 15, 1786, then demised to said John Den from the 13th April last past, for five years. Charles Mundine afterwards on 1 May in the year last, entered and ejected the said John Den. Charles, by John Dickinson his attorney, says he is not guilty ... Cause was continued from term to term until this term, at which day comes the plaintiff by his attorney and confesses that he intends no longer to prosecute. Defendant may depart and recover his costs. [pp301/302]

Saturday, Nov. 17, 1804

John Den lessee of Thomas Hickman
    vs   [In Eject. Appeal]
John Ward
This day came the parties by their attornies and a Jury - Thomas Williamson, William Lancaster,

James Boyd, Joseph Hopkins, Charles Hudspeth, Duncan Stuart, John McDonald, David Jones, Richard Puckett, William Griffin, Griswold Latimer & James S. Wilson and say the defendant is not guilty of the trespass and the defendant to recover the costs of his defense. [See 153] [pp302/303]

The Grand Jury again appeared into Court and having nothing further to present was discharged. [p303]

The Grand Jury proved their attendance and received Tickets:

	Days	Miles	Ferriages
Robert Edmiston, foreman	6	18	
William Haggard	6	180	2
Peter Looney	6	45	2
James Vincent	6	60	2
William Alexander	6	100	2
Buckner Killebro	6	100	2
Zacheus Wilson	6	60	2
Thomas Strain	6	60	2
William Tease	6	100	-
Grant Allen	6	90	2
James Yates	6	60	2
Robert Searcy	6	100	2
Alexander Patton	6	16	-
Absolum Hooper	6	20	2
Josiah Fort	6	70	2
Archibald B. Steel, constable	6		

[p303]

John Den, Lessee of John McNairy
         vs   [In Eject]
Matthias Hoover
John Den, by John Dickinson his attorney, filed his declaration Nov. Term 1803 - complains of Matthias Hoover. Whereas John McNairy on 16 October 1803 demised to John Den 3 cottages and 2560 acres of land in the county of Smith, lying on Wolf Creek, the waters of Cany Fork for a

term of fifteen years and whereas Matthias Hoover ejected the said John Den. Matthias Hoover, by Thomas Stuart his attorney, says he is not guilty and the cause was continued from term to term until this term at which day comes the plaintiff and confesses that he intends no further to prosecute and the defendant assumes the costs. [p303/304]

Francis Weatherel
    vs   [In Case]
Robert King

Nov. Term 1801 a capias at the suit of Francis Weatherel of Sumner county against Robert King in a plea of trespass was returned by the sheriff of Knox county that he found not the said Robert King and at the term last mentioned, on the motion of the plaintiff by his attorney an attachment is awarded him against the estate of Robert King, returnable here at the next court at which Term, to wit, May 1802, the Sheriff of Roane county made return on the Writ 'no property found this 3rd May 1802' and at the Term last mentioned, an alias attachment is awarded him returnable here at the next Court, at which Court, Nov. 1802, the sheriff of Roane made return 'no property to be found in my county ... May 1803 the Sheriff of Washington county made return on the writ aforesaid 'received 8 March 1803 and levied on one gray gelding, a saddle, bridle, one case of pistols and holsters, the property of the within named Robert King, 10 March 1803, Joseph Brown, deputy sheriff, Washington county... Cause continued until this Term, May 1804, came plaintiff by Jenkin Whiteside his attorney, and filed his declaration. 'Robert King, of the county of Roane in the District of Hamilton was attached on a plea of trespass...promised to convey to said Francis between that day and the spring of the year 1801 good land lying on the south side of Cumberland river on Smiths fork of Cany ...value of $416.66 in exchange of a gray horse named Tanner... Jury - Theophelus Bass, John

Payton, James McCuiston, Henry Rutherford, Russell Gower, Robert Thompson , John White, John Parks, Alexander Read, Joshua James, Robert Weakley and William Thomas and find for the plaintiff for $416.66 and costs. [pp305/306]

Robert F. N. Smith took the oath to support the constitution of the United States, of the State of Tennessee and for Attorney at law - admitted to practice as an attorney is this court. [p307]

The State
    vs   [Scifa]
John Harris
To the Sheriff of Wilson County: Whereas John Harris was summoned under penalty of $125.00 to appear at the Superior Court in May 1804 to give evidence on our behalf against Samuel Inman who stood indicted for horse stealing, and being called, came not, it was therefore considered he be fined $125.00 unless he show sufficient cause, command you to make known to him that he be before the Judges on the second Monday of November next... Sheriff of Wilson County made return to Nov. Term 1804 'Executed 27 August' and now came the defendant and on his affidavit is is ordered the forfiture be set aside and John Harris pay the costs. [p307]

John Den lessee of James Stuart & Hugh F. Bell
    vs   [Ejectment]
Robert Cooper
Robert Cooper was attached to answer John Den lessee of James Stuart and Hugh F. Bell, he broke and entered the close of the said John Den in the County of Montgomery, damage $500 - John, by Thomas Stuart his attorney, filed his declaration May Term 1804; whereas James Stuart & Hugh F. Bell demised on 9 March 1804, one tenement and two lotts of land containing about half an acre each situate in the Town of Clarksville and distinguished on the plan of said Town as Lots #61 & #62, to have from 8 March last past for the term of ten years.

Robert Cooper, by John Overton his attorney, says he is not guilty. Cause was continued until this term, at which day comes James Stuart, one of the plaintiffs and says he intends no further action. Defendant may go and recover his costs against the plaintiffs. [pp307-309]

The State
   vs   [Felony]
John Garrett
Be it remembered that in November 1803, before the Honorable David Campbell, Andrew Jackson and Hugh L. White, by the oath of James Menees, foreman, Samuel Gray, James Taylor, Stephen Childress, John H. Hyde, Richard Strother, John Baldridge, William Yandle, Jordan Bass, John Hutcheson, Christopher Stump, Thomas Dillahunty, Asa Woodworth, William Murry and James McMurry, on their oath present that John Garrett, late of the county of Williamson, on 13 October 1803, intending to maim one Thomas Harding, then and yet being a citizen of the State of Tennessee, at Nashville in the County of Davidson...with the teeth of said John, the right ear of the said Thomas Harding, and unlawfully and feloniously did bite off ... J. Whiteside, Atty Gen'l
Whereupon it is ordered that process issue against Garrett to compel him to appear at the next Court. May 1804. Said Garrett did appear and says he is not guilty as the indictment alledged and the trial was continued ...At next Court, came a jury - Joseph Scoby, John Brooks, Peter Looney, Archibald Lytle, Thomas Williamson, William Lytle, Thomas Bradley, Andrew Greir, Joseph Hopkins, John McDonald, John Dawson and William Wilson, who having heard the evidence, say that Garrett is not guilty of the felony, therefore said John Garret be acquitted and discharged. [pp309-310]

Richard Polk
   vs   [In Debt]

Alexander Hopkins
Alexander Hopkins was summoned to answer Richard Polk on a plea of Debt of $333.33. Richard by John Dickinson filed his declaration Nov. Term 1804 ... 'said Alexander on 12 Oct. 1803, at Franklin in the County of Williamson, by his certain writing obligatory, to pay within three months. Defendant, having been called, came not. The Court therefore considers that the debt be paid with interest and costs. [pp310-311]

Monday, Nov. 19, 1804

Andrew Ewing, James Mulherrin & John Overton,
   Executors of Thomas Molloy, Dec'd
         vs   [In Debt]
William Betts
Plaintiffs, Andrew Ewing, James Mulherrin & John Overton, Executors of Thomas Molloy, dec'd, by John Dickinson & John Overton, their attorney filed their declaration May Term 1803 - Whereas William on 14 June 1800, at the County of Davidson, by his certain writing obligatory, now shown, promised to pay $320.00 to the said Thomas in his lifetime or to the said Andrew, James & John after after the decease of the said Thomas. William Betts by Thomas Stuart his attorney, says he paid ... that Molloy was indebted to him for meat, drink, washing, provided by said William. Cause was continued from term to term and the plaintiffs confess they intend no further action and it is ordered plaintiffs pay costs. [pp311-314]

Andrew Ewing, James Mulherrin, & John Overton
   Executors of Thomas Molloy deceased
         vs   [Debt]
William Betts
   [duplication of above case. [pp314-317]

Woolsey Warrington
      vs   [Scifa]

Michael Montgomery & Robert King
To the sheriff of Davidson County: Whereas Woolsey Warrington hath recovered against William L. Lovely $316.82 for debt and $14.13 for costs and whereas Michael Montgomery and Robert King are his bond, and whereas Lovely hath not paid nor surrendered his body to prison, you make known to Montgomery & King to be before the Judges of our Superior Court in May next. signed Randal McGavock Nov. 1803. Sheriff of Davidson County returns that the said Michael Montgomery and Robert King are not found in his county; Warrington came by his attorney, John Dickinson. Ruled the plaintiff to recover against the defendants the debt and his costs. [pp317/318]

Oliver Johnston
    vs   [Scifa]
Elizabeth Cummins, James Cummins & John Hoover
  Administrators of John Cummins, deceased; bail for Evans Moore
To the Sheriff of Rutherford County: Whereas Oliver Johnston recovered against Evans Moore $16.01 for his costs about his defense ... Execution remains and whereas John Cummins was prosecution bail for Evans Moore ... penalty of $200 ... John Cummins has departed this life and goods, chattels, rights and credits committed to Elizabeth Cummins, James Cummins & John Hoover, make known to them that they be before our Court ... At which day comes Oliver Johnston by his attorney, John Dickinson and the Sheriff of Rutherford returns that he had notified the said Elizabeth, James & John but they came not but made default; considered by the Court that Oliver may recover against Elizabeth, James & John for $16.01 and costs. [pp318/319]

Willie Barrow
    vs   [Covenant]
William Pace

William Pace to answer Willie Barrow on plea of covenant broken to his damage of $500.00. Now come the parties and mutually agree to submit all matters in controversy between them to the determination of Thomas Rutherford & Charles Parker.
   ---do award to Barrow $25.00 and costs. 19 Nov. 1804   signed Charles Parker, Thomas Rutherford. [pp319/320]

Philip Duke & Josiah G. Duke, administrators of Richard Myrick, deceased
    vs   **[In Debt]**
William Homes
William Homes was attached to answer Philip Duke & Josiah G. Duke, administrators of the goods and chattels...of Richard Myrick, deceased, render unto them $320.00, plaintiffs by their attorney, Perry W. Humphreys ... Homes, together with C. Stump on 21 Jan. 1803, in the County of Davidson, did made their certain writing obligatory to John Duke administrator. Defendant, by Jesse Wharton his attorney, comes into court ... Cause continued until this term, at which day come the plaintiff by his attorney and confesses they intend no further to prosecute and the defendant assumes the costs. [p320/321]

The State
    vs   **[AB Appeal]**
Mathew Williams
The motion was continued until this term at which day came the attorney for the State, and also Mathew Williams by his attorney ... arguments being heard it is ordered the State recover against Williams $75.00, the fine assessed by the Jury, and that Williams pay the costs of the prosecution. [See 104} [pp321/322]

Tuesday, Nov. 20, 1804

The State

       vs   [Ind't AB Appeal]
John Coffee
On 12 Nov. 1804 an appeal from the County Court of Davidson was filed in the office of the Clerk of the Superior Court for the District of Mero - 'The Grand Jury for the State of Tennessee say that John Coffee, late of the County of Davidson and merchant at Haysborough, did on 3 June 1804, make an assault on the body of Zacklin McIntosh. Jesse Wharton Solicitor for Davidson County. The Grand Jury, by Benjamin Drake, their foreman, endorsed a 'true bill'. Defendant pleaded 'not guilty' .. jury of William Sneed, John Cockrell, Thomas Wilcox, John Deathrige, Wm Lintz, Stephen Bean, Richard Boyd, Allen Brewer, Foster Sayres,, Peter H. Bennett, Alexander Laird & Henry Guthrie who find the defendant Guilty, assign his fine to $55.00 ... defendant obtained an appeal to Superior Court. At this Term of the Superior Court, came a Jury: Thomas Williamson, William Lancaster, Theophilus Bass, James Boyd, Joseph Hopkins, Charles Hudspath, James S. Wilson, Duncan Stuart, John L. Martin, David Jones, William Griffin & Griswold Latimer who find the said John Coffee guilty of the Assault and Battery and assess the fine to $55.00 and costs. [pp322/323]

The State
   vs   [Larceny]
John H. Jones
Be it remembered that on Thursday, the 15th of November, this present Term, by the oath of twelve men, it was presented that John H. Jones, late of the County of Rutherford, Shoemaker, on 13 April 1804, at the County of Davidson twenty pair of leather shoes of the value of thirty dollars, thirty sides of upper leather for shoes of the value of eighty dollars, five dressed calf skins of the value of ten dollars, and five sides of Soal leather for shoes of the value of fifteen dollars of the goods of one Zachariah Betts. J. Whitesides

John H. Jones was led to the bar in custody of the sheriff of Davidson County... came a Jury: James Doherty, George McCormack, Peter Looney, Joseph McKain, John Maclin, William Blackamore, William Hall, Thomas Harney, Joseph Scoby, Henry Belote, William Nash & William Caldwell, who say that John H. Jones is not guilty, therefore it is considered by the court that he be acquitted and discharged. [pp323/324]

William Simpson [In Error of a Judgment rendered by the Justices of the County Court for the County of Davidson at July Sessions 1804]   vs   Edley Ewing
Whereas in the record and proce4ss and also in rendering Judgment in a certain action of debt between Edley Ewing plaintiff and William Simpson defendant, whereby it was considered by the said Court that Ewing recover against said Simpson ...plaintiff represented by Nathaniel A. McNairy his attorney - defendant represented by Thomas J. Overton April Sessions 1804/ defendant represented by Perry W. Humphreys July Sessions 1804. In Superior Court Edley represented by Jesse Wharton, his attorney. - plaintiff in error confesses he intends no further to prosecute his writ, therefore it is considered by the Superior Court that the Judgment of the County Court be affirmed ... defendant recover against the plaintiff $201.82 and costs. [pp324-326]

William Sample
**   vs   [In Case]**
Peter Looney
William Sample by Thomas Stuart, his attorney, filed his declaration Nov. Term 1802; whereas the plaintiff on 30 March 1802 at the county of Sumner sold and delivered a certain negro girl slave named Milly to said defendant and promised defendant that said negro girl was sound to the best of plaintiffs knowledge and defendant promised to pay $337.50 before 1 August 1802 and whereas the said Peter Looney was indebted to

said plaintiff $337.50 for a certain other negro girl slave named Milly before that time, said defendant has not paid ... The defendant by John C. Hamilton his attorney said he did not ... cause continued until this term at which time came a Jury - Thomas Williamson, William Lancaster, Joseph Hopkins, Charles Hudspeth, James S. Wilson, David Jones, Richard Puckett, William Griffin, Griswold Latimer, Duncan Stuart, John L. Martin & Theophilus Bass and jury finds for the defendant and assess damages to $70.00 besides costs, except the costs of John Dawson and William Giles, witnesses on behalf of plaintiff. [327/328]

John Parker & Alexander Rowing
  vs   **[Covenant Broken]**
John White
John Parker & Alexander Rowing filed their declaration by John C. Hamilton, their attorney, Nov. Term 1802; whereas John White on 3 Feb. 1798 in the County of Davidson, made his writing obligatory, whereas White had before that time sold to Parker & Rowing a certain tract of land lying on N side of Cumberland river, at the mouth of Buffalo run, granted to Benjamin Jones, assignee of Ezekiel Linton, said deed to be made as soon as the land paid for, to be made in two separate deeds of 320 acres each, as soon as the said John Parker and Alexander Rowing paid for the same & Parker & Rowing say that on 1 Jan. 1799, at the county aforesaid, they did fully pay and White has not made them a deed. Defendant, by Jesse Wharton, his attorney. Cause continued from term to term until now comes a Jury - James Boyd, Henry Rutherford, John Payton, Samuel Barton, Thomas Bradley, Stephan Cantrell, Ezekiel Douglas, Thomas Hickman, David Vaughn, Martin Cross, Joel Rice & Thomas Bradley, who say the defendant has broken his covenant and assess the plaintiffs damages to $135 and costs. [ppp329/330]

John Den, lessee of Lazarus Cotton

                vs   [In Ejectment]
James Dickinson
James Dickinson was attached to answer John Den, lessee of Lazarus Cotton on a charge of trespass; ejected said John Den in the County of Sumner from his farm, [640 acres, situate on north side of Cumberland river, beginning half a mile below Patons rockhouse spring ... granted by the state of North Carolina, bearing date 26 Sept. 1801 to Evan Jones, heir of Thomas Jones and from him descended to Sarah Earls, a widow, the only child and heir of said Evan Jones and her heirs and conveyed by Sarah Earls to said Lazarus Cotton by indenture bearing date 3 Feb. 1802 and unto John Den for term of ten years from 19 August 1802] whereupon John Den by his attorney Thomas Stuart ...
James Dickinson, by Jenkin Whitesides, his attorney, comes and defends ... cause continued until this term, when came the parties by their attornies, and the plaintiff confesses he intends no further to prosecute and each party assumes the payment of his own costs. [ppp331/332]

Stephen Jett
                vs   [AB Appeal]
Elisha Cheek
Be it remembered that on 18 October 1804, an appeal from the County Court of Robertson was filed in the Superior Court. Jett, on 24 Sept. 1803, obtained a writ; signed by Thomas Johnson, Clerk. Feb. Sessions 1804 Jett, by his attorney Bennet Searcy, filed a plea of Trespass, Assault and battery against Elisha Cheek. Defendant, by John C. Hamilton his attorney, 'not guilty' ... cause continued until May Term 1804 when came a jury - James Sawyers, John Krisel, William Edwards, Nicholas Conrod, Shadwick Rawls, Peter Fiser, Levi Noyes, Joseph Fry, Bazel Borin, William Briscoe, Joseph Wimberley & Joseph Robertson, who find for the defendant, from which verdict the plaintiff prays an appeal to

the Superior Court, gave bond with Bennet Searcy and Charles Miles his securities.

At this Term of the Superior Court, come the parties by their attornies and the plaintiff confesses he intends no further to prosecute and the defendant by his attorney assumes the costs. [pp332/333]

The State
     vs   **[Indictment AB]**
John Anderson
On Wed., 14 Nov., the present Term, by the oath of twelve Jurors, it was presented that John Anderson, late of the county of Smith, on 2 June1804, did make an assault upon the body of James McBride...did strike him with a stone betwixt the eyes with intent to kill and murder ...J. Whiteside, Atty Gen'l
John Anderson saith he is not guilty as charged; whereupon came a Jury - Thomas Williamson, William Lancaster, Theophilus Bass, James Boyd, Joseph Hopkins, Charles Hudspeth, James S. Wilson, Duncan Stuart, John L. Martin, David Jones, Richard Puckett and William Griffin who say that John Anderson is guilty of the assault and battery; it is ordered by the Court that John Anderson pay a fine of ten dollars, be imprisoned two calendar months, without bail, and there to remain until the fine and costs are paid. [pp333/334]

The State
     vs   **[Scire facias]**
Josiah Hallum
To the Sheriff of Wilson County - Whereas Josiah Hallum was summoned to appear at our Superior Court on the 2nd Monday of May 1804, to give evidence in our behalf against Samuel Inman who stood indicted for horse stealing, and the said Hallum, came not, it is considered that said Hallum be fined $125 ... command you to make know to said Hallum.. and now, the day first mentioned, for reasons appearing to the Court -

it is ordered that the forfiture be set aside and Hallum pay the costs. [p334/335]

Samuel Wilson
    vs   [Debt Appeal]
Samuel Hill
On 17 April 1804, an appeal from the County Court of Williamson was filed; Samuel Wilson, assignee of Edmund Barker, assignee of Thomas Masterson & Co. Nicholas Perkins Hardiman, Clerk Feb. 1803. Frederick Davis became Samuel Wilsons security, Thomas Stuart his attorney. Firm of Thomas Masterson & Co., [Masterson, Robert Stothart & George Bell, partners] Hill says he is not the person, Samuel Hill, he is known always as Samuel Sugars Hill, ... cause continued until this term when came the following Jury: Tristran Patton, Abraham Walker, William Willets, John Blackemore, Moses Robinson, Bird Nance, Isaac Nance, Bennet Philips, John Baldrige, Charles Taylor, Lewis Stephens & Bradley Gamble who say the defendant is known as Samuel Hill as well as Samuel Sugars Hill; Defendant by his attorney, John Dickinson ... cause continued until Nov. Sessions 1803 and came a Jury - John Farmer, Benjamin Jordan, Andrew Goff, Joseph B. Porter, William Stephens, John Reed, Thomas W. Stockill, Benjamin Shumate, Isaac Crow, John Edmiston, Henry Rutherford & John Spencer, who find for plaintiff his debt and costs ... defendant appealed to Superior Court ... came this term and pleas relinquested / judgment for debt & costs. [pp335-340]

Sat., Nov. 24, 1804

The following Jurors proved their attendance and received tickets:

	days	miles	ferriages
Thomas Williamson	12	20	
David Jones	13	50	2
Richard Puckett	12	35	
Theophilus Bass	13	40	
John L. Martin	13	100	2

Griswold Latimer	13	45	2
James S. Wilson	13	60	2
William Griffin	13	32	
William Lancaster	13	120	
Joseph Hopkins	12	10	
James Boyd	13	46	
Duncan Stuart	13	110	2
John McDonald	9	260	4
Charles Hudspeth	11	220	4
David Trimble, Constable	15		

[p340]

Monday, Nov. 26, 1804

John Lancaster, Admr of John Lancaster, dec'd
    vs   **[Cov't]**
Micajah Barrow
The plaintiff acknowledges satisfaction for $716.38, part of his judgment and agrees to stay the execution for the balance until the next Court [See 282] [p340]

Wed., Nov. 28, 1804
John Sevier, Governor of the State of Tennessee
    vs
James Menees, Collector & William Armstrong & Philip Parchment his Securities
On the motion of Thomas Crutcher, Treasurer for the District of Mero, it appears that James Menees, Collector of the County of Robertson for the year 1803 has failed to pay to the Treasurer $455.27 State Tax. Considered by the Court that John Sevier, Governor recover that amount plus costs against the collector and his securities. [pp340/341]

John Sevier, Governor of the State of Tennessee
    vs
Nathaniel Perry, Collector & Blake Rutland, John Bradley & Richard Anderson, his Securities
On the motion of Thomas Crutcher, Treasurer of the District of Mero, it appears that Nathaniel Perry, Collector of the County of Wilson for the

year 1803, has failed to pay to the Treasurer the sum of $379.56, the State Tax for the year aforesaid. It is considered by the Court that John Sevier, Governor, recover said sum and costs against Nathaniel Perry, Collector, & Blake Rutland, John Bradley & Richard Anderson, his securities. [p341]

The State
    vs   **[Scifa]**
Thomas Harding
To the Sheriff of Williamson County - Thomas Harding was bound by recognizance in the penalty of $500.00, for his appearance at our Superior Court for the District of Mero in May 1804, to present and give testimony on our behalf against John Garrett who stands indicted for felony and the said Thomas Harding was called and came not, it was considered that the recognizance is forfeited. We therefore command you to make known to said Thomas that he be before the Judges on the second Monday in November next, to shew cause. signed Randal McGavock, Clerk. And the said Harding appeared in Court - and in his affidavit it is ordered the forfiture be set aside and said Thomas to pay costs. [ppp341/342]

Godfrey Carriger
    vs   **[Debt Appeal]**
John Maclin
On Nov. 12, 1804 an appeal was filed from the County Court of Davidson, in the office of the clerk of the Superior Court in the case of Godfrey Carriger vs John Maclin on a charge of debt of $112.17. For the prosecuting of which writ, Robert Searcy became the plaintiffs security and writ was returned to July Sessions 1803 by John Boyd. Plaintiff represented by Bennet Searcy and says that on 2 Oct. 1802 in the County of Davidson, the said Maclin made his certain writing obligatory; whereupon Maclin acknowledged himself indebted and promised to pay within four months ... defendant has not paid. Defendant represented by Jesse Wharton,

says he has paid ... came a Jury: Jonas Maniffee, John McConnell, David Allen, David P. Monroe, James McCuiston, David McGavock, William Smith, John May, John Harman, William Rains, John Glass, & Stephen Bean - find for the plaintiff - whereupon the defendant filed his reasons of appeal.

And now come the parties by their attornies and the appeal in his cause not having been filed within the time prescribed, on motion of the plaintiff by his attorney, it is considered that the judgment of the County Court be affirmed with twelve and one half per cent interest thereon against the defendant and Moses Eakin and R. Henry Dyar, his securities and that plaintiff recover his costs. [pp342/344]

Benton Harris
    vs   **[Debt Appeal]**
William Smith

On 2 May 1804 an appeal from the County Court of Davidson was filed with the Clerk of the Superior Court for the District of Mero.

transcript - William Smith to answer charges of Benton Harris, assignee of Joseph Erwin of a debt of $96.00, writ issued 8 June 1803, signed Andrew Ewing. Edley Ewing became the plaintiffs security; sheriff made return to July Sessions; plaintiff represented by Thomas Stuart, stated that Smith promised to pay a certain Joseph Erwin or order the sum of $96.00; it being for the hire of a negro man named Josh, which commenced on 1 Jan. and to be ended on the last day of December. Joseph Erwin assigned the note to Benton Harris and notified William Smith; defendant although often required hath not paid. Cause continued and then found for plaintiff, whereupon defendant filed appeal with Superior Court - and now comes the plaintiff by Thos Stuart and Defendant by Parry W. Humphrey and this appeal not having been brought within the time prescribed by law, it is considered that the decision of the County Court be confirmed and that Benton Harris recover against the said

William Smith and Martin Smith and Thomas Sappington, his securities. [ppp344-346]

The State
          vs   **[Scifa]**
Golfin Minor
To the Sheriff of Sumner County - Golfin Minor was bound by recognizance in the penalty of $100.00 for his personal appearance at our Superior Court, at the Courthouse in Nashville on the second Monday of November 1803 to prosecute on our behalf against John Reid alias Shaw who stood committed for felony and Golfin was called and came not, therefore it was considered by the Court that the recognizance be forfeited ... therefore we command you to make known to said Minor that he be before the Judges of the next Court ...signed Randal McGavock, Nov. 1803. Sheriff made return that Golfin Minor is not in his county. Nov. 1804 comes J. Whiteside, attorney for the state and the sheriff as aforesaid returns that said Golfin Minor is not found within his county - and the said Minor was called and came not therefore on motion of the attorney the state it is considered the state may have execution for $100.00 and costs. [pp346/347]

The State
          vs   **[Scifa]**
Robert Caruthers
To the Sheriff of Sumner County - Whereas Robert Caruthers was summoned to attend the Superior Court in May 1804 as a Juror and having been called, came not, whereupon a conditional judgment was made against him ... execution still remains to be made. You are commanded to make known to said Caruthers that he be before the Judges at the next Session of our Superior Court. On this day comes J. Whitesides, atty for the State and the sheriff of Sumner County returns that he has notified Robert Caruthers - and the said Robert, alto called, came not but made default. It is considered that the state

have execution against the said Robert for twenty five dollars, the penalty prescribed by law, and the costs. [See 370] [pp347/348]

The State
    vs   **[Scifa]**
Daniel Perkins
To the Sheriff of Williamson County - Daniel Perkins was bound by recognizance in the penalty of $250.00 for the personal appearance of Thomas Harding at a Superior Court held May 1804 to prosecute and give testimony on our behalf against John Garrett, who stands indicted for felony, and the said Daniel Perkins having been called to bring into court the body of the said Thomas Harding came not. It was therefore considered that the recognizance was forfeited. We therefore command you to make known to said Perkins that he be before the Judges on 2nd Monday of November next. On which writ S. Childress, Sheriff of Williamson returns that he had made the same known to Daniel Perkins. And now, it appearing to the Court for reasons, the forfiture shall be set aside and Perkins pay the costs of the Scifa. [p348]

James McElyea
    vs   **[Petition for Divorce]**
Elizabeth McElyea
On 19 Nov. 1800 James McElyea exhibited his petition to the Judges of the Superior Court for the State of Tennessee: "on 9 July 1797 by mutual consent separated from his wife Elizabeth; cause of separation was petitioner having caught a certain Peter Spence in bed with the said Elizabeth and said Peter having admitted having carnal knowledge with the said Elizabeth and after the separation the said Elizabeth took up with a certain William Prince and since that time to the present has lived as man and wife, petitioner has not had any communication as a husband with Elizabeth from the time of the date of the bond; petitioner states Elizabeth has removed herself from here

and lives in Powels Valley in the State of Virginia with the aforesaid William Prince. Petitioner prays your honour to grant to him a bill of divorce ...

   This day personally appeared in open court James McElyea and made oath that the facts contained in the within petition are true. 19 Nov. 1800

   Elizabeth commanded to appear and answer said petition on 2nd Monday in May 1801, on which day came the petitioner by S. Donelson, his attorney, and no return being made an alias spa was awarded and on Nov. 1801 comes petitioner by his attorney and the sheriff returns that the said Elizabeth is not found ... repeated May 1802 and continued from Term to Term and the said petitioner not further prosecuting his petition the same is discontinued and petitioner to pay the costs of the petition. [pp349/350]

Brice Blair
    vs   [Scifa]
John Rawlings & Peter McNamee [bail for Adam Moore]

   To the Sheriff of Washington County - Whereas Brice Blair late in our Superior Court for the District of Mero recovered against Adam Moore four dollars and thirty five cents for his costs ... execution still remains to be made. John Rawlings and Peter McNamee were bail ...
Nov 1803 comes Brice Blair by Jesse Wharton his attorney and the Sheriff of Washington County returns that the said John Rawlings & Peter McNamee are not found in his county and though called came not - considered the plaintiff to recover against them his costs and costs of the Scifa. [p351]

Henry Rutherford
    vs   [Scifa]
Joseph Johnston, bail for Isaac Johnson

   To the Sheriff of Davidson County - Whereas Henry Rutherford late in our Superior Court,

District of Mero, recovered against Isaac Johnston twenty five dollars, eighty eight and one half cents for his costs ...payment remains to be made.   Sheriff   reports that Joseph Johnston was not found in his county ... Ruled by the Court that the plaintiff recover against the said defendant his costs and costs of Scifa. [p352]

James Bowers & Isaac Dorris
         vs
Joseph Anthony & Israel Anderson,
bail for David Enocks & wife
To the Sheriff of Robertson County - Whereas James Bowers and Isaac Dorris recovered against David Enochs and Sarah his wife, Executors of Benjamin Enochs deceased, seven dollars and eighty cents for their costs ...execution still remains to be made . Bowers and Dorris represented by Jesse Wharton, their attorney. Sheriff of Robertson County said Joseph Anthony and Israel Anderson are not found in his county. Judged by the Court that plaintiffs may have execution against defendants for seven dollars and eighty cents and their costs.[p353]

Alexander Moore
       vs   **[Scifa]**
George Smith, bail for Samuel Barton
To the Sheriff of Sumner County - Whereas Alexander Moore recovered against Samuel Barton thirty dollars & ninety two and one half cents for his costs - still remains to be paid. Moore represented by Jenkin Whiteside, his attorney. Sheriff of Sumner County returns that he had notified the said George Smith and said George was solemnly called but came not. Court ruled that Alexander may have execution for $30.92 and his costs. [p354]

Joseph Barnes
       vs   **[Scifa]**
Harrison Boyd, bail for John Boyd, Senr

To the Sheriff of Williamson County - Whereas Joseph Barnes recovered against John Boyd, Senr, $6.29 for his costs and still remains to be made ... came Joseph Barnes by Thomas Stuart, his attorney and Sheriff of Williamson County returned that he had notified Harrison Boyd and Boyd called but came not - Court rules that Barnes may have execution against Boyd for $6.29 and costs of the Scifa.[pp354/355]

David Havert
    vs   [Scifa]
Hugh Henry & David Hoouser, bail for George Briscoe
To the Sheriff of Robertson County - Whereas David Havert recovered against George Briscoe $20.81 for costs ...$6.95 remain to be paid ... May 1804 comes David Havert by Thomas Stuart, his attorney and the Sheriff of Robertson reports he has notified Henry & Hoouser and the same day they were called and came not. Court ruled they should pay $6.95 and the costs of the Scifa. [pp355/356]

Thomas Dillon
    vs   [Scifa]
Stockly Donelson
To the Sheriff of Davidson County - Whereas Thomas Dillon recovered a judgment against Stockly Donelson for $13,493.38 with legal interest from the date of judgment against Donelson in the District Court of the United States in the State of Virginia, 5 June 1799, and also $10.90 costs ... make known to said Donelson that he appear in our Court Nov. next and shew cause ...
Nov. 1804 comes Thomas Dillon, by his attorney, J. Wharton, Donelson having acknowledged the service of the Scire facias, and alto called, came not but made default. Considered by the Court that the plaintiff may have execution against Donelson for $13,493.38 with legal interest from 5 June 1799 and $10.90, and also the plaintiff recover his costs. [pp356/357]

State of Tennessee: Mero District

At a Superior Court of Law, held for the District aforesaid, at the Courthouse in Nashville on the second Monday, being the thirteenth day of May in the year 1805, and of the independence of the United States the twenty ninth -

Present, the Hon. David Campbell, Hugh L. White, John Overton

The following persons were elected and Sworn a **Grand Jury of Inquest** for the body of this District: Henry Tooley, foreman, Nimrod Manifee, Yancy Thornton, John R. Bedford, James Blackwell, George Stubblefield, John Edmiston, John Neville, Samuel Weakley, David Frazier, John Brown, William Wootton, William Johnston, John B. Crisp, .and Alexander McCrabb. [p357]

The State
    vs   [Scifa]
John McKinney an absent Juror
To the Sheriff of Williamson County - Whereas John McKinney was summoned to attend a Superior Court, held for the District of Mero, the 2nd Monday in November 1804, as a Juror and having being called, came not, whereupon it was considered he be fined twenty five dollars and costs, you are therefore commanded to make known to him he be before the Judges on the 2nd Monday in May next... On which writ, S. Childress, sheriff of Williamson county made return that he had made the same known to the said McKinney on 9 Feb. 1805.

And now comes the defendant and on his affidavit it is ordered that the forfeiture be set aside and defendant pay the costs of the Scifa. [pp357/358]

John Den, lessee of Thomas Hickman
    vs   [In Eject Appeal]
Absolom Hooper

On 11 October 1802 an appeal from the County Court of Davidson was filed ...
Whereas Thomas Hickman on 16 Jan. 1801, had demised and let a farm to John Den for 10 years, 2560 acres of land lying in the County of Davidson on the waters of Whites Creek and on the north side of Cumberland River. Beg. at the NE corner of David Shannons preemption ..N boundary of Joseph Kencaids tract, N boundary of Phillip Walkers tract, ...Daniel Johnstons S boundary ... John Marshalls line, John Mears line, crossing the Creek, it being a tract originally granted by North Carolina to Martin Armstrong & Anthony Crutcher by Patent No. 1255 bearing date Dec. 10, 1790. Thomas Stuart, attorney for the plaintiff.

Notice to Absalom Hooper - I am informed you are in possession of a claim title to the premises mention in this declaration .. On which notice Joseph Johnston, Sheriff of Davidson County made report to April Sessions 1801 that he had delivered a copy to Absolom Hooper on 5 March 1801 to which session Absalom Hooper appeared and by Howel Tatum, his attorney, moved he be made defendant ... plead not guilty ... cause argued and by the consent and choice of the parties, the court then appointed Thomas Harney to survey, make and return to the county court ...continued until July Sessions 1802 when came into court a Jury: Samuel Weakley, Matthew Talbott, Anderson Tate, David Dobbins, James Cummins, Thomas Wilson, Geo. Blackamore, William Pettiweay, William Caldwell, Andrew Cassellman, John Cassellman and Owen Edwards who say they find the defendant not guilty, determined by the Court that the defendant do recover against the plaintiff his costs ...plaintiff obtained an appeal to the Superior Court for the District of Mero ... cause continued from term to term until this term and Thomas Hickman confesses that he intends no further to prosecute and it is considered by the Court that the defendant recover against the lessor of the plaintiff his costs. [pp358-361]

Tuesday, May 14, 1805

Edward Douglass
    vs   [In Covenant]
Stockly Donelson
And the enquiry of the damages aforesaid was continued from term to term until this term, to wit, May 11804, at which time came the plaintiff by his attorney and on motion it is ordered that the judgment by default had in this cause be set aside - and this day, Nov. Term 1804, comes the plaintiff by his attorney and the defendant not appearing tho called, it is ordered by the court that the plaintiff recover against the defendant his damages sustained by reason of the non performance of the covenant, to be enquired of at next court. At which court comes the plaintiff by his attorney and a Jury: William Lyons, David Childress, William Tait, Edmund Owens, Thomas Lofton, William Wilson, Isaac Phillips, Thomas Edmiston, Robert McNairy, Abner Henly, James Lauderdale & William Lane, who say the plaintiff has sustained damages of $600.00 besides his costs. [See Book A, page 341] [p361]

Nathaniel Floyd & Israel Tully
    vs   [In Covenant]
Thomas Hickman
May Term 1801 the service of a writ of capias at the suit of Nathaniel Floyd against Thomas Hickman of a plea of covenant broken was acknowledged by Thomas Hickman in open court and the cause was continued to May 1802, at which time the plaintiffs by their attorney J. Whiteside, filed their Declaration: ... whereas Thomas Hickman oif Davidson County, North Carolina, on 24 September 1790 covenanted and obligated himself as follows - Thomas had two judgments obtained in Davidson county, one James Cole Montflorence against Thomas Smith for one hundred and seven pounds North Carolina currency of which Smith had paid twenty eight pounds, sixteen shillings, the other Samuel Martin

against Thomas Smith for eight pounds, twelve shillings, North Carolina currency, Thomas Hickman had sold the balance to the above named plaintiffs and obligated himself to be answerable to said plaintiffs if they should fail to recover the sum of money from Thomas Smith ... said plaintiffs have altogether failed to recover the said money ... signed J. Whiteside.

Defendant, by his attorney said that Thomas Smith paid said money on 1 January 1792 ... issue was continued from term to term until this term, at which time came the parties by their attornies and a Jury; Simpson Harris, Robert Searcy, Joel Holland, William Billings, James Dupree, Ezekiel Douglas, John L. Martin, Archibald Donahoe, Thomas Kieff, Thomas Harding, William Snoddy and James Winchester and find for the defendant and the defendant may recover against the plaintiffs his costs, [pp362-365]

Patrick Lyons
  vs   **[In Covenant]**
Bennet Searcy

Patrick Lyons, by John Dickinson his attorney, filed his Declaration May Term 1803, complains of Bennet Searcy of a plea of Covenants broken ... whereas on 12 March 1802, in the county of Davidson, Searcy did make his writing obligatory...Bennet was indebted to said Patrick in the sum of $252.00 to be discharged upon the following conditions - Patrick was to view sundry tracts of land held by Searcy and after viewing Patrick was to notify Bennet which of said tracts of land he would take in discharge of the debt ... to be viewed afterward by a man chosen by each ... Patrick chose 274 acres of land at the mouth of Johnson's creek below Harpeth about four miles ... Bennet Searcy chose Richard C. Napier and Patrick Lyons chose John Parks to value said tract ... whereas said Napier & Parks did value the land at fifty cents per acre ... Nevertheless said Bennet has not made a deed of conveyance altho often requested.

Bennet by Jinken Whiteside, his attorney, says he has not broken his contract ... that in July 1802 he did appoint a certain Sterling Brewer on his part and Patrick chose a certain Weakley and that said Sterling and Weakley did not agree on the value of the land ... and the cause was continued from Term to Term until Nov. 1804 at which day came the parties by their attornies and a Jury - Griswold Latimer, Joel Rice, Henry Rutherford, John Johnston, Gray Washington, William Betts, James McCuesten, Samuel Crockett, William Simpson, David Beaty, Zenus Baldin & John Holt who say the defendant hath broken his covenant and assess the plaintiffs damages to $277.35 besides his costs And on the motion of the defendant by his attorney, and for reasons appearing to the court it is ordered that the verdick be set aside and that a new trial be held at the next court. At which court came the parties by their attornies and a Jury - Edmond Owens, William Wilson, Isaac Phillips, Thomas Edmiston, Robert McNairy, Abner Henley, James Lauderdale, David Childress, Thomas Lofton, Sherwood Green, William Axum & James Cannon who say the defendant had not broken his covenant and further say defendant did not choose said Napier on his part ...defendant may depart and recover against the plaintiff his costs. [pp365-369]

The State
    vs   **[Scifa]**
John Burgan, a Juror
To the Sheriff of Dickson County - Whereas John Burgan was summoned to attend a Superior Court for the District of Mero at the Courthouse in Nashville on the 2nd Monday in November 1804 as a Juror, and having been called, came not... a conditional judgment against him for a fine of twenty five dollars and costs ... On which writ, R. Weakley, sheriff of Dickson county returns 'made known to John Burgan on 4 May 1805. And now comes the said John Burgan, and on his

affidavit it is ordered that the forfiture be set aside and he pay the costs. [p370]

On the affidavit of Robert Caruthers, it is ordered that the fine entered against him at the last court for nonattendance as a Juror be remitted. [See 347] [p370]

Wednesday, May 15th 1805

Andrew Ewing, James Mulherrin & John Overton
  Executors of Thomas Molloy, deceased
        vs   [Plea of Trespass]
William Betts
Whereupon the plaintiffs by their attorneys, John Dickenson & John Overton, filed their declaration May 1803. Whereas on 7 July 1796, in the county of Davidson, the said William made a note and did acknowledge himself to be indebted to the said Thomas in the sum of eighty dollars ...later indebted for one hundred dollars for certain work and labour done ... money has not been paid before his death nor to the said Andrew, James & John as executors. Defendant, by Jesse Wharton & Thomas Stuart, his attornies, puts himself upon the county ... and the cause was continued from term to term until this term and comes a Jury - David Childress, Isaac Phillips, James Cannon, James Lauderdale, John Buchanan, John Anderson, William Lane, Joel Holland, Simpson Harris, John L. Martin, Robert Prince & Alexander Patton, and the plaintiffs not further prosecuting their action, the Jury aforesaid are discharged, and on motion of the Defendant it is considered by the Court that the plaintiffs be not suited and defendant pay his costs. [pp370-373]

Andrew Ewing, James Mulherren & Overton
  Executors of Thomas Molloy
        vs   [In Debt]
William Betts

Andrew Ewing, James Mulherren & John Overton, Executors of Thomas Molloy, deceased, complain by attorney, plea that he render to them three hundred and twenty dollars ...on 7 July 1796 at the county of Davidson the said William made his certain writing obligatory to pay Thomas Molloy $320.00 as soon as a certain Elisha Rice should make a title to 640 acres on the first bluff south side Cumberland river below Harpeth river ...Dickinson & Overton for plaintiffs.

And the defendant, by Jesse Wharton & Thomas Stuart, puts himself upon the county. Now comes a Jury: David Childress, Isaac Phillips, James Cannon, James Lauderdale, John Buchanan, John Anderson, William Lane, Joel Holland, Simpson Harris, John L. Martin, Robert Prince & Alexander Patton. Jury find for the plaintiff the debt of $320 and assess their damages of $148.80. [pp373-377]

John Den, lessee of Ezekiel Douglass
    vs   [In Ejectment]
Zenus Baldwin & Thomas Harrison

John Den, lessee of Ezekiel Douglass, by Thomas Stuart his attorney, filed his declaration Nov. Term 1802 - complains of Zenus Baldwin & Thomas Harrison on a plea of trespass. Whereas Ezekiel Douglas on 1 October 1802 in the county of Davidson granted and let to John Den one tenement and 640 acres, being in the county of Davidson on the south side of Cumberland, and on the north side of Big Harpeth river about one mile and a half below the mouth of Turners creek on a buffalo road that leads to Fletchers lick...being a track of land granted by the state of North Carolina to said Ezekiel Douglass by patent dated the 27th of November 1793, No. 451., to the said John Den from 30 September 1802 for ten years.

Defendants, by Jenkin Whiteside, their attorney, say they are not guilty and put themselves on the county. The cause was continued until this Term when came the parties by their attornies and a Jury - David Childress, Isaac Phillips,

James Cannon, James Lauderdale, John Buchanan, John Anderson, William Lane, Joel Holland, Simpson Harris, Thomas Edmiston, Robert Prince & Alexander Patton who say the defendants are not guilty, therefore it is considered by the court that the defendants may depart and recover their costs against the plaintiff. [377-378]

The Grand Jury returned into Court and presented an indictment against Thomas Massingale, blacksmith, late of the county of Stuart, and District of Mero, for horse stealing "a true bill"
  Also an indictment against James Massingale, laborer, late of the county of Stuart, and District of Mero for horse stealing, "a true bill." [See book C, page 56] [p378]

Benjamin Joslin
        vs   [In Case]
Christopher Oxberry
And now comes the plaintiff into court and confesses that he intends no further action. It is considered by the Court that the defendant may depart and recover against the plaintiff his costs. [p379]

Edmund Jennings
        vs   [In Covenant]
Joel Dyer
Joel Dyer was attached to answer Edmund Jennings of a plea of covenant broken, damages five hundred dollars. And now comes the plaintiff by Jesse Wharton, his attorney, and confesses that he intends no further to prosecute. It is considered by the Court that the said defendant may depart and recover against the plaintiff his costs. [p379]

Thursday, May 16, 1805

David McGavock
        vs   [Trespass G.C.F.]

Christopher Stump

Christopher Stump was attached to answer David McGavock of a plea of tgrespass, damage five hundred dollars. Whereupon the said David by Jenkin Whiteside, his attorney, filed his declaration ... Christopher Stump on the 20th day of December 1803 did trespass 'with his feet in walking and his horses in riding' over the said grass and the fence of him the said David, twenty pannel of fence of the value of forty dollars, threw down and prostrated and the rails of his said fence, to wit, two hundred rails of the value of ten dollars...place near Nashville, in the county of Davidson. Christopher, by Thomas Stuart his attorney, saith he is not guilty. This cause was continued until this term and the plaintiff confesses that he intends no further to prosecute - and the said defendant assumes the costs of suit. [379-380]

Thomas H. Perkins
vs   [In Case]
Owen Stratton

Owen Stratton was attached to answer Thomas H. Perkins of a plea of trespass on the case, damage five hundred dollars. Thomas by John Dickinson his attorney, filed his declaration November Term 1803; whereas on the fourth day of January 1801, at Nashville in the county of Davidson ... that he the said Owen should hire and rent of the said Thomas a plantation of him the said Thomas lying ... he the said Owen would work upon the said plantation as a laborer and oversee the slaves to be placed on the said plantation and that he the said Thomas should provide and furnish two negro men slaves to work on said plantation as laborers under the management .....but the said Owen refused the two negro men slaves ... hath not delivered to Thomas the two thirds of the produce raised on said plantation amounting to 900 bushels of Indian corn, 200 bushels of rye, 120 bushels of wheat, four tons of hay and 200 bushels of oats.

Defendant by Thomas Stuart, his attorney ... cause continued from term to term until this term and agree to mutually submit all matters to the determination of Henry Tooly and Henry Childress and the arbitrators find a balance of three hundred and twenty nine dollars and four cents, this 16 May 1805. Considered by the Court that the plaintiff recover against the said defendant $329.04 and his costs.[pp381-384]

John Garret
    vs   [In Case]
Thomas Harding
The defendant on this cause being dead, on the motion of the plaintiff by his attorney it is ordered that a Scire Facias be issued against the representatives of the said Thomas Harding returnable to the next court. [p384]

Elmore Douglass
    vs   [I n Covenant]
John Payton
Elmore Douglas, by Robert Whyte his attorney, filed his declaration May Term 1804. Douglas complains of John Payton of a plea of covenant broken; whereas John on the fifth day of April 1798, at Sumner County, by his certain writing vovenanted and agreed that he would make a deed for 640 acres of land lying on Dicksons Creek where Thomas Lacy now lives, and it was further covenanted by said John that he the said John should make to the said Elmore right as agent for Ephraim Payton. The defendant, by his attorney Thomas Stuart says he is not guilty and the cause was continued from term to term until this term and the plaintiff says he intends no further to prosecute. [pp384-386]

Thursday, May 16, 1805

Joseph Williams
    vs   [In Debt]

Yancy Thornton

Yancy Thornton was was summoned to answer Joseph Williams for a debt of $282.25 and damage of $100.00. Joseph, by Thomas Stuart his attorney, filed his declaration November Term 1804; Yancy Thornton is in custody of the Sheriff of Stuart County for a plea of debt ... Yancy Thornton by his writing obligatory made at Smith County on 30 November 1802. Defendant, by Nathaniel A. McNairy his attorney, and defends ... and now comes the plaintiff and confesses that he intends no further to prosecute his actions, therefore it is considered the defendant may depart and recover against the plaintiff his costs. [pp386/387]

Thomas H. Perkins
vs   [In Covenant]
John Turner

John Turner was attached to answer Thomas Harden Perkins in a plea of covenant broken, whereas on 11 November 1802 at Nashville he signed this article of agreement to sell to the said John 523 acres of land, lying on the west fork of Payton's creek, adjoining the tract whereon Michael Murphy then lived at the price of two dollars per acre and agreed to pay to the said Thomas $500 as soon as he made to him, the said John, a good title, and also to pay him the said Thomas Harden two young breeding mares, not to exceed the value of eighty dollars each; also to pay the balance within 12 months... says further that on 26 April 1804, he executed a deed of conveyance and that the said John has not paid to him the $500 or the two young breeding mares ... Dickinson, attorney for plaintiff, Jesse Wharton, attorney for defendant. The cause was continued until this Term, at which day came the parties and the plaintiff confesses that he intends no further to prosecute his action and the defendant, by Jesse Wharton, assumes payment of the costs. [pp387-389]

Brooking Burnett & Reuben Burnett

vs   [In Case]
Peter LeGrand
Peter LeGrand was attached to answer Brooking Burnett & Reuben Burnett on a plea of trespass. ... and now to wit, come the plaintiffs into Court and say they intend no further to prosecute their said action and the defendant assumes the payment of the costs. [p389]

James B. Reynolds, gentleman, took the oath to suppert the consitution of the United States, of the State of Tennessee and the oath of an attorney at Law, he is therefore admitted to practice as an attorney in this court. [p389]

Friday, May 17, 1805

The **Grand Jury** return into court and presented an indictment against Jonathan Stump, late of the county of Davidson, yeoman, for felony "a true bill" and again withdrew to consider of further presentiments. [p389]

Saturday, May 18, 1805

William Gunn
    vs   [In Covenant]
James McCuston
Be it remembered that in May 1803 a writ of certiorari issued from the Superior Court for the District of Mero, directed to the Justices of the Court of Pleas and Quarter Sessions for the county of Davidson commanding the Justices to send and certify the record and proceedings in a certain action between William Gunn and James McCueston ... which action was filed in the said Superior court on 11 October 1803. Writ issued to April Sessions 1802 and signed Edley Ewing, D.S. '...at which sessions plaintiff appeared in prosecution of his suit by Jesse Wharton his attorney .. William Gunn complains of James McCuistin if a plea of covenant broken... says that on 2 July 1801 at

Nashville, by his certain writing obligatory agreed to deliver before 1 December next $150.00 worth of good cotton for value received. ... James has not performed as requested.. At April Sessions the defendant appeared by Joseph Hindon, his attorney. Cause continued Term to Term until April Sessions 1803 when came the plaintiff by his attorney aforesaid and the defendant by John Dickinson, his attorney in the place of Joseph Hindon, his former attorney. Came a Jury - John Costillo, Obediah Davis, John Harman, Drury Alsop, Bennet Blackman, Micajah Barrow, William Douglass, Nicholas Raymond, Frederick Stump, George Burnet, Lewis Perkins and Jacob Reader who find in favour of the plaintiff and assess his damages to $162.37 and also the costs of suit.... Andrew Ewing

And the cause was continued in the Superior Court until this term, May 1804, at which day came the parties by their attornies and a Jury: Joseph Collins, Beal Bosley, Micajah Woodward, Wilson Gibson, Cary Felts, Andrew Grier, John Stump, Thomas Mitchel, Benjamin Totton, Aaron Rawlings, William Farr and Arthor Hogan who find for the plaintiff ... the defendant hath not performed the covenant ... assess the plaintiffs damages to $181.12 and costs. Whereupon, on the motion of the defendants attorney, and for reasons appearing to the Court, rule the verdict be set aside and that a new trial granted ... at which Court - to wit, November Term 1804 come the parties by their attornies and a Jury - William Lyons, David Childress, William Tait, William Axum, Edmond Owens, Thomas Lofton, William Neeley, Isaac Phillips, Henry Hide, Thomas Edmiston, Robert McNairy, and Sherwood Green who find for the plaintiff and assess his damages to $134.02 and costs. [pp390-393]

John Den lessee of Sampson Williams
    vs   **[In Ejectment]**
Richard Fen, Job Carter & Daniel Fox
Richard Fen of the county of Jackson was attached to answer John Den of a plea of

trespass ... he entered into a tract of land being in the county of Jackson on the south side of Cumberland River, containing six thousand acres, Beg. at some sycamore trees and a beech tree marked I.D.I.S. and other letters standing on the bank of Cumberland River where the line lately called the Virginia line ... thence running East on said State line, then running at right angles - and running South .... which said tract of land with the appurtenances Sampson Williams demised to the said John Den for a term which is not yet expired and ejected him ... The said John Den by John Dickinson his attorney ...
And the cause was continue until this term at which day comes the plaintiff by his attorney and it appearing to the court on affidavit that copies of the declaration in Ejectment and notice thereto annexed were read and delivered to Job Carter and Daniel Fox - a writ of possession is awarded to the plaintiff returnable here at the next court. [pp393-395]

Saturday, May 18, 1805

Jaramah Claypole
    Vs   **[Covenant Appeal]**
John Boyce
On 11 October 1803 an appeal from the County Court of Sumner County was filed in the office of the clerk of the Superior Court in the following words: 'Pleas before the Court of Pleas and Quarter Sessions of the County of Sumner at the town of Gallatin ...1st Monday of July 1803 ... To the sheriff of Sumner - have John Boyce before the Justices of said County on 1st Monday in January next to answer Jaramah Claypole on a plea of covenant broken. D. Shelby, Clerk. 24 Dec. 1802 Sheriff made return 'not to be found in this county. Thos. Maston, DS Writ again issued in January of 1803. Plaintiff by his attorney, John C. Hamilton ... complains of John Boyce, to wit, on 4 August 1795 in the county of Sumner made and entered

into a certain writing obligatory… covenanted with the plaintiff to pay or cause to be paid unto Jeramah Claypole forty eight pounds, twelve shillings, equal to one hundred and sixty two dollars, and has not paid.

Defendant, by Samuel Donelson & Thomas Stuart, his attornies, pleaded "covenant performed" and a Jury was called: James S. Wilson, William Beard, Matthew Cartwright, Richard King, John Weathered, Mark Richmond, Reuben Douglass, Thomas Barrett, John Woods, Daniel Trigg, John Mitchell and Hardy Bloodworth, who find for the plaintiff and assess his damages at two hundred and thirty six dollars and fifty two cents plus costs. Whereupon the defendant by Thomas Stuart prayed an appeal to the Superior Court and filed reasons, entered into bond .. know that we John Boyce, William Moore and Henry Lyon are held and firmly bound unto Jeremiah Claypole.. 8 July 1803

And the cause was continued from term to term until this Term, when came the parties by their attornies and a Jury: William Snoddy, Abner Henley, Robert Searcy, James Cannon, James Lauderdale, William Lane, Joel Holland, Gideon Pillow, William Gunn, James McCuiston, Samuel Hanness, Edward Jennings who say the defendant hath not performed his covenant and asses damages by occasion of the nonperformance to $23.58 & costs. [pp395-397]

William T. Lewis
    Vs   [Scifa Appeal]
Anne Hay, administratix of David Hay, dec'd
Be it remembered that on 11 October 1803 an appeal from the county court of Davidson was filed I with the clerk of the Superior Court of the District of Mero: Whereas William Terrell Lewis in our Court of Pleas & Quarter Sessions for the county of Davidson, July Sessions 1798 obtained judgment against David Hay for the sum of twenty eight pounds, thirteen shillings and eight pence and costs … sundry writs of scifa filed …April 1800 Joseph Johnston made return

that the costs endorced and satisfied ... and whereas sometime after judgment was obtained the said David Hay departed this life leaving this Judgment unsatisfied ... January Sessions 1801 On application made to the Court Letters of Administration was granted to Anne Hay on the Estate of the said David Hay, dec'd. signed Andrew Ewing, Clerk January 1802 March 1, 1802 Scifa issued to Anne Hay, signed Edley Ewing, D.S. April last the plaintiff appeared by his attorney Thomas Stuart, also the defendant by Bennet Searcy, her attorney and the cause continued until July term 1803 and for plea saith that since the last continuance she has settled with the court her administration and saith that she has fully administered and of the goods and chattels which were of the aforesaid David Hays at the time of his death, all that remain in her hands are one dollar and sixty six cents.

Thomas Stuart for the plaintiff and the defendant by Bennet Searcy, her attorney. And came a Jury - Thomas James, James McCuiston, William Scott, Samuel Weakley, William S. Mullen, Samuel Kerr, James Hamilton, Samuel Blair, William Hall, William Thomas, William Perkins, and Alexander Walker who find for the plaintiff according to the prayer of the scifa with a credit thereon of twenty seven dollars and eighty five cents and also find that the defendant has fully administred as stated in her plea. Therefore it is considered by the court that the plaintiff do recover of the defendant the sum of one dollar and sixty six cents. From which judgment the plaintiff obtained an appeal to the Superior Court having given bond with Joel Lewis & Thomas Crutcher his securities. Andrew Ewing

And the cause was continued from term to term until this term when came the parties by their attornies and Jury - William Snoddy, Abner Henley, James Cannon, James Lauderdale, William Lane, Joel Holland, Gideon Pillow, William Gunn, James McCuiston, Samuel Hannes, Edmund Jennings and Simpson Harris who say the defendant did not fully administer the goods and chattels of the said David Hay … judgment against Anne Hay for $71.70 & costs. [pp398-400]

Richard Smith, lessee of William P. Anderson
    Vs   [In Eject Appeal]
Amos Moore

On 13 April 1804 an appeal from the County Court of Rutherford was filed in the office of the Superior Court for the District of Mero - Be it remembered that on 25 June 1804 the following writ was issued out of the office of the Clerk of the Court of Rutherford county - To the sheriff of Rutherford county 'you are hereby commanded to take the body of Amos Moore if to be found in your county and have his body before the Justices of our court of Rutherford at Jefferson on the first Monday in July next to answer Richard Smith, lessee of William P. Anderson . Joseph Herndon, Clerk Issued 25 June 1804 answered - 'came to hand the same day it issued and executed', Sam'l McBride sheriff

  Richard Smith, by his attorney, complains of William Stiles of a plea of trespass and ejectment. … whereas William P Anderson on 2 March in the year aforesaid demised to the said Richard one cottage and six hundred and forty acres of land situate on the East fork of Stones river about four miles above the mouth, granted to John Reed by the state of North Carolina by Patent #943, bearing date 18 May 1789, for the term of twelve years which is not yet expired. July session 1804 the said Amos Moore appeared and entered himself defendant in this action and pleaded not guilty …action continued from Session to Session until April 1805 and the parties then appeared by their attorneys and a Jury - James Doherty, Robert Hanna, Travis? C. Nash, Grifford Cathey, Henry Davis, William McKnight, Lewis Banton, Hiram Jenkins, Samuel Oliphent, Cader Dement, James Hamilton and Joseph Thompson, who find the defendant guilty and assess the plaintiffs damage to one cent and costs. Said defendant obtained an appeal to the Superior Court and gave bond with Josiah Payne his security.

I Joseph Herndon Clerk of the Court of Pleas and Quarter Sessions of Rutherford county, do certify the foregoing to be a true transcript.

And now at this term of the Superior Court and the appeal not having been brought within the time proscribed by law. Ordered the judgment of the county court be affirmed against the appellant and Josiah Payne and that he recover against the appellant and Josiah Payne his security in the said appeal his costs. [pp400-402]

The Grand Jury again returned and presented an indictment against James Campbell for forgery 'a true bill' and having nothing further to present were discharged. (see 417) [p402]

Nelly Harris
     vs   [AB Appeal]
Thomas Gore

On 29 April 1805 an appeal from the County Court of Jackson was filed in the office of the Superior Court for the District of Mero: transcript abstract - At a county court of quarter sessions for the county of Jackson, Nelly Harris obtained a writ against Thomas Gore 'to have him before the Justices at the county court to be held at the dwelling house of John Bowen on 1st Monday in September next to answer Nelly Harris of a plea of Trespass Assault and battery ... March 1804 signed John Bowen clk by A. Rawlings which was indorsed the 4th June 1804. At Sept sessions 1804 Wyley Huddleston, Depy Sheriff, made return that he had executed the same and plaintiff made her declaration: ' in the year 1804 the said Thomas with force and arms an assault did make on the body of the said Nelly and did beat and ill treat and did unlawfully imprison and detain the said Nelly for a long time, to wit, for the space of twenty days to her damage $3,000. J. C. Hamilton, atty for pltf.

And the defendant put in the following, 'and the said Thomas Gore by his attorney, Redmond D. Barry, comes and defends and for plea says that the said Nelly Harrius mentioned in the Declaration is a slave, and cannot maintain her action, therefore prays judgment that the same may be quashed - And the plaintiff for replication says she ought not to be precluded from having her action against him because she says she is not a slave and puts herself on the County and the Defendant likewise. Suit was continued in December and in March 1805 came the said Nelly Harris & Thomas Gore and prayed the Court for a venire which was awarded them: John Dale, James Parris, Joseph Gunnels, Andrew Phillips, William Allen, Hezekiah West, Francis Seyport, William Chisum, Robert Seypert, Stephen Mayfield, James Richardson, & Isham Bradley who say they find that the plaintiff is free and assess her damage to six cents and recover her costs of the suit. Thereupon the Defendant prayed an appeal which was awarded him.

And now at this Term of the Superior Court comes the said Nelly Harris by her attorney John C. Hamilton, and the appellant not having brought forth the appeal within the time prescribed by law, the Court considers that the Judgment of the County Court be affirmed. [pp403/404]

Jesse Beasley
    vs   [In Debt]
Joel Dyer

Be it remembered that on the 13th day of May 1805 an appeal from the County Court of Smith was filed. transcript - 'To the sheriff of Smith County - take the body of Joel Dyer if to be found in your county and him have before the Justices of our next Court of Pleas and Quarter Sessions to be held at Bledsoes borough on the 2nd Monday in December ... to answer Jesse Beasley in a plea athat he render unto him the sum of $80 dollars which to him he owes .. and damages of $40. signed Sampson Williams, clerk Sept. 1804

... said Joel at the County of Smith on 22 August 1800 made his certain writing obligatory and bound himself to pay the said Jesse the sum of forty dollars before the 25th day of December 1801 for value received and the said Joel also on same date did make his writing obligatory bound himself to pay the said Jessee the sum of forty dollars on or before the 25th day of December 1802 for value received; nevertheless the said Joel altho often requested did not pay the aforesaid. Wharton, Atty

Defendant, by his attorney, pleads payment and at March Term following came the parties by their attornies and a Jury: John Sanders, James Smith, Thomas Draper, Andrew Greer, Jeffery Litten, Hugh Stephenson, William Simpson, James Gibson, Francis Patterson, John Miles, Jeremiah Taylor, and John Campbell who find for the plaintiff the debt besides damages of $13.57 and the defendant prayed an appeal which was granted and entered into bond with Andrew Greer & Gay Renolds for securities. Sampson Williams, Clerk.

And now at this term of the Superior Court comes the said Jesse Beasley by his attorney and the appellant not having brought up the appeal within the time prescribed by law, it is considered the judgment of the county court be affirmed and that the plaintiff recover against the defendant and his securities his costs.[pp404-406]

James Scott
     vs   [Case Appeal]
John Grissum

On 13 May 1805 an appeal from the county court of Smith county was filed with the Clerk of the Superior Court for the District of Mero; December 1803 a capias was filed bearing words - 'To the Sheriff of Smith county - have John Grissum before the Justices of our court of pleas and quarter sessions to be held at tthe House of William Walton, March next, to answer James Scott in a plea of Trespass, damages of $150.00. signed Sampson Williams, clerk of said court. March Term 1804, John Douglass, Sheriff, made the following return "Kept off by force" whereupon by motion of plaintiffs attorney a Judicial attachment was issued - '...John Douglass, Sheriff, having made return that the said defendant kept him off by force and would not suffer said writ to be executed ... whereupon a judicial attachment should issue against the Estate of the said defendant to the amount of the plaintiffs damages ...'that the same may be liable to further proceedings thereon to be had at our next court to be held at Peter Turneys in June next ...' S. Williams, Clk

At the term next following came the plaintiff by his attorney, filed declaration that defendant was indefted to plaintiff for divers work and labour done and performed before that time ... signed Wharton, for plaintiff.

To which declaration defendant came into court by his attorney, plead non assumpset, set off and statute of limitation, suit continued until December Term 1804, when came the parties and the following Jury - James Wallace, Thomas Jones, Thomas Banks, Randolph Wren, Edmond Jennings, Thomas Jimerson, John Will, John Morris, Godfred Sherrer, Henry Danier, William Pendares, & Lewis Corder who find for the plaintiff and assess his damages to twenty one dollars and costs; from which judgment the defendant prayed an appeal, which was granted with Redmond D. Barry and Joel Dyer for Securities.

And now comes the said James Scott by his attorney and the appellant not having filed within the time prescribed by law, it is considered by the court that the judgment of the county court be affirmed. [pp406-408]

Edmond Jennings

vs   [Debt]
Joel Dyer
On 13 May 1805 an appeal from the county court
of Smith was filed in the Superior Court for the
District of Mero: June 1804   ...to the Sheriff
of Smith County - take Joel Dyer if to be found
in your county and have him before the Justices
of our next court of pleas and quarter sessions
to be held at Col. William Waltons on second
Monday in September next to answer Edmond
Jennings on a plea he render to him $100.00
which he owes and damages of $50.00. signed
Sampson Williams. At September sessions 1804
came the plaintiff by his attorney and filed his
declaration - that Joel Dyer at the county of
Smith on 24 April 1800 made his certain writing
obligatory to pay Jennings on or before the last
day of August next ... though often asked has
not paid all or any part. signed Wharton
At the same time came the defendant by his
attorney and plead the plea of payment. December
Term following came the defendant by his
attorney and withdraws his plea - Judgment was
entered with interest from the date and costs of
suit. From which judgment the defendant prayed
and obtained an appeal giving bond with Daniel
A. Burford and William Penny his securities.
And now at this term of the Superior Court comes
the said Edmond Jennings by his attorney and the
appelant not having brought his appeal in this
issue within the time prescribed by law. On the
motion of the plaintiff it is considered by the
court here that the judgment of the county court
be affirmed. [pp408/409]

Edmund Jennings
        vs   [In Case Appeal]
Joel Dyer
On 13 May 1805 an appeal from the county court
of Smith was filled with the Superior Court for
the District of Mero - transcript: To the
Sheriff of Smith county - ...take the body of
Joel Dyer if to be found in your county & have
him before the Justices at the next court of

152

pleas and quarter sessions to be held for the county of Smith at the house of Peter Turneys on second Monday of June next to answer Edmond Jennings. Sampson Williams, Clerk. June Term 1804 Edmond Jennings by his attorney complains of Joel Dyer of a plea of trespass on the case ... said Joel at the county of Smith on 14 April 1800 made a certain note by which note said Joel promised to pay said Edmond the sum of fifty dollars to be discharged in trade or work on or before the last day of March next following the date of the note. Note has not be paid.

March 1805 came the parties by their attornies and a Jury - John Sanderson, James Smith, John Campbell, Jeffery Sitton, Thomas Draper, Andrew Grier, Hugh Stephenson, William Simpson, James Gibson, Larkin Bethel and Moses Ashbrook who find for the plaintiff. & assess his damages to sixty one dollars, seventy five cents and costs. Defendant prayed an appeal which was granted and entered into bond with Andrew Greer and Renolds his securities.

And now at this Term came Edmond Jennings by his attorney, and the appellant not having brought up the appeal within the time prescribed by law on the motion of the plaintiff, it is considered the Judgment of the county court be affirmed. [pp409-411]

Robert C. Foster & George Gray
vs   [Debt Appeal]
Thomas Mitchell

On 13 May 1805 an appeal from the county court of Rutherford was filed in the office of the clerk of the Superior Court for the District of Mero - 4 June 1804 a writ was issued out of the clerks office for the county of Rutherford 'To the Sheriff - you are commanded to take Thomas Mitchell if to be found in your county and have him before the Justices of our court of pleas and quarter sessions July next at Jefferson, to answer Robert C. Foster and George S. Gray, merchants trading under the firm of Foster & Gray in a plea that he render to them the sum of two hundred and fifteen dollars eighty seven and one halfcents which to them he owes and damages of one hundred dollars. Joseph Herndon, Clerk At July Term 1804, the foregoing writ was returned "came to hand 13 June 'not found'" Writ was reisisued July Term and October Term 1804 the foregoing writ was returned with the following "came to hand the same day issued - executed 16th day of August 1804, Samuel McBride, Shrff October Term the said plaintiffs by their attorney, Jesse Wharton, filed declaration - ... said Thomas Mitchell on 25 May 1803 at the county of Rutherford made his certain writing obligatory for value received but the same to pay has wholly neglected.

And the defendant, by William Smith his attorney pleaded payment and issue was continued to January Term 1805 when came the parties by their attornies and a Jury - Thomas Blair, Josiah Davidson, John Davidson, Samuel McCleary, William Edwards, Cader Dement, James Norman, Samuel Long, Adam Woods, Thomas Yardley, Alexander Moore and Reed Miller who find for the plaintiff the debt and seven dollars fifty five cents damages for detention. Court find plaintiff to recover from the defendant the debt, damages of seven dollars and fifty five cents plus costs of suit. From which Judgment the said Mitchell prayed and received an appeal to the Superior Court. Joseph Herndon, Clerk of the court of pleas and quarter sessions for Rutherford county.

And now at this term come the plaintiffs by their attorney and the appellant not having brought the appeal in the time prescribed by law, on the motion oof the plaintiffs it is considered by the court her that the judgment of the county court be affirmed and recover against the defendant and Mark Mitchel and Peter LeGrand his securities. [pp411-412]

Edmund Jennings
    vs   [In Debt Appeal]
Joel Dyer

On 13 May 1805 an appeal was filed in the office of the clerk of the Superior Court of the District of Mero ... Be it remembered that a capias against Joel Dyer dated in June 1804 to sheriff of Smith county ...to have Joel Dyer before the Justices of our Court second Monday in Sept. next to answer Edmund Jennings assignee of Gay Reynolds in a plea that he render unto him the sum of one hundred dollars which he unjustly detains to his damage of fifty dollars...Edmond Jennings by his attorney complains of Joel Dyer that Dyer at the county of Smith on 12 June 1804 made his certain writing obligatory to pay to Gay Reynolds one hundred dollars one day afterwards which said writing obligatory being due & unpaid, the said Gay Reynolds by endorsement on the back of said note, assigned the contents of said note to Edmond Jennings for value received, of which said Joel had notice. signed Wharton, atty for pltf Ruled by court plaintiff to recover from defendant which judgment the said defendant by his attorney prayed and was granted an appeal with Daniel H. Burford and William Penny his securities.

And now at this Term of the Superior Court came Jennings by his attorney, and the appellant not having filed his appeal within the time prescribed by law, considered by the court that the judgment of the county court be affirmed and that the plaintiff recover against the defendant and his securities the amount of his judgment and the costs of suit. [pp113-114]

Pines Ingram
         vs   [In Debt]
Thomas Bedford
On motion it is ordered that this suit be revived against John R. Bedford, administrator of the said Thomas Bedford, deceased.

The Grand Jury proved their attendance and received Tickets:

Name	Days	Miles	Ferriages
Henry Tooly foreman	6	110	2
Nimrod Manifee	6	60	
Yancy Thornton	6	120	
John R. Bedford	6	40	
James Blackwell	6	66	2
George Stubblefield	6	82	2
John Edmiston	6	80	2
John Neville	6	84	2
Samuel Walker	6	80	
Daniel Frazier	6	18	2
John Brown	6	60	2
William Wootton	6	120	4
William Johnston	6	60	2
John B. Cross	6	220	4
Alexander McCrabb	6	120	4
Robert Thomas Constable	6		

[p414]

Jabes Fitzgerald
    vs
Benjamin Totton
On the affidavit of the said Jabes Fitzgerald a writ of certiorari and supersedias are awarded him to certify the record and procedures from the county court of Jackson wherein Benjamon Totton is plaintiff and the said Jabes Fitzgerald defendant. [p415]

Monday, May 20, 1805

The State
    vs   **[Indictment for Murder]**
Samuel Forrister
Be it remembered that at a court held for the Distrist of Mero at the courthouse in Nashville on the second Monday in November 1804, before the Judges of the said court by the oath of Robert Edmiston foreman, William Hazzard, Peter H.Looney, James Vinson, William Alexander, Buckner Killebru, Zachius Wilson, Thomas Strain, William Tease, Grant Allin, James Yates, Robert Searcy, Alexander Patton, Absolam Hooper and Josiah Fort. November Term 1804, the Jurors for

the State empannelled, sworn and charged to enquire for the body of the said District of Mero, upon their oath present that Samuel Forrester, late of the county of Jackson, in the District aforesaid, labourer, not regarding the laws of the State, on the twenty sixty day of March in the year of one thousand, and eight hundred and three, with force and arms, at the said county of Jackson, in and upon a certain female negro slave named Mille, the property of a certain Garrett Fitzgerald, and the said Samuel Forrester a certain Riffle gun of the value of ten dollars loaded with gunpower and one leaden bullet, which Riffle gun, he said Samuel Forrester, in both his hands, then and there had and held against and upon the said slave named Mille and then and there feloniously, wilfully and with malice aforethought did shoot and discharge, and that the said Samuel Forrester, ... did shoot one shot in and upon the left side of the belly of the said Mille near the short ribs of the said slave named Mille ... mortal wound of the debth of six inches breath of half an inch, from which said mortal wound said slave named Mille, did languish from the twenty sixth day of March until the fourth day of April in the year aforesaid ...

Jurors aforesaid upon their oath do say that Samuel Forrester, the said female negro slave named Mille, did with malice aforethough kill and murder.

Samuel Forrester was led to the bar in custody of the Sheriff of Davidson county and thereupon being charged and pleaded not guilty to the indictment aforesaid and for his trial put himself upon the county - and on the affidavit of Jabes Fitzgerald the prosecutor, the trial is continued until the next Court and it is ordered the said Forrester be removed to Jail. ...and now at this term came a jury - John Kennedy, William Snoddy, Henry Hide, James Lauderdale, James Neeley, George Blackamore, David Parker, Thomas Shute, William Hall, John Brooks, John

Dew and Alexander Walker who find him guilty of murder as charged and it ordered the said Samuel Forrester be remanded to jail. [pp415/416]

The State
    Vs   [Indt for Horse Stealing]
Thomas Massingale
Be it remembered that on Wednesday, the fifteenth day of May, this present term, by the oath of twelve Jurors it was presented that Thomas Massingale, late of the County of Stewart, blacksmith, on 7 February 1805, in the said county of Stuart, did steal one young mare of a bay colour of the price of eighty dollars and one young mare of a roane colour of the price of one hundred dollars of the goods and chattels of a certain Jeremiah Norrod. J. Whiteside, Atty General. Massingale was led to the bar and plead not guilty and put himself upon the county. A jury - Joel Holland, John Lancaster, William Lyons, Thomas Cox, John Sedgety, Gideon Pillow, Henry Hide, Daniel Evans, William Lane, Oliver Williams, Robert Searcy and William Snoddy who find the said Massingale not guilty of the horse stealing as charged, therefore it is ordered that he be acquitted and discharged [See 378] [p416]

The State
    vs   [Ind't for Forgery]
James Campbell
Be it remembered that on Saturday, 18 May of the present Term, by the oath of twelve Jurors it was presented that James Campbell, late of the county of Davidson, laborer, did deceive and defraud a certain Greenwood Paine and with the intention of compelling said Paine to pay for sundry goods James Campbell wished to procure from a certain William Easton, and falsely forged a certain writing on paper purporting to be an order drawn by said Paine on said William Easton in favour of said James Campbell. And Campbell was led to the bar in custody of the Sheriff of Davidson county and being charged

pleaded not guilty. Whereupon came a Jury - Edmond Owens, Thomas Lofton, William Neeley, Isaac Phillips, Thomas Edmiston, Robert McNairy, Sherwood Green, Abner Henley and James Cannon who find the said James Campbell guilty as charged on two counts and not guilty or two counts …it is considered by the Court that Campbell pay a fine of twenty five dollars, that he be imprisoned three months without bail and there to remain until the fine be paid. [See 402] [pp417/418]

February May 21, 1805 Pleas at the Courthouse in Nashville

Andrew Ewing, James Muherrin and John Overton, Executors of Thomas Malloy, deceased
   Vs
William Betts
Plaintiffs by John Dickinson, their attorney, filed their declaration … complain of William Betts that he render to them three hundred and sixty dollars; whereas William on 14 June 1800, made his certain writing obligatory to Thomas Molloy for the sum of $320 on or before 14 June 1803 for value received … Betts, by Jesse Wharton, his attorney, says he has paid. Cause was continued from term to term until this term at which day came the parties and a Jury: William Lyons, David Childress, William Axum, Thomas Lofton, Edmund Owens, William Neelly, William Wilson, Henry Hide, Thomas Edmiston, Robert McNairy, Sherwood Green and William Tait who find for the plaintiffs and assess their damage to to $48.16 and costs. [pp419/420]

Benjamin John
   Vs   **[In Covenant]**
James Berry, Senr & James Berry, Junr
James Berry Senior & James Berry, Junior were attached to answer Benjamin John of a plea of covenant broken to the damage of two thousand dollars. Benjamin, by Thomas Stuart his

attorney, filed his declaration Nov. Term 1803; whereas James Berry Junior and James Berry Senior on 12 September 1798, by their certain writing obligatory … would make a sufficient and lawful title to the said Benjamin John, for a certain tract of first rate land with a good spring on it containing 200 acres which the said James Berry Junior bought of John Carns in the State of Kentucky below Saleen Creek and about six or seven miles from Cumberland River … title to be agreeable to the laws and customs of the state of Kentucky . Plaintiff says that the said defendants have kept their said covenant. Defendants by Jesse Wharton, their attorney, came into court and defend their plea … and the trial was continued until this term, May 1804, at which day came the plaintiff by his attorney and James Berry Senr, one of the Defendants being dead, on motion a Scifa was awarded. This Term comes the plaintiff and the defendant, by their attornies, and a July: Isaac Philips, Robert Searcy, James Cannon, James Lauderdale, William Lane, Joel Holland, John McMurry, Edmond Jennings, Robert Nelson, William Lancaster, Chapman White and John Brooks who find for the plaintiff and assess his damages to $267/60 and costs. [pp420/421]

James Latham
    Vs   **[AB Appeal]**
James Menees
On 16 April 1804 an appeal from the county Court of Robertson County was filed in the office of the clerk of the Superior Court of the District of Mero; On 20 January 1803 James Latham obtained a writ to have James Menees 'if to be found in your county,'
Before the Justices of our county court of pleas and quarter sessions to answer James Lathan in a plea of Trespass, Assault & Battery and false imprisonment, damages of $1000.00 Thomas Johnson, Clerk January 1803; executed March 12, 1803, D. Holman, Coroner. Proceedings were continued until Oct Term 1803 at which time came

into court the plaintiff by Thomas Stuart and Matthew Lodge, his attornies. Likewise came the defendant by Bennet Searcy & William Smith, his attornies and a Jury - Isham Rogers, Isaac Dorris, Edward King, Joseph Robertson, Nimrod McIntosh, John Siglar, William Wills, Charles Wheaton, John Chatham, Bazel Brown, John Wilson & William Sale, who find for the plaintiff and assess his damages to twenty five cents, from which verdict the Defendant prayed and obtained an appeal. Thomas Johnson, Clerk of Robertson County.

And the cause was continued from term to term until this term, at which time came the parties by their attornies, and a Jury - Robert Searcy, James Cannon, James Lauderdale, William Lane, Joel Holland, John McMurry, Edmund Jennings, Robert Nelson, William Lancaster, Chapman White, John Brooks & Henry Gutherie who find the Defendant not guilty and it is considered by the court that the defendant may depart and recover against the plaintiff his costs. [pp421/423]

Jacob Scott
    vs   **[Case Appeal]**
Richard Brown
On 21 Aprpil 1804 an appeal from the county court of Williamson was filed in the office of the Superior Court. transcript 'To the sheriff of Williamson county - 'You are hereby commanded to take the body of Richard Brown if to be found in your county and have him before the Justices of our court of pleas and quarter sessions to be held for the county of Williamson at the court house in Franklin on the first Monday in November to answer Jacob Scott of a plea of trespass' signed Nicholas Perkins Hardiman, clerk August 1803; and for the prosecution of which writ Philip Maury became the plaintiffs security, which writ was issued 14 Sept 1803, executed 22 Sept 1803. Jacob Scott by John Dickinson his attorney, complains that whereas on 15th day of April in 1800 at Franklin in the county aforesaid it was agreed between them the

said Jacob and Richard that Richard should put nine mares to a stud horse owned and kept by Jacob known by the name of *Goldfinder* and as the satisfaction for the service of said stud horse, he the said Jacob should have and receive one of the colts to be begotten ... when Jacob asked to see the mares and colts to make his choice as per their agreement Richard hath and still doth refuse. And also on 10 August 1803 at Franklin the said Richard was indebted to Jacob in the sum of $200 for the covering of sundry other mares and tho often requested Jacob hath not paid him.

The Defendant by Thomas Stuart his attorney, at the Nov. 1803 Session put himself upon the county. Cause was continued until April Sessions 1804 when the parties came into court by their attornies and a jury - James Davis, Spencer Hill, Elisha Dotson, John Blackman, Jacob Wright, Moses Chambers, John Mckinny, Ruffin Brown, John Cluck, Bazel Berry, William Edmondson and John Hicks, who find for the plaintiff and assess his damages to fifty five dollars and costs. The plaintiff being dissatisfied obtained an appeal. The cause was continued from term to term to this term and came a Jury: William Syms, David Childress, William Tait, William Axum, Edmund Owens, Thomas Lofton, William Neelly, William Willson, Isaac Philips, Henry Hide, Thomas Edmiston and Robert McNairy who find for the plaintiff and assess plaintiffs damages for $55.00 , Judgment to forty five dollars besides his costs. [pp423-426]

John Walker & Jenny Walker,
   Exors of Philip Walker
       vs   **[Case Appeal]**
Simpson Harris

On 14 May 1804 an appeal from the county court of Davidson was filed in the office of the clerk of the Superior Court for the District of Mero. transcript - To the sheriff of Davidson County 'You are commanded to take the body of Simpson

Harris if to be found in your county and have him before the Justices of our Court to be held at the Town of Nashville on the second Monday in January to answer John Walker and Jinny Walker, Executors of the last will and testament of Philip Walker, deceased, in a plea of trespass, damages $250.00. Andrew Ewing, clerk Oct. 1803. Jesse Wharton became the plaintiffs security. Executed the 3rd day of November 1803 and bail taken, signed Edley Evins. Walkers complain by their attorney that whereas on the 13th day of May 1801, the said Simpson Harris made a certain note, by which note Simpson promised to pay to Philip Walker the sum of $178.25, and afterwards in the county of Davidson the said Philip Walker departed this life and by his last Will and Testamend did appoint John Walker, executor and Jinny Walker, executrix who did qualify as such. At the January 1804 Sessions the defendant appeared by Bennet Searcy, his attorney ... continued until April Sessions 1804, at which time come the parties by their attornies and a Jury - Benjamin Drake, Andrew Hays, George Farmer, James Byrns?[ink spot], John Morris, Frederick Stump, Churchwell Hooper, John Harman, Laurence McCormack, George W. L. Marr, Elliott Hickman & Claiborne Gentry who find for the defendant. Therefore is considered that the defendant do recover against the plaintiffs his costs of defense - from which judgment the plaintiffs prayed and obtained an appeal to the Superior Court for the District of Mero, having given security as required. Andrew Ewing, Clerk

And the cause continued from term to term until this date at which day came the parties by their attornies and a jury, to wit: Sherwood Green, William Snoddy, James Cannon, James Lauderdale, William Lane, Joel Holland, John McMurry, Richard Brown, Willis Jones, John Lancaster, Abner Henly, and Henry Rutherford who find for the plaintiff and assess damages to $220.27 and costs. [pp426-427]

Patrick Campbell
    vs   [Cov't Appeal]
Nancy Benton, Executor of Jesse Benton
Be it remembered that on 24 April 1804 an appeal from the county court of Williamson was filed. transcript - Patrick Campbell is plaintiff vs Nancy Benton, the only acting and surviving Executrix of Jesse Benton, deceased To the Sheriff of Williamson County 'you are to take the body of Nancy Benton if to be found in your county and have her before the Justices of our Court ...town of Franklin, county of Williamson in a plea of covenant broken, damage eight thousand dollars ... Nicholas P. Harding, Clerk May 1803

    Bennet Searcy becamne the plaintiffs security// sheriff made return to August session 'executed 25 July 1803.' Patrick Campbell complains of Nancy Benton, the only acting and surviving executrix of Jesse Benton, deceased ... whereas the said Jesse Benton in his lifetime - together with a certain John Rice (now also deceased) - on the 24th day of October in 1783 at the county of Williamson by his certain writing obligatory, did acknowledge himself, his heirs, executors ... jointly to which writing obligatory the condition was annexed that whereas the said John Rice had received and sold to the said Patrick a tract of land to contain one thousand acres in the western part of this state (meaning the State of North Carolina and included in the District of Mero) to be equal in quality to the tract of land Rice had purchased from Major Absalom Tatum ... and also the said Jesse was to locate for the said Patrick five thousand acres of land on the most fertile and convenient which was best known to the said Jesse, Deceased ... and if the said Jesse, deceased made good the agreement the said writing obligatory was to become void otherwise to remain in full force and the said Patrick saith a grant hath been issued by the State of North Carolina for the land aforesaid and the said Patrick saith the said track of one thousand acres has not been neither did the said Jesse, deceased, nor his executors or heirs, convey the land that Jesse bought of Absalom Tatum. B. Searcy & Dickinson for the plaintiff. Original agreement entered and read … signed by John Rice and Jesse Benton; witnessed by James Galloway & Charles Bruce. Nancy said she hath fully adminstered the goods of Jesse Benton.

Nov. Session 1803 came the parties by their attornies and a Jury - Joseph B. Porter, John Reed, Isaac Crow, John Edmiston, Andrew Goff, John Farmer, Thomas W. Stockett, Benjamin Jordan, John Wilson, David Squires, Joseph Mairs and John Williamson who could not agree on a verdict and by consent of the parties there was a mistrial. January Sessions 1804 came the parties and a Jury - William Childress, John Parks, George Poe, Samuel Snoddy, Martin Standley, Henry Rutherford, Edmond Cook, John West, Joseph German, William Pillow, Ephraim Brown and John Jordon who find for the plaintiff and assess his damages to five hundred and twenty five dollars and costs of suit and the plaintiff being dissatisfied prayed and obtained an appeal to the Superior Court of the District of Mero. Nicholas Perkins Hardiman, Clerk of Williamson County, TN.

And the cause was continued until this Term, at which time came the parties by their attornies and a Jury - Sherwood Green, William Snoddy, Abner Henley, Robert Searcy, James Cannon, James Lauderdale, William Lanes, Joel Holland, John McMurry, Richard Brown, Willis Jones and John Lancaster who find the defendant has fully adminstered all goods and chattels which were of the said Jesse Benton at the time of his death and they do assess the plaintiff damages to four thousand dollars besides his costs and upon various arguments cause continued until the next court for argument. [See book C page 203] [pp428-433]

Wednesday, May 22, 1805

John Lawrence
  Vs   [Covenant]
Francis Hall, Andrew Jackson & Francis R. Nash
November Term 1803 a Capias ad respondentuin, at the suit of John Lawrence against Francis Hall, Andrew Jackson and Francis R. Nash of a plea of Covenant broken, damage one thousand dollars was returned by the Sheriff of Davidson County – 'executed on Andrew Jackson & Francis R. Nash and Francis Hall 'not found'. And at the term last mentioned the said Francis Hall in Court here acknowledged the service of he writ … The plaintiff, by Thomas Stuart his attorney, filed his declaration May Term 1804. …that whereas the defendants by their certain writing obligatory made in the county of Davidson on 4 April 1800 and to the Court now shown .. date is the same day but aforesaid writing that whereas Bennet Barrow of the State of North Carolina and Edgecomb County authorised and impowered said Francis Hall by a special power of Attorney to sell and convey a certain tract of land containing six hundred and forty acres lying on Round Lick Creek, granted to John Haywood, and conveyed by Haywood to the said Bennet Barrow and whereas the said Francis Hall sold and conveyed the said tract of land jointly to Ezekiel Bass, Jourdan Bass and the said John Lawrence who severally paid the said Francis in manner following: Ezekiel Bass paid $245; Jourdan Bass paid $150 and the said John Lawrence paid $245 – said land being rated at one dollar per acre and also reciting that whereas the said land had been conveyed by the said Francis not strictly agreeably to said power of attorney and apprehensions arising that the said land would be taken by an older entry therefore for the safety of the joint purchasers of said tract the said defendants bound themselves and understood that said Francis Hall faithfully should make application to Bennet Barrow for another power of attorney … it was discovered that there was a priority of entry to the said land by the prior entry of John Howell

whereof said defendants had notice. Thos. Stuart for Plaintiff. John Dickinson the attorney for the defendants who say they have not broken their covenant… The cause was continued until this Term at which day came the parties by their attornies and a Jury – William Lyons, David Childress, William Tait, William Axum, Edmond Owens, Thomas Lofton, William Neelly, William Wilson, Isaac Phillips, Henry Hide, Thomas Edmiston and Robert McNairy who find for the plaintiff --judgment for $327.88 and costs. [pp433-435]

Edward Douglass & Robert Ewing
    Vs   **[In Debt]**
Matthew Tolbot
The Sheriff having returned the Scirefacias made known to Thomas Tolbot, Robert Weakley and David McGavock, Executors of Thomas Tolbot, deceased. It is ordered that this suit be revived against the said Exectors. [See 350] [p435]

Stephen Cantrell
    Vs   **[In Debt]**
Andrew Davis, Executor of John Blackamore
Andrew Davis, Executor of the last will and testament of John Blackamore, deceased was summoned to answer Stephen Cantrell of a plea that he render unto him $540. Stephen, by Thomas Stuart his attorney, filed his declaration November Term 1803. John Blackamore in his lifetime by his certain writing obligatory made at the county of Davidson on 28 November 1797 to pay Stephen Cantrell or his assigns on or before 25 December next the sum of $140 for value received. And also another writing obligatory dated 24 Dec. 1799 for $400 for value received. This debt was not paid by John Blackamore in his lifetime nor by his executors …
Defendant, by Parry W. Hunphrey his attorney, defends says that Blackamore did pay in August 1799 – cause continued until this Term when came a Jury – William Lyons, David Childress, William

Axum, Edmund Owens, Thomas Lofton, William Neelly, William Wilson, Isaac Phillips, Henry Hide, Thomas Edmiston, Robert McNairy & Sherwood Green who find for the plaintiff for $540 debt & $200 damages. [pp435-437]

Bolling Felts
Vs [In Debt]
John Caffery & Thomas Harney

John Caffery and Thomas Harney were summoned to answer Bolling Felts of a plea of seven hundred and forty six dollars which to him they owe. Bolling by Thomas Start his attorney filed his declaration as follows - Caffery & Harney by their certain writing obligatory made in county of Davidson on 24 July 1801, and to the Court now here shown bound themselves to pay said Bowling on or before first day of March 1802 and lawful interest from the date … and also a certain wriiting obligatory made and same date to pay Bowling the sum of two hundred dollars on or before 25 December 1802, it being for value received for a total of $746. Thos Stuart for plaintiff and Jesse Wharton for defendants. And the cause was continued until this term at which day come the parties by their attornies and a lawful Jury - William Tait, William Snoddy, Abner Hinley, Robert Searcy, James Cannon, James Lauderdale, Henry Rutherford, William Lane, Joel Holland, John McNairy, Henry Guthrie and Cooper Vick who said the defendants have not paid the debt of $746 and assess his damages to $154.58. [pp437/438]

Thursday, May 23, 1805

Jesse Wharton & Thomas Stuart
Vs [In Covenant]
John Carter

Plaintiffs filed their declaration May Term 1804; Jesse Wharton & Thomas Stuart complain of John Carter, a citizen of Carter County, in the District of Washington of a plea of covenant broken. John Carter, at Nashville, on 14

February 1803 made his covenant in writing by which covenant he covenanted to deliver to Thomas Stuart and Jesse Wharton on or before the second Monday in May next, a good likely young horse to be valued at $125.00 and said Stuart & Wharton say Carter hath not kept his said covenant. Wharton, atty for plaintiffs. And the defendant not appearing though called it is therefore considered by the Court that the plaintiffs recover their damages … to be inquired of by a Jury at the next court at which Court {November Term 1804] came the following Jury – William Tait, William Snoddy, Abner Henley, Robert Searcy, James Cannon, James Lauderdale, Henry Rutherford, William Lane, Joel Holland, John McMurry, Cooper Vick & Willis Jones who find for the plaintiff and assess his damages to $140.20 besides their costs. [pp438-439]

Thomas Gore
    Vs   **[Detinue Certiorari]**
Rueben Searcy

Be it remembered that in May 1804 a writ of certiorari issued from the Superior Court for the District of Mero directed to the Justices of the Court of Pleas & Quarter Sessions of Sumner County commanding said Justices to send and certify the record and proceedings in action between Thomas Gore, plaintiff, and Reuben Searcy, defendant…which record was filed in the clerks office of the Superior Court of Mero on 28 October 1804.

Transcript – Pleas before the Court of Pleas & Quarter Sessions – Sumner County at the Courthouse in the Town of Gallatin on third Monday in June 1804 … to answer Thomas Gore of a plea wherefore he unjustly detains a negro woman named Nell price three hundred and fifty dollars and a negro boy named Harry worth two hundred and fifty dollars and a negro boy named Sam worth two hundred dollars to his damage two thousand dollars. D. Shelby, Clerk, Issued 23 September 1802. Whereupon the sheriff made

return to October Term 'came to hand 23rd Sept, Executed 28th' Thomas Maston D.S. And at the term last aforesaid the plaintiff by John C. Hamilton his attorney filed his declaration. Defendant, by Thomas Stuart his attorney then pleaded and parties joined issue after which the cause was continued from term to term until the term first above mentioned when came the parties by their attornies and a Jury – Edward Maxey, Peter Lemmons, William King, James Franklin, Nathan Edwards, Alexander Kirkpatrick, Richard Alexander, Hugh Caruthers, Edward Cage, Laurence Whitsett, Alexander Cathey and James Hamilton who find for the plaintiff and assess his damages to $40 & costs; rule for new trial entered, argued and overruled.
…we Thos Gore & J. C. Hamilton are bound unto Reuben Searcy in the sum of two hundred and fifty dollars to be void on condition that the said Thos Gore doth with effect prosecute a suit by him this day commenced against Reuben Searcy otherwise pay and satisfy all costs & damages. 23 Sept 1802 Thos Gore   J. C. Hamilton Test: Thos. Donnell
And the cause continued in the Superior Court until this term at which day comes the said Reuben by his attorney and the said Thomas Gore not appearing though called, neither is his suit further prosecuted, therefore it is considered by the court that the plaintiff be nonsuited and pay to the defendant his costs. [pp439-441]

Thomas Stuart
     Vs   **[In Debt]**
Benjamin Holland
Benjamin Holland was summoned to answer Thomas Stuart … that he render to him the sum of $445 which he unjustly detains. Thomas by Jesse Wharton his attorney made his declaration May Term 1804 …that whereas Holland at Nashville on 1 July 1803 made his certain writing oblgatory for $445 for value received … nevertheless said Benjamin altho often requested has not paid. The defendant by Nathaniel A. McNairy his

attorney, says he has paid and the cause was continued until this term when came a Jury – William Lyons, David Childress, William Axum, Edmund Owens, Thomas Lofton, William Neelly, William Wilson, Isaac Phillips, Henry Hide, Robert McMurry, Thomas Edmiston & Sherwood Green who find for the defendant for his debt of $325 and assess damages of $36.83 and costs. [pp441-442]

Samuel Cummins
    Vs   [In Debt]
Peter Edwards

On 16 October 1804 an appeal from the county court of Williamson was filed in the office of the Clerk of the Superior Court for the District of Mero. *Transcript* – To the Sheriff of Williamson County – ordered to have Peter Edwards before the Justices of our Court for the County of Williamson at the Courthouse in the Town of Franklin on the second Monday in April next to answer Samuel Cummin, assignee of Robert & William Searcy in a plea the he render unto him the sum of $150 and damages of $75. Nicholas P. Hardiman, Clerk. John Dickinson became the plaintiffs security. Whereas said Peter on 1 April 1803 at Franklin in the County aforesaid by his certain writing obligatory … has not paid … signed Dickinson, attorney for pltff. Defendant at April Sessions 1804 by Jesse Wharton his attorney, says he has paid – continued until July Session 1804 at which time came the parties into court by their attornies and a Jury – Thomas Barnet, David Nolin, George Oldham, Jordan Soloman, James Love, Robert Page, Joseph Ralston, Richard Polk, David Campbell, Harrison Boyd, John C. Ervin & George Wrenn who find for the plaintiff. The defendant being dissatisfied prayed and obtained an appeal to the Superior Court for the District of Mero. And the cause was continued in the Superior Court until the date first mentioned at which day came the parties by their attornies and a Jury – William Tait, William Snoddy, Abner

Henley, Robert Searcy, James Cannon, James Lauderdale, Henry Rutherford, William Lane, Joel Holland, John McNairy, Cooper Vick, and Willis Jones who find for the plaintiff - to recover his debt of $150, damages of $12.17 and costs. [pp442-444]

William Bowen
    Vs   [Covenant]
Thomas Watson
The plaintiff in this cause being dead, on motion, it is ordered that the suit be revived in the names of John H. Bowen, Executor of the said William Bowen, deceased. [p444]

Joseph T. Elliston
    Vs   [Debt Appeal]
William German & James Caldwell
On 20 October 1804 an appeal from the County Court of Davidson County was filed ~ *transcript:* To the Sheriff of Davidson County - have William German and James Caldwell before the Justices of our Court of pleas and quarter sessions to be held for the county of Davidson at the Courthouse in the town of Nashville January next, to answer Joseph T. Elliston in a plea of Debt of $227 and damages of $200. Andrew Ewing, Clerk Oct. 1803 - Issued 30 Dec. 1803. Parry W. Humphreys became security for the plaintiff. Return was made to the Justices of said County Court January 1804 'came to hand 5 January and executed the same day. Signed Rich'd Boyd, D.W.

    January Sessions last appeared the plaintiff by his attorney, Parry W. Humphreys who brings with him his certain bill … said defendants on 20 October 1802 in county and state aforesaid by promisory note signed by their hands to pay or cause to be paid to Benjamin Gains before 25 December next and the said note being due and unpaid the said Benjamin Gains did on 26 July 1803, by endorcement on the said note to the said Joseph T. Elliston for value received. Defendants appeared by their attornies, Bennet

Searcy and Jesse Wharton … entered 'thus payment accord and satisfaction.' Cause continued to April 1804 at which time came into court the plaintiff and the defendants and thereon came a Jury ~ Benjamin Drake, John Sommerville, Christopher Connelly, Enoch Douge, John Marlin, James Byrns, John Morris, Thomas Rutherford, James Jackson, Josiah Morris, Neal Thompson & William Easton who find for the plaintiff his debt and the sum of $18.23 and ½ cents damages. From which Judgment the defendant prayed and obtained an appeal to the Superior Court.

And the cause was continued in the Superior Court until the day above mentioned at which time come the parties and a Jury ~ William Lyons, David Childress, William Axum, Edward Owens, Thomas Lofton, William Neally, William Wilson, Isaac Phillips, Henry Hide, Robert McNairy, Thomas Edmiston & Sherwood Green who say the defendants have not paid the debt ~ considered by the Court that the decision of the County Court be affirmed and the plaintiff recover his costs against William German & James Caldwell and John Raines, James Garrett & Cooper Vick, their securities. [pp444-446]

David Beaty
    vs   **[Debt Appeal]**
Henry Gutharie

On 22 October 1804 an appeal from the County Court of Davidson was filed ~ *transcript* To the Sheriff of Davidson County – have Henry Gutherie before the Justices of our Court to be held for the county of Davidson at the Courthouse in Nashville April next to answer a plea of debt of $52.00, damage $30.00. Signed Andrew Ewing. Jan. 1804 Nathan Ewing became the plaintiffs security. April Sessions the plaintiff appeared by William Smith, his attorney. On 11 October 1803 Henry Gutharie made his certain writing obligatory and promised to pay fourteen days after date, it being for value received. Defendant appeared, Bennet Searcy, his attorney,

and saith that he paid said debt. Cause continued until July Sessions 1804, at which time came the parties by their attorneys and a Jury ~ Jacob Dickinson, William Lintz, John Cockrell, George Green, Nathaniel McCreary, Thomas Harding, John Gordon, Jonas Maniffee, John Deathrige, Cooper Vick, John Brownlee & John Harrisson who find in favor of the plaintiff - plaintiff has not paid the debt and also the sum of two dollars and twenty nine cents interest as damages plus costs of suit. From which judgment defendant prayed and requested an appeal.
The Cause was continued until this day when came a Jury ~ William Lyons, David Childress, William Axum, Edmund Owens, William Neelly, William Wilson, Isaac Phillips, Henry Hide, Robert McNairy, Thomas Edmiston, Sherwood Green & Rob't Searcy who find the defendant has not paid the debt and it is considered by the Court that the judgment of the County Court is affirmed. [pp446/447]

William Parker
vs [Case Appeal]
Henry Gutherie

On 22 October 1804 an appeal from the County Court of Davidson was filed: *transcript* ~ To the Sheriff of Davidson County - have Henry Gutherie before the Justices of the Court of pleas and quarter sessions April next to answer William Parker of a plea of Trespass. January 1803. Nathaniel McNairy became the plaintiff security. ..return was made at April Sessions 1803 'came to hand the 27th of February 1803, Executed by me Richard Boyd D.S. 3 March 1803.' The plaintiff appeared by Thomas Stuart his attorney; the defendant by Bennet Searcy, his attorney. Cause continued until July 1803 and then continued to October Sessions 1803 … Defendant in debt $100 for work & labor performed before that time by the plaintiff … in year 1802 plaintiff built a chimney with five fireplaces part of stone and part of brick and two stone pillars seven feet high and tho often requested hath not paid. April 1804 came the parties by their attornies and a Jury ~ Frederick Foster, Christopher Stump, Robert Dean, Wittshire P'Pool, Matthew Brooks, Aaron Everett, Francis Campier, Foster Sayres, Chartes Cabiness, Joseph Mott, James McBride and James Hamilton who find for the plaintiff and considered he recover the sum of forty two dollars, also his costs of suit. The defendant moved for a new trial which the court refused to grant, the defendant then prayed and obtained an appeal to the Superior Court. Andrew Ewing 4 May 1804

And the cause was continued until this Term at which time come the parties by their attornies and a Jury ~ William Tait, William Snoddy, Abner Henly, Joel Rice, James Cannon, James Lauderdale, Henry Rutherford, William Lane, Joel Holland, John McMurry, Cooper Vick & Willis Jones who find for the Defendant. Therefore it is considered by the Court that the defendant may depart and recover against the plaintiff his costs of defence. [pp448/449]

David Beaty
    Vs   **[Debt Appeal]**
Henry Guthrie
On 22 October 1804 an appeal from the County Court of Davidson was filed in the Superior Court: *transcript* ~ To the Sheriff of Davidson County – have Henry Gutherie before the Justices of the Court of Pleas & Quarter Sessions April next to answer David Beaty on a plea that he render to him the sum of $66 which he unjustly detains. Andrew Ewing January 1804 Nathan Ewing became Security for the plaintiff. Sheriff made return that he had on 10 Feb. executed the same. Whereas on 24 March 1803 Henry Gutherie made his certain writing obligatory to pay said David Beaty or assigns the sum of sixty six dollars on or before 1 August … debt has not been paid. At April Sessions the defendant appeared by Bennet Searcy his attorney and saith that he paid the

obligation. ... cause continued until July 1804 at which time came the parties and a Jury ~ Jacob Dickinson, William Lintz, John Cockrell, George Greer, Nathaniel McCrary, Thomas Harding, John Gordon, Jones Manifee, John Deathrige, Cooper Vick, John Brownlee and John Harrison who find in favor of the plaintiff the debt of sisty six and interest of three dollars and ninety cents. And costs of suit. - from which Judgment the defendant obtained an appeal to the Superior Court of Mero District.

And the cause was continued in the Superior Court until this date at which time came the parties by their attornies and a Jury ~ William Tait, William Snoddy, Abner Henly, Robert Searcy, James Cannon, James Lauderdale, Henry Rutherford, William Lane, Joel Holland, John McMurry, Cooper Vick and Willis Jones who say the defendant hath not paid the debt, therefore on the motion of the plaintiff by his attorney, it is considered by the court here that the Judgment of the County Court is affirmed and that the plaintiff recover against the said Henry Gutherie and Bennet Searcy and Robert Searcy his Securities together with interest and his costs about his suit. [pp450-452]

Andrew Morris
    Vs   [Scifa]
Nathaniel M. Baker & George McCormack
  Bail for Ezekiel Able

To the Sheriff of Davidson County - Whereas Andrew Morris, lately in our Superior Court, at November term 1803, recovered against Ezekiel Able one hundred and sixty seven dollars as well for damages he sustained by reason of the nonperformance of a covenant and whereas Nathaniel M. Baker and George McCormack were his securities and whereas said Able hath not paid therefore make know to Baker and McCormack that they be before the Judges of our Court ... Randal McGavock, May 1804

On which day comes the said Andrew Morris by Bennet Searcy his attorney, and the Sheriff of

Davidson returns that Baker is not found in his county and McCormack by Jesse Wharton, his attorney comes into court and says he has surrendered Ezekiel Able, in discharge of himself. Plaintiff charges – comes a Jury ~ William Tait, William Snoddy, Abner Henly, Robert Searcy, James Cannon, James Lauderdale, Henry Rutherford, William Lane, Joel Holland, John McMurry, Cooper Vick & Willis Jones who find that McCormack did not surrender up the defendant/ find that defendant has not paid plaintiff and the sheriff having returned the second writ of Scifa and Nathaniel M. Baker was not to be found - [See Book C, p368] [pp452/453]

Searcy & Carvin
Vs   [Case Appeal]
Peter Edwards

On 25 October 1804 an appeal was filed from the County Court of Williamson: *transcript* ~To the Sheriff of Williamson County – have Peter Edwards if to be found in your county before the Justices of our Court of pleas and quarter sessions to be held at the Courthouse in the town of Franklin February next to answer Robert Searcy and William Carvin, merchants and copartners trading under the firm of *Searcy & Carvin.* Nicholas P. Hardeman, Clerk Nov. 1803 – William Searcy became the surity for the plaintiffs.

Sheriff made return 'executed 24 December 1803; and at January Session 1804 the plaintiffs, by John Dickinson their attorney, appeared in prosecution on a plea of trespass; whereas Peter Edwards on 10 October 1803 at Franklin, in the County of Williamson, was in debt to the plaintiffs for $250 for goods, wares and merchandize and also said Peter was indebted to Joseph Coleman and the said Robert, lately partners in trade using the title of *Coleman & Searcy,* for $194.25 for goods and merchandise. Cause continued until 8 October 1804 at which time came into Court the parties by their

attornies and a Jury ~ Britain Adams, Isaac
Philips, John More, John West, Henry Walker,
Henry Petty, Joel Dilliard, Ruben Parks, James
Robert Orr, Abram Maury Degraffenreed, James
Dowing and Newton Cannon who find for the
plaintiff and assess their damage to $199.25 and
costs of the suit; defendant dissatisfied with
judgment prayed and obtained an appeal to the
Superior Court for the District of Mero.

And at this Term of the Superior Court, come the
parties by their attornies and the defendant
puts himself upon the Country and came a Jury ~
William Lyons, David Childress, William Axum,
Edmund Owens, William Neely, William Wilson,
Isaac Phillips, Henry Hide, Robert McNairy,
Thomas Edmiston, Sherwood Green and John Payton
who find for the plaintiff and judgment of the
County Court is affirmed and damages of 12 ½
percent interest from the time Judgment passed
in the County Court. [pp454-456]

Daniel Frazier
Vs [Covenant]
John White

John White was attached to answer Daniel Frazier
of a plea of covenant broken to his damages of
three thousand dollars. Whereupon the said
Daniel by Thomas Stuart filed his declaration
November Term 1804; John White in custody of the
Sheriff of Williamson County; whereas John White
by his certain writing obligatory made in the
County of Williamson 22 February 1800 covenanted
himself to make unto said Daniel Frazor deed to
500 acres of land lying on Salt Lick Creek in
Smith County, which five hundred acres was to be
an equal half in qualify of one thousand the
choice of three corners of said 'large' survey
and said deed was to be made to said Frazor in
twelve months after the date of said writing
obligatory and tho often asked has not been
made. Defendant, by Jesse Wharton his attorney,
says he has performed the covenant and the
matter was continued until this term, when came
the parties by their attornies and a Jury

~William Lyons, David Childress, William Axum, Edmond Owens, William Neelly, William Wilson, Isaac Phillips, Henry Hide, Robert McNairy, Thomas Edmiston, Sherwood Green & Robert Searcy who find for the plaintiff and say the defendant has broken his covenant; assess his damages to $500.00 and costs. [pp356/457]

Roger B. Sappington
    Vs   **[In Debt]**
Joseph Hays
May 23, 1805 service of a writ at the suit of Roger B. Sappington against Joseph Hays of a plea of debt for $260 was acknowledged and declaration was filed … whereas the said Joseph at Nashville in the District of Mero on 23 May 1804 made his certain writing obligatory to pay within six months the sum of $260 and interest – said Joseph Hays confesses that he cannot deny the debt and damages and agrees to pay and the plaintiff agrees to stay the execution of this judgment six months. [p458]

Andrew Ewing, James Mulherrin & John Overton
    Vs   **[Debt]**
William Betts
William Betts was summoned to answer Andrew Ewing, James Mulherrin & John Overton, executors of the testement and last will of Thomas Molloy, deceased on a plea he detains $320.00 to their damage of one hundred dollars. Plaintiffs, by John Dickinson their attorney, filed their Declaration November Term, 1804 ~ whereas said William Betts on 14 June, 1800, in Nashville, by his certain writing obligatory, bound himself to pay said Thomas on or before 14 June 1804 and debt has not been paid and said William has and does refuse to pay to the said Andrew, James & John since the death of Thomas Molloy. The defendant by his attorney, Jesse Wharton, says he has paid the debt. The trial was continued until this day come the parties, by their attornies, and a Jury ~ William Lyons, David Childress, William Axum, Edmund Owens, William

Neely, William Wilson, Isaac Phillips, Henry Hide, Robert McNairy, Thomas Edmiston, Sherwood Green & Robert Searcy who find for the plaintiffs the debt of $320 and assess their damages to $18.00 plus costs. [pp458/459]

James Moore
    Vs   [In Case]
John Billingsley
John Billingsley was attached to answer James Moore in a case of trespass, to his damage four thousand dollars. James, by Jesse Wharton his attorney, filed his Declaration November Term, 1804 …said defendant is indebted in the sum of four thousand dollars for merchandize sold and delivered to the defendant. Plaintiff sold to defendant and agreed to convey to defendant   acres of land lying in Smith County and one other tract of land lying in Sullivan county in the state of Tennessee, containing one thousand acres. Defendant though often requested has not conveyed said tract by Deed of Conveyance. Defendant, though solemnly called, came not ~ therefore considered by the Court that said James Moore recover against the said John Billingsley his damages … to be enquired of by a Jury at the next Court; at which Court the said James by his attorney comes, and a Jury ~ William Lyons, David Childress, William Axum, Edmund Owens, William Neelly, William Wilson, Isaac Phillips, Henry Hide, Robert McNairy, Thomas Edmiston, Sherwood Green & Robert Searcy who find for the plaintiff, damages of one cent besides his costs. [pp460/461]

Thomas Hardeman
    Vs   [In Debt]
Daniel Allen
Daniel Allen was summoned to answer Thomas Hardeman of a plea that he render to him $730 which to him he owes and unjustly detains, to his damage of four hundred dollars. Thomas, by John Dickinson his attorney, filed his Declaration November Term 1804. The defendant,

by William Smith his attorney, defends and says he has paid the debt. And the trial was continued until this day when comes the parties, by their attornies, and a Jury ~ William Lyons, David Childress, William Axum, Edmund Owens, William Neilly, William Wilson, Isaac Phillips, Henry Hide, Robert McNairy, Thomas Edmiston, Sherwood Green and Robert Searcy who say the defendant hath not paid the debt of $730 and assess the damages to $46.59 besides his costs. [pp460/462]

King, Carson & King
Vs   [Debt Appeal]
John Caffery

On 23 January 1805 an appeal was filed from the County Court of Davidson: To the Sheriff of Davidson County ~ have John Caffery if to be found in your county, before the Justices at the Courthouse in the town of Nashville April next to answer William King, Charles S. Carson and James King, copartners in the firm of *King, Carson & King*, debt of $490.22, damages of two hundred dollars.

Andrew Ewing. Alson Edney became the plaintiffs security. Edly Ewing, Deputy Sheriff made return to April Sessions 1804 that he had 'executed same on 30 January 1804.

Whereas on 16 June 1802 at Nashville John Caffery, by his certain writing obligatory, promised to pay two months after date for value received, with lawful interest from the date of the said writing obligatory. Debt has not been paid, therefore they bring suit. John Dickinson, attorney for the plaintiffs. Defendant, by Thomas Stuart his attorney, craves oyer of the endorsements on the said writing obligatory as follows: 'Received August 19, 1803, three hundred dollars of the within note in a Negro girl' . . . Rec'd Nashvill, January 14, 1803 of Capt Jno Caffery, James Mulherin's receipt for cotton to the amount of sixty five Dollars . . . . King, Carson and King August 26th 1804 then signed the within note on John Caffery the amount to Eli Hammond for one hundred and sixty one Dollars and the interest on the note and Eighty one cents and three fourths. Witness Zachariah Tait

Thus were the plaintiffs and defendant at issue and the cause was continued to July Sessions 1804 at which time comes the plaintiffs by their attornies and comes a Jury ~ John Harrison, Alexander Laird, John Skinner, Matthew Williams, Joel Pace, Nathan Skinner, C. Stump, David McGavock, William Murry, James Moore, William Gordon and Kemp Holland who find in favor of the defendant - after which the plaintiffs by their attorney prayed and obtained that the cause should be again reheard, and it was continued to October Sessions 1804 at which time came the parties by their attornies and thereupon came a Jury ~ William Scott, Greenwood Payne, William Thompson, Francis Sanders, William Mullin, John Harrison, Junr, John Payne, Samuel Caldwell, Andrew Work, George Bell, William Tait and Sylvenus Cassellman who find for the plaintiffs their debt remaining due principal and interest $172.51. Defendants requested another trial which was refused; defendant requested and obtained an appeal to the Superior Court. Andrew Ewing 5 December 1804

And now at this term of the Superior Court come the parties by their attornies and a Jury ~ William Lyons, David Childress, William Axum, Edmund Owens, William Neilly, William Wilson, Isaac Phillips, Henry Hide, Robert McNairy, Thomas Edmiston, Sherwood Green and Robert Searcy who say the defendant did not pay to the plaintiff one hundred and sixty six dollars and seventeen and one half cents parcel of the Debt and assess the plaintiffs damages to sevewnteen dollars and forty three cents and their costs. [pp462-465]

Roger B. Sappington
    Vs   [In Debt]
Joseph Hays

On this day, May 23, 1805, a writ at the suit of Roger B. Sappington vs Joseph Hays of a plea of Debt for $700.00 was acknowledged in open Court by the said Joseph Hays; declaration filed by Hays attorney as follows ~ Joseph (together with William Dickson who is not in custody) in the District of Mero on 18 of July 1803 made his certain writing obligatory, by which Hays and Dickson promised to Sappington the sum of $700.00 on or before 1 September 1804 for value received. Mr. Smith, atty.

Hays confesses that he cannot deny the plaintiffs action for seven hundred dollars, also thirty one dollars and ten cents damages. Therefore, with the assent of the plaintiff, it is considered that he recover against the said defendant and damages and his costs and the plaintiff agrees to stay the execution of this judgment. [pp465/466]

Henry Hide
   Vs   **[Debt Appeal]**
Roger B. Sappington

On 27 March 1805 an appeal from the County Court of Davidson was filed with the clerk of the Superior Court. *Transcript* ~Sheriff of Davidson County directed to have Roger B. Sappington before the Justices of the Court of Davidson County to be held July next to answer Henry Hide on a charge of debt of $328.54 and damages of fifty dollars. Signed Andrew Ewing April 1804 and issued May 18, 1804. Sheriff made return to July Sessions 1804 'executed 22 May 1804 and bail taken. Signed J. Boyd, shff At July sessions the plaintiff appeared by Jesse Wharton, his attorney, and made his declaration – on 16 April 1803 said Roger made his certain writing obligatory and promised to pay on or before the 1st January next; yet tho often requested the debt has not been paid. At July Sessions the defendant appeared by William Smith, his attorney, and says there is a varience between the said writing obligatory and the declaration. Cause continued to Octoer

Sessions 1804 at which time came the parties by their attornies and again continued to January Sessions 1805 at which time came the parties and a Jury ~ Stephen Bean, Robert Edmondson, Eli Garrett, William Simpson, Benjamin D. Wills, William Gordon, John Milligin, John P. McConnell, Benjamin Bashaw, Jonathan Downey, David Allen, & Calvin Wheaton who find for the plaintiff; should recover his debt plus twenty one dollars and eighteen cents damages; making the whole debt $349.72 and his costs of suit. From which judgment the defendant prayed and obtained an appeal to the Superior Court.
And now at this Term of the Superior Court come the parties by their attornies and a Jury ~ William Lyons, David Childress, William Axum, William Neelly, William Wilson, Isaac Phillips, Robert McNairy, Edmund Owens, Thomas Edmiston, Sherwood Green, John McMurry and Abner Henley who find for the plaintiff. Therefore on the motion of the plaintiff by his attorney, it is considered that the Judgment of the County Court be affirmed and that the plaintiff recover against the said Roger B. Sappington and William Smith, his securities, with twelve and ½ per cent interest thereon from the time Judgment passed in the County Court until this day and his costs of suit and plaintiff agrees to stay the execution of this judgment if debt and damages are paid within six months. [pp466-469]

Friday, May 24, 1805

Henry Hide
    Vs   **[Debt Appeal]**
Roger B. Sappington
On 27 March 1805 an appeal from the County Court of Davidson was filed ~*transcript:* To the Sheriff of Davidson - have Henry Hide before the Court of Pleas & Quarter Sessions July Sessions to answer Henry Hide in a plea that he render unto him $328.44 ..Issued May 18, 1804 ~ signed Andrew Ewing July Sessions 1804 plaintiff appeared by Jesse Wharton, his attorney and

filed his declaration; said Roger made his certain writing obligatory on 16 April 1803 to pay said Henry the sum of $328.54 on or before the fifteeth day of July next. Nevertheless tho often requested debt has not been paid. Defendant, by William Smith his attorney, defends ... cause continued to October Sessions 1804 at which time comes into Court both plaintiff and defendant by their attornies and cause was continued to January sessions 1805 when comes a Jury ~ Stephen Bean, Robert Edmondson, Eli Garrett, William Simpson, Benjamin D. Wills, William Gordon, John Maliegin, John P. McConnell, Benjamin Bashaw, Jonathan Downey, David Allen & Calvin Wheaton who find for the plaintiff principal and interest computed as damages of detention the sum of one hundred and ten dollars and fifteen and three fourth cents evidence of sundry payments indorsed in the declaration mentioned, also his costs of suit at which time defendant Sappington prayed and obtained an appeal to the Superior Court.

And now at this term of the Superior Court come the parties by their attornies and a Jury ~ William Lyons, David Childress, William Axum, Edmund Owens, William Neelly, William Wilson, Isaac Phillips, Robert McNairy, Thomas Edmiston, Sherwood Green, John McMurry and Abner Henry who find for the plaintiff; therefore on the motion of the plaintiff by his attorney, it is considered by the court here that the Judgment of the County Court be affirmed and that the plaintiff recover against Roger B. Sappington and William Smith and Nathan Ewing, his securities. [pp469-471]

Joseph McKean
    Vs   **[Debt Appeal]**
Henry G. Kearney
On 16 April 1805 an appeal from the County Court of Williamson County was filed in the Superior Court: *transcript* ~ To the sheriff of Williamson County – you are hereby commanded to have Henry

G. Kearney, if to be found in your county, before the Justices of our court of pleas and quarter sessions for the county of Williamson at the courthouse in the town of Franklin, to answer Joseph McKean of a plea of debt of $75.81 and damages. July 1804 signed N. P. Hardiman Sheriff made return to October Court; executed 4 August 1804. Plaintiff appeared by his attorney, Thomas Stuart .. that whereas Henry G. Kearney on 9 April 1804 his certain writing obligatory to Joseph McKean and promised three days after date to pay, nevertheless though often requested hath not paid said debt. The defendant, by J. Wharton his attorney, saith the defendant has paid said debt; cause continued until January session 1805 at which time came the parties by their attornies and a Jury ~ William Legate, William Perry, Thomas L. Robertson, Daniel McMahan, Matthew Johnston, John Johnston, Charles Brown, Moses Oldham, Ambrose Powel, Martin Standley, William McKnight and Joel Stephens who say the defendant did not pay the plaintiff the debt and assess the damages to three dollars and thirty six cents besides his costs, with which judgment the defendant being dissatisfied prayed and obtained an appeal to the Superior Court for the District of Mero.

And now at this term of the Suerior Court come the parties by their attornies and a Jury ~ Henry Hide, James Cannon, James Lauderdale, William Lane, Joel Holland, William Tait, Thomas Lofton, James Franklin, James Frazier, Edmund Jennings, Washington Jackson and Henry Bradford who say the defendant has not paid they debt and assess the plaintiffsto three dollars and thirty six cents besides his costs. Therefore on the motion of the plaintiff by his attorney, it is considered by the court here that the Judgment of the County Court be affirmed and that the plaintiff recovered against the said Henry G. Kearney and Peter R. Brooker, Joseph Mairs, his securities, together with twelve and an half per cent interest from the day Judgment was passed in the county until this day. [pp471-474]

King, Carson & King
Vs [Debt Appeal]
Peter Edwards

On 16 April 1805 an appeal was filed from the County Court of Williamson County in the Superior Court of the District of Mero.

Transcript ~ To the Sheriff of Williamson County - you are to have Peter Edwards before the Justices of our County court of pleas and quarter sessions at the courthouse in the town of Franklin in October to answer James King, Charles S. Carson and William King, trading as merchants under the firm of *King, Carson & King*, of a plea of debt of $86.87. signed Nicholas P. Hardiman, Clerk, July 1804, which writ was issued 13 September 1804; whereupon sheriff made return to October Session, 'executed same day came to hand.' The plaintiffs, by their attorney John Dickinson, made their declaration - whereas said defendant on 6 January 1804 at Franklin in the county of Williamson, by his certain writing obligatory, bound himself to pay the plaintiffs three days after the date of said writing for value received, yet said debt nor any part thereof has yet been paid. The defendant, by Jesse Wharton his attorney, says the debt has been truly paid … cause continued until January sessions at which time came the parties by their attornies and the following Jury ~ William Ligate, William Perry, Thomas L. Robinson, Daniel McMahan, Matthew Johnston, John Johnston, Charles Brown, Moses Oldham, Ambrose Powel, Martin Standley, William McKnight and Joel Stephens who find the debt has not been paid and assess their damages to five dollars thirty cents and costs of the suit. The defendant being dissatisfied prayed and obtained an appeal to the Superior Court for the District of Mero.

And now at this Term of the Superior Court come the parties by their attornies and the following

Jury ~ William Lyons, David Childress, William Axum, Edmund Owens, William Neelly, William Wilson, Isaac Phillips, Robert McNairy, Thomas Edmiston, Sherwood Green, John McMurry & Abner Henly who say the debt has not been paid and on motion of the plaintiffs by their attorney it is considered by the Court here that the judgment of the county court be affirmed and that the plaintiffs recover against the said Peter Edwards & Henry G. Kearney and Isaac Crow his securities the debt with damages and 12 ½ per cent interest from the day Judgment passed in the County Court until this day. [pp474-476]

William McKey
     Vs   **[Debt Appeal]**
John Maclin
On 16 April 1805 an appeal from the County Court of Davidson was filed in the Superior Court – *transcript:* To the Sheriff of Davidson County – have John Maclin, if to be found in your county, before the Justices of our court of pleas and quarter sessions to be held at the courthouse in the town of Nashville October next, to answer William McKey of a plea that he render to him $131.00. Andrew Ewing,   Issued September 1, 1804
Thos Stuart became the plaintiffs security .. Sheriff made return to October Sessions 'came to hand the same it issued; executed the same day it came to hand, signed Edly Ewing, D.S. - and at which sessions the plaintiff appeared by Thomas Stuart his attorney; William McKey complains of John Maclin; whereas said John Maclin by his certain writing obligatory made on 17 April 1804, bound himself to pay Willie Barrow $131 with interest from date, it being for value received; said Willie Barrow afterwards, on said 15 May 1804, did endorse said writing obligatory and assigned the said note to William McKey, for value received. John Maclin then and there had notice   ... nevertheless said debt has not been paid. The defendant appeared by Jesse Wharton, his

attorney … cause continued to January Sessions 1805 when came the parties by their attorneys and the following Jury ~ Philip Pipkins, William Gordon, William Wilkinson, Edward Collins, Lackland McIntosh, John Davis, Samuel Buchanan, John Blackman, Alexander Lird, William Homes, Charles Hays and Lazarus Gatlin who say the defendant has not paid and assess his damages to nineteen dollars making the whole debt & damages $150 and costs from which judgment the defendant prays and obtains an appeal.

And now at this term of the Superior Court come the parties by their attornies and the following Jury ~ Henry Hide, James Cannon, James Lauderdale, William Lane, Joel Holland, William Tait, Thomas Lofton, James Franklin, James Frazier, Edmund Jennings, Henry Bradford, and Robert Searcy who say the Defendant hath not paid the debt and it is considered by the Court here that the plaintiff recover against the defendant his debt together with his damages and costs. [pp476-478]

James Titus
    Vs   **[Debt Appeal]**
John Gordon

On 16 April 1805 an appeal from the County Court of Davidson was filed in the Superior Court: *transcript* – To the Sheriff of Davidson County – Have John Gordon before the Justices of our court of pleas and quarter sessions at the courthouse in the town of Nashville July next, to answer James Titus assignee of Arthur Turner in a plea of debt of $65 – issued June 15, 1804 and signed Andrew Ewing. John Boyd, sheriff, made return to July Sessions 'came to hand June 16, 1804. Executed 21 June 1804'. At July Sessions the plaintiff appeared by Parry W. Humphreys his attorney, and presented his bill as follows – James Titus complains of John Gordon … defendant on 10 April 1804 made his certain writing obligatory to a certain Arthur Turner and promised to pay said Arthur Turner or his assignee one day after date of said note, for value received ... said Arthur Turner by the name of Arthur H. Turner on the 10th of May 1804 endorsed said note to Titus and defendant had notice.   Defendant appeared by Bennet Searcy his attorney and maintains he has paid note. Cause continued to October Sessions 1804 at which time came the parties by their attornies and a Jury ~ David Hays, Foster Sayers, Neal Thompson, Joseph Hopkins, Daniel A. Dunam, Joseph Brown, William Harvey, William Probart, Matthew Williams, William Corbit, Jonathan Downey and Hugh McNeely who find for the plaintiff the debt is not paid and assess his damages to $210 and costs of the suit. Defendant prayed and secured an appeal.

And now at this term of the Superior Court come the parties and a Jury ~ William Lyons, David Childress, William Axum, Edmund Owens, William Neely, William Wilson, Isaac Phillips, Robert McNairy, Thomas Edmiston, Sherwood Green, John McMurry and Abner Henly who find for the plaintiff therefore on motion of the plaintiff by his attorney it is considerd that the judgment of the county court be affirmed. [pp478-480]

Jackson & Hutchings
    Vs   **[Debt Appeal]**
John Gordon
On 16 April 1805 an appeal was filed in the Superior Cour of the District of Mero from Davidson county court ~ *transcript* - To the sheriff of Davidson county - 'you are commanded to have John Gordon if to be found in your county, before the Justices of our court of pleas & quarter sessions to be held at the courthouse in the town of Nashville on 3rd Monday in July next to answer Andrew Jackson and John Hutchings, merchants trading under the firm of *Jackson & Hutchings*, assignee of James Irwin, assignee of Jesse Dawson, that he render unto them seventy six dollars and sixty cents which he owes to them' April 1804 signed Andrew Ewing; issued June 6, 1804. John Boyd, shff returned

same 'came to hand the same day issued, executed this 21st June 1804. Signed John Boyd, shff.

Plaintiffs appeared at aforesaid sessions by Thomas Stuart, their attorney. Whereas John Gordon by his certain writing obligatory made at the county aforesaid on 29 April 1804, and by endorsement on the back of the said writing obligatory signed in the proper hand of the said Jesse Dawson assigned the note to James Irwin, whereof the said John Gordon had notice; James Irwin afterwards, 4 June 1804, indorsed the said note to Jackson & Hutchings, whereof John Gordon had notice. The defendant appeared in the defense by Bennet Searcy, his attorney, says debt has been paid. The cause was continued until October Sessions when came the parties by their attornies, and came the following Jury~ David Hays, Foster Sayres, Neal Thompson, Joseph Hopkins, Daniel A. Dunam, Joseph Brown, William Harvey, William Probst, Matthew Williams, William Corbett, Jonathan Harvey & Hugh McNeely who find for the plaintiffs, considered by the court the plaintiffs to receive their debt + damages for total of seventy eight dollars and thirty two cents plus costs. The defendant prayed and obtained an appeal to the Superior Court, having given bond …

And now at this term of the Superior Court come the parties by their attornies and a Jury ~ Henry Hide, James Cannon, James Lauderdale, William Lane, Joel Holland, William Tait, Thomas Lofton, James Franklin, James Frazier, Edmund Jennings, Henry Bradford & Robert Searcy who find for the plaintiffs - therefore considered by the Court that the judgment of the County Court be affirmed and that the plaintiffs recover against the said John Gordon and Jonas Manifee and Bennet Searcy, his securities. [pp481-483]

Robert Stephens
    Vs   [Debt Appeal]
John Nichols

On 17 April 1805 an appeal from the County Court of Davidson was filed – *transcript* – 'To the Sheriff of Davidson County – You are commanded to have John Nichols, if to be found in your county, before the Justices of the Court of pleas and quarter sessions to be held at the court house in the town of Nashville … to answer Robert Stevens on a plea that he render to him $586.75 which he owes plus damages .. June 30, 1804 Andrew Ewing. And whereon Edly Ewing, then Deputy Sheriff, made return July Sessions 'came to hand 4 July 1804, Executed 7 July 1804' and at which Sessions of July the plaintiff appeared by his attorney, John Dickinson. Whereas the said John on 13 October 1803 at Nashville, made his certain writing obligatory and promised to pay the sum of $586.75 on or before the first day of January next. John did not pay the said Robert although often requested. July Sessions came the defendant by his attorney, Jesse Wharton; cause continued to October Sessions 1804 when came the parties into court, by their attornies and thereon comes a Jury ~ David Hays, Foster Sayers, Neal Thompson, Daniel A. Dunam, William Harvey, Joseph Hopkins, William Probat, Matthew Williams, William Corbett, Jonathan Harvey & Hugh McNeely, who say they find that defendant has paid $165 of the debt but the residue is unpaid and they assess the plaintiff damages to twenty one dollars and eighty nine cents. Therefore it is considered the plaintiff do recover the said residue of the debt plus the damages and costs of the suit. From which Judgment the defendant prays an appeal to the Superior Court, having give bond and security.

And now at this term of the Superior Court come the parties by their attornies and a Jury ~ William Lyons, David Childress, William Axum, Edmund Owens, William Neelly, William Wilson, Isaac Phillips, Robert McNairy, Thomas Edmiston, Sherwood Green, John McMurry and Abner Henly who find for the plaintiff. It is considered by the Court that the judgment of the County Court be affirmed and that the plaintiff recover against the said John Nichols and William Lytle, Junr and Joseph McKean, his securities. The debt aforesaid and damages together with twelve and one half per cent interest from the time Judgment passed in the County Court. [pp483-485]

John Overton
    Vs   [Debt Appeal]
Thomas H. Perkins

On 23 April 1805, an appeal from the County Court of Williamson was filed to the Superior Court of the District of Mero. *Transcript* ~ To the Sheriff of Williamson County - ..have Thomas H. Perkins, if to be found in your county, before the Justices of our Court of pleas and quarter Sessions to be held at the courthouse in the town of Franklin the second Monday in January next to answer John Overton on a plea of $552.50 with damage of $200.00. signed Nicholas P. Hardiman, Clerk   October 1804   John Dickinson became the plaintiffs security. The sheriff made return to January Sessions 1805 'Executed'   Plaintiff appeared by John Dickinson, his attorney. Whereas the defendant on 21 October 1802, at Franklin, made his certain writing obligatory for the said sum of $552.50 to be paid one year from the date of the said note, for value received, yet the defendant did not and has not paid the debt. Cause continued until April Session 1805, at which time came the parties by their attornies and a Jury ~ Joseph B. Porter, Alexander Crawford, Edward Swanson, William Willet, Andrew Corvisar, Joel Riggs, William McEwen, William Pillow, Joseph Philips, Samuel Wilson, Rhodin Poe & Matthew McGaugh who say the defendant did not pay the debt and assess the plaintiffs damages to $81.95 besides his costs; Defendant dissatisfied prayed and obtained an appeal to the Superior Court.

And now at this term of the Superior Court come the parties by their attorney and a Jury ~ Henry Hide, James Cannon, James Lauderdale,

William Lane, Joel Holland, William Tait, Thomas Lofton, James Franklin, James Frazier, Edmond Jennings, Henry Bradford and Robert Searcy who find for the plaintiff. [pp486-488]

John P. McConnell
    Vs   [Case Appeal]
William German

On 20 May 1805 an appeal from the county court of Davidson was filed with the Superior Court for the District of Mero: *transcript* ~ To the Sheriff of Davidson County – have William German, if to be found in your county, before the Justices of the court of pleas & quarter sessions at the courthouse in the town of Nashville July next to answer a plea of trespass. June 2, 1804 Andrew Ewing & Jacob Garret became plaintiffs security. And at July Sessions plaintiff appeared by John Dickinson, his attorney. John P. McConnell complains that on 16 May 1804 at Nashville William German did publish and make known a certain scheme or plan for the sale or disposal of sundry articles of personal property of him the said William commonly called 'a lottery' did offer for sale 326 tickets at the price of $1.50 each … ticket to be drawn on or about the 18th of July. William bought five the said tickets … numbers #77, #78, #193, #322 & #323; afterwards on 29 of same month the said William proceeded to draw and the prize of a horse of value of $100 was drawn against the number #323 …has not delivered horse or value thereof. John Dickinson represented the plaintiff and Jesse Wharton the defendant. Cause was continued until January at which time came the parties by their attornies and a Jury ~ Harris Ogilvie, James Gordon, William Caldwell, William Curry, James Gatlin, Thomas Dillon, Nathan Gatlin, Thomas Warron, Mark Thomas, William Davidson, Daniel Wooton and Jesse Maxel who find for the plaintiff. From which judgment the defendant prayed and obtained an appeal to the Superior Court. 27 March 1805   Andrew Ewing

And now at this term came the plaintiff by his attorney and the appellant not having brought up the appeal in this cause within the time prescribed by law, it is considered by the court here that the decision of the county court be affirmed and recover against the appellant and William Porter & Maclin Cross, his securities. [pp488-491]

John Summerville
    Vs   [In Debt]
Stockley Donelson

Stockley Donelson was summoned to answer John Sommerville in a plea of Debt of $1582.34 and damages of $500.00. Whereupon the said John by Bennet Searcy, his attorney filed his declaration November Term 1803 - Whereas on 25 February 1801 in the county of Davidson the said Stockley made his certain writing obligatory for $792,17 before the first of May next ensuing - said Stockley did not pay on or before said date therefore became liable to pay the sum of $1,582.34 according to said writing obligatory. Defendant by Robert Whyte his attorney, says he paid the debt. Cause was continued from term to term when come the parties and the Defendant confesses that he cannot deny the plaintiff action for $791.17 and legal interest, therefore with the assent of plaintiff it is considered that he recover against the defendant the said sum and his costs. [pp491-493}

Roger B. Sappington
    Vs   [Debt]
William Dickson

On this day, May 24, 1805, a writ at the suit of Roger B. Sappington against William Dickson of a plea of debt for $700, damage $100, was acknowledged in open court by the said William Dickson; whereupon the said Roger by his attorney filed his declaration ~ William Dickson, together with a certain Joseph Hays who is not in custody, at Nashville on 18 May 1803 made his certain writing obligatory. . bound himself to pay to said Roger $700.00 on or before the first of September 1804, for value received. Nevertheless the said William hath not paid - And the said William confesses that he cannot deny the plaintiffs action for seven hundred dollars, also thirty one dollars and ten cents damages. Therefore with the assent of the plaintiff, it is considered by the court that he recover said amount and his costs and plaintiff agrees to stay the execution of this judgment for the principal for six months. {p493}

Samuel Forrester, late of the County of Jackson, who stands convicted of Murder, was again led to the bar in custody of the sheriff of Davidson county, and thereupon it be demanded of the said Samuel Forrister if any thing for himself he had or knew to say why the Court here to judgment and execution of and upon the premises should not proceed, said he had nothing but what he had before said; whereupon all and singular, the premises being seen and fully understood. It is considered by the Court that the said Samuel Forrister be taken to the Jail from whence he came, and there to remain until the fifteenth day of June next, and from thence to the public gallows of Davidson County, there to be hanged by the neck until dead - and that execution of this Judgment be made and done upon him the said Samuel Forrester, by the Sheriff of Davidson County on Saturday the fifteenth day of June next between the hours of twelve in the morning and four in the afternoon of the same day. [See p301/p415][p494]

Saturday   May 25, 1805

The following Jurors proved their attendance and received tickets:

Name	days	miles	ferriages
William Lyons	12	110	4
David Childress	12	170	2
William Tait	11		
William Axum	12	90	2
Edmund Owens	12	10	
Thomas Lofton	12	26	
William Neelly	12	51	
William Wilson	9	50	
Isaac Phillips	12	80	2
Henry Hide	9	10	2
Thomas Edmiston	11	28	
Robert McNairy	12	120	
Sherwood Green	12	36	
William Snoddy	12	50	2
Abner Henly	12	144	6
Robert Searcy	11		
James Cannon	12	80	2
James Lauderdale	12	76	2
William Lane	12	120	4
Joel Holland	12	120	2
John McMurry	5	70	2

[p494]

Perry W. Humphrey
    Vs   [O Atta]
John Verrell

On 19 Oct 1804 Parry W. Humphreys obtained an attachment against the estate of John Verrell for $1560.00 to be discharged by the payment of $725.00 with interest, returnable to November Term 1804. The Attachment is in these words: .. Sheriff of Smith county ~whereas Parry W. Humphreys hath complained on oath to me, John Lancaster Esquire a Justice of the Peace of the county aforesaid, that John Verrill is indebted …we command you that you attach the estate of the said Verrell, if to be found in your county, to satisfy the said debt and costs. And such estate so attached to secure, that the same may be liable to further proceedings to be held for the District of Mero at Nashville. The sheriff of Smith County made return to November Term

1804 that he had "levied the within on a stud horse – and summoned Richard Brittain garnishee the 25th of October 1804. Lee Sullivan" November Term 1804 came the plaintiff by John Dickinson his attorney ... ordered proceedings be stayed for six months and now at this term comes the plaintiff and confesses that he intends no further action. It is therefore considered the plaintiff pay the costs of this suit. [p495]

Nancy Paxton by her next friend Jesse Wharton
    Vs   **[Petition for Divorce]**
Thomas Paxton
On 29 January 1803, Nancy Paxton by her next friend Jesse Wharton exhibited her petition to the Judges of the said Court against Thomas Paxton, which said petition follows: 'To the Honorable the Judges of the Superior Court of law and equity for the State of Tennessee. The petition of Nancy Paxton alias Nancy Thomas, by her next friend Jesse Wharton , respectfully represents to your honors that sometime in the month of February 1800, she was married to a certain Thomas Paxton, that the said Paxton lived with her only about eight months and then absented himself and left the State without any just cause and carried away with him two negroes which he got by his intermarriage with the petitioner and that he has not as yet returned – that she has been informed and verily believes that the said Paxton was at the time of his intermarriage with this petitioner, a married man, and that his lawful wife was then, and now is living. That he now is as she believes, living with his first wife in the Mississippi Territory - requests the court will set aside, and forever disannul the bands of matrimony – State of Tennessee. Davidson County – 16 February 1803 This day personally appeared before me, Andrew Jackson, one of the Judges of the Superior Courts of law and equity for the State of Tennessee, Nancy Paxton alias Nancy Thomas, and made oath that the above petition is true ... 29 January 1803   Andrew Jackson

And process of subpoena having being granted commanding the said Thomas to appear ... Sheriff of Davidson County having returned that the said Thomas was not found and now at this term, May 1803, it is ordered that an alias subpoena be served commanding the said Thomas to appear at November Term. And the cause was continued from Term to Term until this term, Nov 1804, at which sheriff reports said Thomas is not to be found, and also appearing that notice has been given in the *Tennessee Gazette* for four successive weeks and said defendant failing to appear and answer and testimony having been heard .. it is ordered that the said bonds of matrimony be dissolved, and that the said marriage be declared null and void... that all the property both real and personal be vested in the said Nancy Paxton and said Nancy to pay costs of this petition. 28 May 1805 John Overton [pp496/497]

Tuesday May 28, 1805

Josiah G. Duke
    Vs   **[petition Appeal]**
William Hargrove, admr of John Hargrove, decd
On 21 July 1803 an appeal from the county court of Davidson was filed for the Superior Court. *Transcript* ~ Davidson County – your petitioner, Josiah G. Duke, of the county aforesaid, saith that sometime in the latter end of the year 1798 a certain John Hargroves departed this life intestate, and at the January Court held for the county in the year 1799 William Hargrove administered on all goods and chattels of the said John, deceased and did render an inventory of the estate of the said deceased and obtained an order to dispose of the perishable estate of the said John, deceased. You petitioner further showeth that sometime previous to the death of the said John Hargroves he intermarried with Sally Hargroves, daughter to the said deceased, and therefore in right of his wife Sally became entitled to a share of the estate of said John, deceased. You petitioner further showeth that

after the death of the said John he did purchase from Thomas Hargrove one of the leggatees of the said his share and part of theestate, that he was or could be entitled to by law, which said contract was made July 1801, at which time said Thomas was of full age and capable of contracting for himself , wherefore your said petitioner being entitled to two shares of the said estate. The amount of said estate amounting to sixteen hundred and fifty two dollars and four cents. Admr had paid nine hundred sixty five dollars ninety seven cents which left a balance of six hundred and eighty six dollars seven cents, petitioner claims his right of two shares … Admr has not made account of other materials received … a matter of iron – 30 bushels of salt received from Kentucky by the hands of Jacob Lovel .. amount of about $30 never accounted for .. never made an account of the increase in the stock .. further states that said administrator kept three negroes belonging to the estate for two years without accounting to the legatees their part of the hire of said negroes but kept it for his own use ..Oct Sessions 1801 Bennet Searcy for the plaintiff Whereon a rule of court was then made writ issued to said William Hargrove to answer as administrator said petition – whereon John Boyd Esquire Sheriff made return to January Sessions 1802 'Decr 8 1801 – I have this day executed the within' Joseph Herndon appeared in behalf of said William Hargroves Thomas Stuart, one of the plaintiffs attornies moved to continue ~ Cause continued until this Term, at which time came the parties by their attornies and the petition being argued, it seems to the Court that said matters in the Petition are not sufficient to compel the defendant to answer and that the said petitioner shall pay the costs. [pp497-502]

Josiah G. Duke guardian of Lucy M. Hargrove
Vs   **[Petition Appeal]**

William Hargrove, admr of John Hargrove, deceased

Be it remembered that on 22 July 1803 an appeal from the County Court of Davidson County was filed with the Superior Court ~ 'To the Court of pleas and quarter sessions – Josiah G. Duke, guardian for Lucy M. Hargrove who now sues as quardian for her 'sometime in the latter end of the year one thousand seven hundred and ninety eight John Hargroves, father to the said Lucy, died intestate at at January court William Hargroves, administered on all the goods and credits of the said John, dec'd and obtained an order to dispose of the perishable estate of the said John .. [same charges as given in preceeding petition]
And the cause was continued in the Superior Court until this term at which day comes the said petitioner by Bennet Searcy his attorney, and confesses he intends no further to prosecute his said action. Considered by the court the same be dismissed and petitioner pay the costs. [pp503-508]

Charles M. Hall
    Vs   [In Case]
John Caffery

John Cafery was attached to answer Charles M. Hall on a plea of Trespass upon the case to his damage $550.00, whereupon the said Charles by Jesse Wharton his attorney filed his declaration ~ whereas the said John Caffery on 7 April 1803 at Nashville made a certain note, commonly called a promisory note in which said John Caffery promised to pay Hall or his assigns ten days after the date of said note $402.80 for value received ... though often requested said note remains unpaid. Caffery, by Thomas Stuart his attorney requests charge be dismissed .. cause continued until this term at which day comes the plaintiff by his attorney and the defendant in person who confesses he cannot deny the plaintiffs action ..therefore with the assent of the plaintiff it is considered that he recover his said debt and the costs of the suit and plaintiff agrees to stay the execution for six months. [pp508/509]

John Sevier Esquire Governor
    Vs
Benjamin Totton collector of the county of Jackson & James Henderson & Henry Reybourn, his securities

On the motion of Thomas Crutcher, treasurer of the District of Mero, and it appearing that Benjamin Totton, collector of the county of Jackson for the year 1804 has failed to pay the treasurer the sum of $545.73 ¾ cents tax for the year and that John Sevier, Governor recover the aforesaid sum and costs. [p509]

John Sevier, Governor
    Vs
Robert Weakley, collector of Dickson County & Samuel Walker & Nathaniel Johnston, his securities

On the motion of Thomas Crutcher, treasurer of the District of Mero, and it appearing to the satisfaction of the court that Robert Weakley, collector of the county of Dickson for the year 1804, has failed to pay to the treasurer the sum of $268.69 ½ cents for the year and that John Sevier, Governor, recover the aforesaid sum and costs. [p510]

John Sevier, Governor
    Vs
Benjamin Menees {*James, in small print*} collector of Robertson County & Benjamin Menees, Senr, Philip Parchment & William F. Ellin, his Securities

On motion of Thomas Crutcher, Treasurer of the District of Mero, and it appearing that Benjamin Menees, collector of the county of Robertson for the year 1804, has failed to pay to the treasurer the sum of $334.28 for the year and that John Sevier, Governor, recover the additional sum and costs. [p510]

Joseph Boyer [In Error - a Judgment rendered by the Justices
Vs of the county court of Davidson - Jan 1804]
William Porter
Whereas in the record and also in rendering Judgment in a certain action of Debt between William Porter plaintiff and Joseph Boyer, defendant, whereby it was consiered by the county court that Porter should recover against Boyer 4298.86 and costs, manifest error hath intervened, and we being willing that the error aforesaid if any, be corrected … signed Randal McGavock Nov 1803
Jesse Wharton became security for plaintiff ,,, charges that said Joseph on 3 July 1793, at Campbell County, VA, made his certain writing obligatory… J. Wharton for plaintiff. Defendant then appeared October Sessions 1802 by Redman D. Barry - cama a Jury ~William Parker, John Gowen, William Ewing, Richard Harman, Nicholas Riter, James Campbell, John Taylor, Jacob Garret, David Earheart, David Cloyd, Joseph Lynn and William Thomas who find for the plaintiff. Defendant moved for a new trial, overruled- defendant, by Robert White, his attorney, filed for reasons of an arrest of judgment .. And now at this Term of the Superior Court May 1804, comes Boyer by Robert Whyte .. And now upon further mature consideration it is determined that the judgment of the county court is affirmed and said William do recover against the said Joseph his costs. [pp510-514]

Matthew Brooks
Vs [On a petition for a ferry]
David McGavock
On 9 May 1804 an appeal from the county court of Davidson was filed in the office of the clerk of the Superior Court for the District of Mero.

April 17, 1804 - Robert Hewitt, Robert Heaton, Daniel Young, Thomas Williamson, Thomas Dillahunty, James Mulherrin, Joseph Phillips, James Dickson, Edmond Gamble, Joel Lewis, James Byrns, Joseph Coleman, John Stump, Thomas Hickman, Thomas Deaderick, and Isaac Roberts, Esquires Justices of the peace in and for the county of Davidson, and then sitting as a court when the following petition was exhibited to them ~ April 1804. To the worshipful court of Davidson county. Greeting - the petition of Matthew Brooks, Junr and others sheweth to your worships that it would be of public utility to have a ferry established at the upper end of Waynesborough at the mouth of Harrys branch called Brook's Landing and in granting said petition your petitioners as in duty bound will pray, and to which petition was marked the following names, to wit, Matthew Brooks etc . . . And the above named Justices then taking the said petition into consideration are of the opinion that the prayer of the same ought to be granted, and that a ferry be established to Matthew Brooks across Cumberland river at the mouth of Harrys Branch below Heatons Old Station agreeable to the prayer of the petitioners. ~ Whereupon David McGavock concerning himself injured by the decision of the said Court in granting said Ferry prayed and obtained an appeal to the Superior Court for the District of Mero having given bond and security. I certify that the before is a true transcript. Andrew Ewing 5 May 1804 And the cause was continued until this term at which day came the petitioner by Thomas Stuart his attorney and the defendant by Jesse Wharton his attorney; arguments were heard - It is ordered by the Court that the Judgment of the county court be reversed and the said petition be dismissed and Matthew Brooks pay the costs of this petition. [pp514/515]

Ethelred Williams
    Vs [Scifa]
Robert Hays & Robert McConnell

Bail for Stockley Donelson
Whereas Ethelred Willians at November Term 1799, in our Superior Court of Mero District recovered against Stockley Donelson five thousand two hundred and fifty four dollars and seventy five cents as well for damages which he sustained by reason of the non performance of a certain covenant between Ethelred and the said Stockley Donelson, nevertheless execution of three thousand nine hundred and sixty four dollars and eleven cents remains to be paid and whereas Robert Hays and Robert McConnell are security; make it known to them that they be before the Judges of our Superior Court May next. Randal McGavock Nov. 1803 On which day comes the said Etheldred Williams by John Dickinson his attorney and the sheriff returns that he has made the same known to Robert Hays, and Robert McConnell not found in his county. The defendants by their attorney Bennet Searcy come into court and defend because they say that they surrendered up said Stockley in discharge of themselves ... above continued until the next court at which time came the parties by their attornies ~ the defendants relinquish their plea, therefore on the motion of the plaintiff it is considered by the court that he may have execution against the said defendants for $3,964.11 and also that the plaintiff recover against the defendants his costs. [pp516/517]

Eley Letner by her next friend, Joseph German
    Vs   **[Petition for Divorce]**
John Christopher Letner
On 11 November 1803 Eley Letner by her next friend Joseph German exhibited her petition to the Judges of our court against John Christopher Letner, which said petition follows ~ 'The petition of Eley Letner wife of John Christopher Letner on the ____ day of November 1799, in the county of Davidson and state of Tennessee and she was then and still is a citizen of the state of Tennessee, but now an inhabitant of the

county of Williamson. You petitioner further states that since said marriage said John Christopher Letner has been guilty of acts and deeds inconsistent with the matrimonial vow by willful and malicious desertion of your petitioner of your petitioner and by absence from her without reasonable cause for more than two years .. Elcy (X) Letner Test: Thos Stuart This day appeared before me Daniel Perkins one of the Justices of the peace for the county of Williamson and State of Tennessee and Elcy Letner made oath that the facts contained in the above petition are true to the best of her knowledge. Elcy (S) Letner 11 Nov 1803 Dan'l Perkins, J.P.

May Term 1804 comes the petitioner by Thomas Stuart her attorney; and the sheriff of Davidson county having returned that the said John C. Letner was not found in his county, and an alias subpoena issued … Nov. 1804 comes the said petitioner by her attorney reports that John C. Letner not found and on motion of the petitioner it is ordered that a decree dissolving the bonds of matrimony be made ~ whereupon it is ordered.This cause coming to be heard this 29 May 1805 before the Hon David Campbell It appearing that an alias subpoena has been and public notice has been given in the *Tennessee Gazette* for four successive weeks and that proclamation has been publicly made by the Sheriff on three several days at the court house during this present term, and the said defendant having failed to appear it is therefore decreed that the bonds of Matrimony be dissolved and that the said John Christopher be divorced from the said Eley Letner and the said Elcy Letner pay the costs. [pp517-519]

Peggy Buford
    Vs   [Petition for Divorce]
Henry Buford
On the   day of March 1804, Peggy Buford, by her next friend Robert Branch, exhibited her petition to the honorable Hugh L. White, one of

the Judges, against Henry Buford which said petition follows: The petition of Peggy Buford by her next friend Robert Branch, respectfully sheweth that on the fourteenth day of December 1801 she was lawfully married to a certain Henry Buford, with whom she lived but a very little time, to wit, for the space of three days, after the celebration of the rites of matrimony before he deserted her and continued absent from her for the space of eight or nine weeks, he then returned and continued with her for about the space of three weeks perhaps not so much after and willfully deserted and left her again stating that he would return within a week – your petitioner states that from that time until the present the said Buford has not returned, that she has received three letters from him, in all which he tells her that he never again will live with her and that she is at liberty to marry again to whom she pleases. She reports that from the letters she has received and what he has told others that it is not his intention ever to live with her as a husband, states that as she is informed and believes that said Buford has been the whole of the time in the Mississippi Territory and that the only occupation he has pursued is that of gaming. *Affidavit* – this day appeared before me Joseph Philips Esquire, one of the Justices of the Peace for Davidson County, Peggy Buford and made oath that the facts are true. Signed Peggy Buford

And process of Subpoena having been granted …May Term 1804, comes the said petitioner by Jesse Wharton her attorney . . On motion alias subpoema issued Nov. Term 1804 .. cause continued 29 May 1805 this cause coming to be heard before the Honorable David Campbell, Judge of the Superior Court ~ publication having passed in the *Nashville Gazette* and proclamation having been made at the court house on three several days during the November Term of this Court 1804 ~ it is therefore ordered that the bonds of matrimony between the said Peggy

Buford and Henry Buford be dissolved and that the said marriage be null and void. Peggy Buford to pay the costs. David Campbell & Jno Overton [pp519-521]

Wednesday May 29, 1805

James Hamilton & Joseph Porter
    Vs
Daniel G. Brown
It appearing to the satisfaction of this Court that Patrick Joyce and John Dun recovered against James Hamilton and Joseph Porter as bail for Daniel G. Brown $173.90 for debt, also $26.55 for costs and it also appearing that the debt and costs were satisfied by the said James Hamilton and Joseph Porter bail. Therefore on motion of the said James Hamilton & Joseph Porter by Parry W. Humphreys their attorney, it is considered the said James Hamilton and Joseph Porter recover against Daniel G. Brown $245.00 the amount of the debt and costs. [p521]

Joseph Porter & William Brown
    Vs
Daniel G. Brown
It appearing to the satisfaction of the court, that James Elder and Co. recovered against Joseph Porter and William Brown $29.00 for debt also $18.35 for their costs ..also appearing from the return of the Sheriff of Williamson County that the debt and costs were paid and satisfied by the said Porter & Brown, bail ~ Therefore on the motion of the said Porter & Brown by Parry W. Humphreys their attorney, it is considered that Joseph Porter & William Brown recover against the said Daniel G. Brown $47.35, the sum of the debt & costs. [p522]

Roger McDaniel
    Vs   [Scifa]
Benjamin J. Bradford

Whereas Benjamin J. Bradford was summoned under the penalty of $125.00 to appear at our Superior Court for the District of Mero November 1804 and give testimony on behalf of Roger McDaniel at the suit of John Overton, James Mulherin & Andrew Ewing, executors of Thomas Molloy, deceased in a matter of controvercy in the said Court between the executors and the said Roger McDaniel. And Bradford, having been called, came not, it is considered by the court that the said Benjamin J. Bradford be fined $125.00 unless he shew sufficient cause of his inability to attend. Randal McGavock On which writ the sheriff of Davidson County made return that he had made known to the said Bradford and the said Bradford appeared in court and on his affidavit it is ordered that this fine be remitted and he pay the costs. [pp522/523]

INDEX

Able
: Ezekiel 34, 176
: Gabriel 20

Adam Shepherd & Co. 51

Adams
: Britain 178
: William 3

Alcorn
: John 7, 24, 25

Alexander
: Henry 35, 91, 105
: Mathew 1, 7
: Matthew 4, 11, 16
: Richard 170
: William 95, 110
: William 156

Allen
: Beverly A. 82
: Daniel 180
: David 107, 125
: Grant 110
: William 149

Allen
: David 185

Allen,
: David 184

Allin
: Grant 95
: Grant 156

Allison
: Andrew 1-3, 14, 20, 22, 23
: David 83, 91

Allison
: Andrew 1

Alsop
: Drury 143

Anderson
: Israel 129
: John 17, 41, 59, 101, 105, 121, 136-138
: Luke 34
: Richard 123
: Timothy 86
: William 76
: William P. 69, 147

Andrew 64

Andrews
: James 2, 3, 5, 11, 16

Anthony
: Joseph 129

Armstrong
: James 33, 94
: Martin 13, 16, 21, 28, 56, 62, 101, 132
: William 123

Armstrongs
: John 3

Arthur
: Charles R. 83

Ashbrook
: Moses 153

Atkins
: Moses 56

Axum
    William 135
    William 143, 159, 162, 167, 171, 173, 174, 178-182, 184, 185, 188, 190, 192, 197

Badgers
    Oliver 25

Baily
    Henry 24

Baker
    Edmund 12

Baker
    Nathaniel M. 176

Balance
    Joshua 9, 49

Baldin
    Zenus 135

Baldridge
    John 34, 40, 60, 113

Baldrige
    John 122

Baldwin
    Zenus 137

Ballow
    James 33

Banks
    Thomas 151

Banton
    Lewis 147

Barfield
    Frederick 16

Barnes
    Joseph 48, 81, 129

Barnet
    Thomas 171

Barr
    Hugh 5, 14, 21, 91
    Patrick 49, 52, 55, 56, 64, 67, 70, 73, 75, 77, 79, 107

Barraw
    Micajah 28

Barrett
    Thomas 145

Barrow
    Micajah 4, 6, 8, 21, 23, 27, 28, 33, 35-37, 39-41, 49, 71, 76, 102, 123
    Micajah 143
    Sharrod 102
    Shearrod 57
    William 23, 37
    Willie 8, 13, 17, 21, 26, 27, 30-32, 34-36, 38-41, 115

Barrow
    Bennet 166
    Micajah 143
    Willie 188

Barry
    Redmond D. 20, 36, 67, 149
    Redmund D. 46, 59

Barry
    Redmond D. 151
Barton
    Samuel 119, 129
Bashaw
    Benjamin 184, 185
Bass
    Ezekiel 24, 98
    Ezekiel 166
    Jordan 34, 40, 60, 113
    Jourdan 166
    Theophelus 111
    Theophilus 96, 103, 104, 106, 117, 119, 121, 122
Batchelor
    Thomas 20, 35
Bean
    Stephen 7, 36, 37, 71, 72, 76, 117, 125
    Stephen 184, 185
Beard
    William 145
Beasley
    Isham 33
    Jesse 28
    Jesse 149
Beasley
    Jesse 150
Beaty
    David 68, 70, 73, 75, 77, 135
    David 173, 175
Beavers
    Joel 65, 66

Bedford
    John R. 131, 156
    Thomas 155
Bell
    George 8, 41, 107, 122
    George 182
    Hugh 87
    Hugh F. 89, 112
    Samuel 17
    William R. 49
    William R. 89
Belote
    Henry 118
Bennett
    Peter H. 117
Benton
    Jesse 164
    Nancy 164
Berry
    Bazel 162
    Redmund D. 44
Berry, Jr.
    James 159
Berry, Sr.
    James 159
Berry, Sr.
    James 160
Bethel
    Larkin 153
Betts
    William 23, 30, 59, 107, 114, 135, 136
    William 159, 179
    Zachariah 105, 117
Bigley
    Patrick 7, 37

Billings
    William 12, 59, 65, 66, 105, 134
Billingsley
    John 180
Billingsley
    John 180
Bird
    Amos 87
Birdwell
    George 50
    William 50
Bishop
    William 25
Black
    William 7, 37
Blackamon
    George D. 5
Blackamore
    Geo 132
    George 157
    John 167
    William 118
Blackbourn
    James 100
Blackburn
    James 33, 90
Blackemore
    John 122
Blackman
    Bennet 56
    Bennet 143
    John 162, 189
Blackman
    Bennet 143
Blackwell
    James 131
    James 156
Blair
    Brice 128
    Samuel 146
    Thomas 154

Blanton
    John 108
Bloodworth
    Hardy 145
Blount
    Jacentha 32
    Jackey 31
    Thomas 31, 55
    William 92
    Willie 15, 101, 102
Blythe
    Andrew 22
    Samuel 22
Boatwright
    Daniel 25
    David 25
Booker
    P. R 11
    P. R. 78
Boren
    Bazel 78
    Stephen 78
Borin
    Bazel 120
Bosley
    Beal 49, 55-57, 67, 72, 74, 75, 78, 79
    Beal 143
    James 19
    John 7
Bounds
    Obediah 49, 58, 63
Bowen
    John H. 172
    William 13, 68
    William 172
Bowen
    John 148

Bowers
    James 129
    Joel 65
Bowman
    Andrew 27
Boyce
    John 144, 145
    Nicholas 21, 23, 26, 27, 30-32, 34, 35, 37-40
Boyd
    Abraham 17, 59
    Andrew 26
    Harrison 129
    Harrison 171
    J. 29
    J. 183
    James 68, 70, 73, 75, 77, 96, 101, 104, 105, 110, 117, 119, 121, 123
    John 76, 80, 90
    John 189
    John, Sr. 48, 129
    Richard 117
    Rich'd 172
Boyd
    Richard 174
Boyer
    Joseph 203
Boyers
    Joseph 65, 66
Boyes
    Barnabas 57
Braden
    Alexander 24

Bradford
    Benjamin J. 6, 38
    Henry 19, 49, 52, 107
    Henry 189
Bradford
    Benjamin J. 208
    Henry 186, 191, 194
Bradley
    John 123
    Richard 49, 58, 64
    Thomas 24, 113, 119
Bradley
    Isham 149
Bradshaw
    William 107
Branch
    Robert 206
Branton
    Levi 84
Bratney
    Robert 107
Brewer
    Allen 9, 117
    Sterling 135
Briarce
    John 46
Bridgment
    Daniel 55
Brigance
    William 68
Briscoe
    George 89, 130
    William 120
Britain
    Thomas 73
Brittain
    Richard 101
    Thomas 68, 70, 77

Briward
    John 44
Brooker
    Peter R. 186
Brookins
    Thomas 22
Brooks
    John 113
    John 157
    Matthew 17, 22,
        73, 90,
        101, 105
    Matthew 175,
        203
    Matthew, Jr.
        204
    Matthew, Sr. 17
Brooks
    John 160, 161
Browder
    John 9
Brown
    Bazel 161
    Charles 186,
        187
    Daniel 70
    Daniel G. 13,
        71, 76,
        95, 208
    Daniel G. 75
    Jacob 19
    Jeremiah 85
    John 131
    John 156
    Joseph 111
    Joseph 190,
        191
    Richard 161,
        163, 165
    Ruffin 162
    William 70, 76,
        95
    William 208

Brown
    Ephraim 165
Browning
    George 78
Brownlee
    John 174, 176
Bruce
    Charles 165
Bryan
    Hardy S. 51
Buchahan
    John 72
Buchanan
    David 63
    George 63
    John 2, 3, 7,
        11, 12,
        16, 71,
        76,
        136-138
    Samuel 7, 33
    Samuel 189
Buckhannon
    Samuel 56
Buford
    Henry 206
    Peggy 206
Bulgin
    James 82
Bun
    Henry 13
Bunn
    Henry 68
Burford
    Daniel A. 152
    Daniel H. 155
Burgan
    John 135
Burnet
    George 143
Burnet
    George 143
Burnett
    George 37, 63

Burnett
    Brooking 141
    Reuben 141
Burnpass
    William 25
Burrow
    John 68
Burrows
    John 6
Burton
    Robert 61
    William 96
Butler
    Pierce 91
Byrnes
    James 17, 56
    James, Jr. 56
Byrns
    James 173, 204
Byrns?
    James 163
Cabiness
    Chartes 175
Caffere
    John 69
Caffery
    Capt Jno 181
    John 50, 69
    John 181, 201
Caffery
    John 168
Caffrey
    John 42-44
Cage
    Edward 33
    Edward 170
    J. 87
    William 36
    Wilson 33
Caldwell
    James 42
    James 172
    Samuel 104
    Samuel 182

William 33, 36,
    37, 71,
    76, 105,
    118, 132
William 194
Caldwell
    James 173
Campbell 1
    David 1, 2, 4,
        6, 8, 15,
        17, 19,
        21, 49,
        91, 95,
        113, 131
    David 171, 207
    George W. 10,
        11, 14,
        15, 30,
        92
    Hugh L. 95
    James 158, 203
    John 153
    Patrick 164
    Samuel 87
    W. 105
Campbell
    David 39
    James 148
    John 150
Campier
    Francis 175
Campior
    Francis 76
Cannaday
    Dennis 31
Cannon
    James 135-138
    James 145,
        146, 160,
        161, 163,
        165, 168,
        169, 172,
        175-177,
        186, 189,

       191, 193, 197
    Miner 35
Cannon
    James 159
    Newton 178
Cantrell
    Stephan 119
    Stephen 167
Capshaw
    Esau 87
Carmick
    Acquila 9
    Acquilla 37
Carns
    John 160
Carper
    Francis 71
Carriger
    Godfrey 124
Carson
    Charles L 8
Carson
    Charles S. 181, 187
Carter
    John 67
    John 168
Carter
    Job 143
Cartright
    Caleb 49
Cartwright
    Matthew 145
    Robert 13
Caruthers
    Hugh 170
    Robert 126, 136
Carvin
    William 177
Cash
    William 9
Cassellman
    Andrew 132

    John 132
Cassellman
    Sylvenus 182
Casselman
    Andrew 19, 33
    John 33
Cassle
    Littleton 24
Castilio
    John 76
Castleman
    Andrew 11, 50
    Slyvanius 57
Cates
    Thomas 7, 71, 76
Cathey
    Grifford 147
Cathey
    Alexander 170
Caveat
    Alexander 65
    Joseph 50
    Richard 50, 65, 66
Caveness
    Charles 105
Chambers
    Moses 162
Chatham
    John 161
Cheatham
    Anderson 88
    Edward 78
    John 97
Cheek
    Elisha 120
Cherry
    Daniel 25
    Willie 24, 49, 58, 64, 68, 70, 73, 75, 77

Childress
    David 133,
        135-137
    David 143,
        159, 162,
        167, 171,
        173, 174,
        178-182,
        184, 185,
        188, 190,
        192, 197
    John 71, 89
    S. 96, 127, 131
    S. 97
    Stephen 34, 40,
        60, 113
    William 165
Childress
    Henry 140
Chism
    Elijah 108
Chisum
    William 149
Claxton
    John 39
Claypole
    Jaramah 144
Clendenon
    James 5
Clinton
    Thomas 3, 87
Cloyd
    David 38, 49,
        64-66
    David 203
Cluck
    John 162
Clynton
    Thomas 3, 5,
        11, 16,
        89
    Thos 2
Cochram
    William 93

Cochran
    Alexander 54
    James 44, 46
    William 54
Cocke
    James A 35
    James W. 27,
        28, 33,
        35-38, 40
    John 97
Cockrell
    John 117
    John 174, 176
Cockrill
    John 9
Coffee
    John 58, 117
Cohia
    Amos 78
Cole
    Joseph 24
Coleman
    Joseph 17
    Joseph 204
Collins
    Edward 189
    John 9
    Joseph 34, 49,
        55, 56,
        67, 72,
        74, 75,
        78, 79
    Joseph 143
Collins
    Joseph 143
Colter
    Levi 52, 53
Connell
    William 87
Connelly
    Christopher
        173
Conrod
    Nicholas 120

Cook
  Edmond 165
Cooke
  Joseph 34
Coonrod
  Nicholas 20, 27, 38, 39, 73, 90
Cooper
  Robert 112
Coots
  John 2, 3, 56
Corbett
  Allen 89
  William 59
  William 191, 192
Corbit
  William 190
Corbitt
  William 71, 76
Corder
  Lewis 151
Cortney
  Nancy 60
Corvisar
  Andrew 193
Costileo
  John 71
Costillo
  John 143
Cotton
  Lazarus 119
Cox
  Thomas 158
Crabtree
  James 2, 3, 7, 9-12, 16
  John 22
  Joseph 88
  William 88
Crafford
  Hugh 5

Craighead
  John B. 7, 68
  Thomas B 3
Crawford
  Alexander 193
Crisp
  John B. 131
Crockett
  Samuel 135
Cross
  John B. 156
  Maclin 8, 76
  Maclin 195
  Marlin 71
  Martin 119
Crow
  Isaac 122
  Isaac 165
Crow
  Isaac 188
Crutcher
  Anthony 20, 56, 62, 86-88, 132
  E. 68, 81, 106
  Edmund 5, 27
  Thomas 8, 123
Crutcher
  Thomas 146
Crutcher,
  Thomas 202
Cryer
  James 36, 107
Cummins
  Elizabeth 115
  James 34, 115, 132
  John 32, 38, 115
  Samuel 171
Curle
  Wilson 80

Curry
    William 194
Curtis
    George B. 9, 37
Dale
    John 149
Danier
    Henry 151
Darden
    Jonathan 81
Darr
    John 9
Davidge
    Rezin 32
Davidson
    John 23, 24,
        27, 28,
        33, 35,
        38, 40,
        83
    William 194
Davidson
    John 154
    Josiah 154
Davidson Academy 47
Davis
    Andrew 167
    David 103
    Frederick 122
    Henry 147
    Isham F. 7
    James 162
    John 17, 36,
        37, 57
    John 189
    Obediah 143
    Robert 63
Dawson
    Jesse 190
    John 113, 119
Day
    Matthew 6, 7,
        21, 23,
        26, 27,
        30-33,
        35-38,
        40, 78
Deaderick
    Thomas 204
Dean
    Joseph 31
    Robert 175
Deason
    Samuel 19
Deathrige
    John 117
    John 174, 176
Debow
    Frederick 28
Degraffenreed
    Abram Maury 178
Dement
    Cader 147, 154
Demos
    Lewis 48
Demoss
    Lewis 9, 39
Den 1
    John 2, 3, 14,
        20-23,
        25, 31,
        35, 39,
        50, 55,
        56, 62,
        64, 65,
        67, 73,
        84, 90,
        91,
        98-100,
        105,
        108-110,
        112, 119,
        131, 137
Den
    John 143
Denman
    Samuel 53

Desha
    James 68, 107
Dew
    John 157
Dickenson 21
    John 136
Dickinson
    Jacob 174, 176
    James 120
    John 5, 27, 43, 44, 62, 71, 74-76, 78, 92, 93, 98, 99, 108, 110, 114, 115, 122
    John 143, 159, 181, 187, 192, 194
Dickinson 141
    John 139, 144, 161, 167, 171, 179, 180, 193
Dickinson,
    John 143
Dickinson, 141
Dickson
    James 17
    James 204
    Thomas 9
    William 77, 83, 94
    William 195
Dickson
    William 183
Dillahunty
    Thomas 17, 34, 40, 60, 113
    Thomas 204

Dilliard
    Joel 178
Dillon
    Thomas 108, 130
    Thomas 194
Dixon
    T. 46
    Thomas 8
    Tilman 28, 33
Dobbins
    David 132
Dodd
    John 87
Doe
    John 23, 84, 94
Dohertie
    James 69
Doherty
    James 70, 118
    James 147
Donahoe
    Archibald 134
Donalson
    Samuel 52, 53
Donelson
    John 19, 71, 76
    S. 128
    Samuel 12, 53, 59, 70, 81
    Stockley 195, 205
    Stockly 130, 133
    William 17
Donelson
    Samuel 145
Donnal
    William 11
Donnel
    Thomas 7
    William 2, 3, 7, 8, 16

Donnell
    Thos. 170
Donnelly
    James 8
Donnelson
    William 11
Doris
    Isaac 78
Dorris
    Isaac 129
    Isaac 161
Dotson
    Elisha 162
Douge
    Enoch 173
Doughertie
    James 69
Dougherty
    James 43, 44, 69
Douglas
    Ezekiel 34, 119, 134
    William 71
Douglass
    Edward 133
    Elmore 140
    Ezekiel 49, 137
    John 82
    John 151
    Reuben 145
    William 63, 76, 107
    William 143
Douglass
    Edward 167
    William 143
Dowing
    James 178
Downey
    Jonathan 184, 185
Downey
    Jonathan 190

Drake
    Benjamin 117
    Benjamin 163, 173
Draper
    Thomas 33
    Thomas 150, 153
Droling
    Harris 57
Duffell
    John, Sr. 33
Duffey
    John 3
Duffield
    John 3
Duke
    John 20, 42, 116
    Josiah G. 21, 42, 92, 93, 116, 199
    Philip 21, 42, 116
Duke
    Josiah G. 200
Dun
    John 208
Dunam
    Daniel A. 190-192
Duncan
    John 71
    Martin 82
Dunn
    John 75, 76
Dunning
    Robert 86
Dupree
    James 63, 64, 134
Dupriest
    Banyon 3

Dyar
    R. Henry 125
Dyer
    Joel 49, 58,
        63, 82
    Joel 138, 149,
        152, 154
Dyer
    Joel 138, 151,
        152
Eakin
    Moses 125
Earheart
    David 203
Earick
    Frederick 1, 2
Earls
    Sarah 120
Earrick
    Frederich 14
    Frederick 23
Easten
    John 17
Eastin
    John 53, 54
    William 54
Easton
    John 8
    William 158
Easton
    William 173
Eaton
    Pinktham 93
    Robert 66
Eckland
    Francis 22
    John 22
Edmiston
    John 122, 131
    John 156, 165
    Robert 1, 17,
        95, 110

Thomas 6, 11,
    133, 135,
    138
Thomas 143,
    159, 168,
    174,
    178-182,
    184, 185,
    190, 192,
    197
Edmiston
    Robert 156
    Thomas 162,
        167, 171,
        173
Edmiston,
    Thomas 143
Edmondson
    Robert 184,
        185
Edmondson
    William 162
Edney
    Alson 181
Edwards
    Nathan 170
    Peter 171, 187
    William 84, 120
    William 154
Edwards
    Peter 177, 188
Elder
    James 70
Ellice 23
    Robert 26
Ellin
    William F. 202
Elliot
    James 27
Elliott
    Lewis 87
Ellis
    Robert 21, 27,
        30, 31,

33,
35-38, 40
Elliston
    Joseph T. 42,
        172
Elm...
    Jerlins 78
Enochs
    Enoch 50
Enocks
    Benjamin 129
    David 129
    Enock 64
    Sarah 129
Ervin
    John C. 171
Erwin
    Joseph 125
Espy
    Robert 19
Etheridge
    Isaac 12
Evans
    Daniel 158
Evens
    John B. 20, 83
Everett
    Aaron 175
Evins
    Edley 163
Ewing
    Andrew 9, 26,
        43, 45,
        72, 104,
        114, 125,
        136
    Andrew 143,
        146, 159,
        163, 179,
        181,
        188-190,
        192, 194,
        209
    E. 83

E. 100
Edley 9, 70,
    125
Edley 142, 146
Edly 181, 188,
    192
Nathan 68, 70,
    73, 77
Nathan 185
Robert 19
Robert 167
William 7, 71,
    76
William 203
Ewing
    Andrew 173,
        175,
        182-184,
        194
    Nathan 173,
        175
Farmer
    George 163
    John 122
    John 165
    Thomas 13, 21
Farr
    William 143
Farris
    Edward 33
Fells
    Cary 49
Felts
    Bolling 168
    Cary 52, 55,
        56, 67,
        72, 74,
        75, 78,
        79
    Cary 143
Fen
    Richard 1, 2,
        23, 25,
        32, 35,

        39, 62,
        74, 90,
        98-100
    Richard 143
Fenton
    Caleb 22
Figures
    Matthew 49, 58, 64
Findley
    Francis 44, 46
Finley
    George 105
Fiser
    Peter 120
Fite
    John 49, 57
    Leonard 4, 49, 57
Fitzgerald
    Garrett 157
    Jabes 156
Fletcher
    Aaron 49, 58, 64
Floyd
    Nathaniel 133
Fly
    John 9
Ford
    James 89
Forrester
    Samuel 109
    Samuel 196
Forrister
    Samuel 156
Fort
    Josiah 22, 27, 28, 30-32, 34-38, 40, 95, 110
    Josiah 156

Foster
    Frederick 175
    Robert 8
    Robert C. 7
Foster
    Robert C. 153
Foster & Gray 153
Fox
    Daniel 143
Franklin
    James 13
    James 170, 186, 189, 191, 194
Frazeir
    James 68
Frazier
    Daniel 18
    Daniel 156, 178
    David 131
    James 1, 70, 73, 75, 77
    James 186, 189, 191, 194
Fry
    Jacob 78
    Joseph 120
Gains
    Benjamin 172
Gallaway
    John 91
Galloway
    John 4, 14, 21, 91
Galloway
    James 165
Gamble
    Bradley 122
    Edmond 17, 59
    Edmond 204

Edmund 33, 35, 38, 40
Edward 36
Gambrell
    Bradley 31
    John 31
Gardener
    Elizabeth 10
Gardner
    Henry 97
Garret
    Jacob 203
    John 113
    John 140
Garret
    Jacob 194
Garrett
    Eli 184, 185
    James 37
    John 113, 124
    Joseph 33
Garrett
    James 173
Gatlin
    James 194
    Nathan 12
    Nathan 194
Gatlin
    Lazarus 189
Gentry
    Claiborne 163
Germain
    William 40, 42
German
    Joseph 165, 205
    William 194
German
    William 172, 173
Gibson
    James 150, 153
    William 55

Wilson 49, 52, 56, 60, 67, 72, 74, 75, 78, 79
Wilson 143
Giles
    William 119
Gillaspie
    George 5
    William 5, 19
Gillespie
    John 107
    William 28, 33, 35
Gillispie
    William 22, 27, 36-40
Glass
    John 125
Goff
    Andrew 122
    Andrew 165
Goodloe
    David S. 100
    Henry 100
    John M. 100
    Robert 100
    William 100
Gorden
    John 38
Gordon
    James 19
    James 194
    John 84
    John 174, 176, 189, 190
    William 184, 185, 189
Gordon
    William 182
Gore
    Thomas 148, 169

Gore
    Thomas 149
Gowen
    John 203
Gower
    Russel 9
    Russell 8-12, 112
    Wm 9
Grace
    Allen 7
Graves
    John 1, 4, 5, 11, 16
Gray
    Deliverance 37, 71, 76
    George 153
    Samuel 34, 40, 60, 113
Grayhams
    John 84
Green
    George 174
    Sherwood 135
    Sherwood 159, 163, 165, 184, 185, 188, 190, 192, 197
    Thomas 9
    William 188
Green
    Sherwood 143, 159, 168, 171, 173, 174, 178-182
Greene
    Thomas 37

Greer
    Alexander 19
    Andrew 39, 52, 55, 56, 75, 78
    Andrew 150
    George 176
Greer
    Andrew 150, 153
Greir
    Andrew 113
Grerr
    Andrew 49
Grier
    Andrew 22, 67, 72, 74, 79
    Andrew 143, 153
Griffin
    William 96, 103, 105, 106, 110, 117, 119, 121, 123
Grissum
    John 150
Gunn
    William 142, 146
Gunn
    William 145
Gunnels
    Joseph 149
Gutharie
    Henry 173
Gutherie
    Henry 174
Gutherie
    Henry 161
Guthrie
    Henry 117
    Henry 175

Guthrie
    Henry 168
Guttery
    Henry 8
Hackett
    John 77
Hadley
    Joshua 69
Hadley & Rawlings 69
Haggard
    William 110
Hall
    Absolom 7
    Charles M. 39,
        56, 59,
        201
    Dan 35
    Francis 166
    William 21, 23,
        27, 28,
        33,
        35-37,
        39, 40,
        50, 55,
        118
    William 146,
        157
Hall
    Francis 166
Hallam
    George 98
Hallum
    Josiah 121
Hamilton
    J. C. 149
    James 9, 11-13,
        32, 72,
        75, 76,
        105
    James 146
    John C. 10, 12,
        24, 78,
        81, 119,
        120, 149

John C. 107
    Thomas 109
Hamilton
    James 147,
        170, 175,
        208
    John C. 144
    Thomas Maston
        170
Hammon
    Eli 32
Hammond
    Eli 21, 27, 28,
        30, 34,
        36, 37,
        40
Hammond
    Eli 182
Hammonds
    Eli 23, 31, 38
Hampton
    Adam 19
Hankins
    Arthur 39
    William 98
Hanks
    John 11
Hanna
    Robert 147
Hannes
    Samuel 146
Hanness
    Samuel 145
Hannum
    Washington L.
        32
Hardeman
    Nicholas P. 177
    Thomas 8
    Thomas 180
Hardiman
    N. P. 92

Nicholas P. 93,
    171, 187,
    193
Nicholas
    Perkins
    122, 161
Hardiman
    N. P. 186
Harding
    Moses 68
    Nicholas 164
    Nicholas P. 164
    Thomas 113,
        124, 127,
        134
    Thomas 140,
        174, 176
Hargrove
    John 199
    Sally 199
    William 199
Hargrove
    William 200
Hargroves
    Hargrove 92
    John 10
    Thomas 92
    William 10, 92
Harman
    John 125
    John 143, 163
    Richard 203
Harney
    Thomas 63, 118,
        132
    Thomas 168
Harris
    Benton 125
    Elmore 13, 68
    John 112
    Nelly 148
    Sampson 17
    Samuel B 38
    Samuel B. 34

Simpson 80,
    134,
    136-138
Simpson 162
Harris
    Nelly 149
    Simpson 147
Harrison
    John 182
    John, Jr. 182
    Thomas 137
Harrison
    John 176, 182
Harrisson
    John 174
Hart
    Lieutenant
        Anthony
        109
Harvey
    John 50
    William
        190-192
Harvey
    Jonathan 191,
        192
Hassell
    John 10
Haton
    Robert 9
Havert
    David 130
Hay
    Anne 145
    David 20
    David 145
Hay
    Anne 147
    David 147
Haynie
    William 33
Hays
    Andrew 60, 63
    Andrew 163

Charles 37
David 190-192
Joseph 179, 182
Robert 56
Robert 205
Hays
    Charles 189
    Joseph 195
    Robert 204
Haywood
    John 166
Haywood,
    John 166
Hazzard
    William 95
    William 156
Heaton
    Robert 8, 10-12, 59, 65
    Robert 204
    Thomas 9
Hedgepeth
    Charles 99
Heeting
    James 52
Henderson
    Bennett H. 96
    John G. 13
Henderson
    James 202
Henley
    Abner 135
    Abner 145, 146, 165, 169, 171
Henley
    Abner 159, 184
Henly
    Abner 133
    Abner 163, 175-177, 197
Henly
    Abner 188, 190, 192
Hennen
    James 77
Hennen & Dickson 78
Henning
    Jones 38
Henry
    Andrew 59
    David 52
    Hugh 130
    James 78, 107
Henry
    Abner 185
Herbert
    Isaac 82
Herndon
    Jo 87
    Joseph 10, 26, 59, 76
    Joseph 147, 154
Herndon
    Joseph 148, 200
Herrod
    Barnabas 91
    Barnard 57
    Barnebas 66
    John 24
Hewit
    Robert 17
Hewitt
    Robert 204
Hibbile
    James 26
Hibbits
    James 27, 33, 35-37, 39, 40
Hibbitts
    James 22

Hickman
    Thomas 8, 17, 19, 53-55, 62, 64, 65, 109, 119, 131-133

Hickman
    Elliott 163
    Thomas 204

Hicks
    John 162
    Zebedie 60

Hide
    Henry 9-12, 60
    Henry 143, 157-159, 162, 167, 168, 171, 173, 174, 178-184, 186, 189, 191, 193, 197
    John H. 34, 40

Hill
    Dan 21, 23, 26, 27, 30-33, 35-38, 40
    Samuel 80, 122
    Samuel Sugars 108
    Samuel Sugars 122
    Spencer 162
    William 1

Hindon
    Joseph 143

Hindon
    Joseph 143

Hinley
    Abner 168

Hinton
    Jeremiah 63

Hitton
    Daniel 44, 46, 50

Hodge
    Francis 27
    James 5

Hodges
    David 62
    Francis 28

Hogan
    Arthur 72

Hogan
    Arthor 143

Holland
    Benjamin 170
    Joel 134, 136-138
    Joel 145, 146, 158, 160, 161, 163, 165, 169, 172, 175-177, 186, 189, 191, 194, 197

Holland
    Kemp 182

Holman
    D. 160

Holt
    John 135

Homes
    Adam 63
    William 116
    William 189

Hood
    George 9

Hooper
    Absalam 95
    Absalom 57
    Absolam 22

Absolom 131, 132
Absolum 110
Churchwell 163
Hooper
    Absolam 156
Hoouser
    David 130
Hoover
    John 115
    Matthias 110
Hope
    John 17
    William 49, 58, 64
Hopkins
    Alexander 114
    Joseph 2, 3, 5, 11, 16, 96, 101, 104, 105, 110, 113, 117, 119, 121, 123
    Joseph 190-192
Horton
    Josiah 17
Houser
    Daniel 9
Houston
    John 95
Howard
    William 48
Howell
    John 98
    Thomas 13, 68
Howell
    John 166
Huddleston
    Wyley 148
Hudson
    Thomas 71, 76
Hudspath
    Charles 96, 117
Hudspeth
    Charles 101, 104, 105, 110, 119, 121, 123
Huey
    Thomas 11
Humphrey 22
    Parry W. 103, 125
    Perry W. 108
    Perry W. 197
Humphreys
    P. W. 76, 94
    P.W. 71
    Perry W. 42, 116, 118
Humphreys
    Parry W. 172, 189, 208
Hunphrey
    Parry W. 167
Hunt
    Gersham 7
Hutcheson
    John 7, 10-12, 16, 40, 60, 113
Hutchings
    John 10, 68
    John 190
Hutchinson 2
    John 2, 3, 8, 9
Hutchison
    John 34
Hyde
    Henry 71, 76
    John H. 60, 113
Hyser 108
Ingram
    Pines 155
Inman
    Samuel 60, 112, 121

Irvin
    John 25
Irwin
    James 190
    John 84
Jackson
    Andrew 14, 15,
        21, 31,
        39, 61,
        94, 113
    Andrew 198
    James 63
    James 173
    Samuel 93
    William 50, 57
Jackson
    Andrew 166,
        190
    Washington 186
Jackson & Hutchings
        190
James
    John 88
    Joshua 63, 112
    Thomas 103
    Thomas 146
James Elder & Co. 71
Jamison
    William
        Caldwell
        86
Jeffers
    Nathaniel 49,
        58, 64
Jenkins
    Hiram 147
Jennings
    Edmond 4, 7, 9,
        10, 50,
        87, 105
    Edmond 151,
        160, 194
    Edmund 2, 4,
        10-12,
        16, 33,
        57
    Edmund 138,
        152, 154,
        161, 186,
        189, 191
Jennings
    Edmond 153
    Edmund 146
    Edward 145
Jennings.
    Edmond 153
Jennins
    Edmond 87
    Edmund 50
Jernigan
    Jesse 23
Jernigans
    Jesse 83
Jett
    Stephen 120
Jimerson
    Thomas 151
John
    Benjamin 159
John B. Evans & Co.
        84
Johns
    John 63
Johnson
    Daniel 55
    John B. 107
    Joseph 44
    Thomas 120
    Thomas 160,
        161
    Thos 51
Johnston
    Abner 60, 61
    Andrew 104
    Danial 62
    Daniel 132
    Isaac 128
    John 70, 135

John 186, 187
Joseph 32, 62,
    65, 66,
    128, 132
Matthew 186,
    187
Nathaniel 202
Oliver 37, 115
Peter 60, 80
Robert 11
Thomas 60, 78
William 131
William 156
Johnston
    Joseph 145
Joice
    Patrick 75
Joiner
    Freeman 102
Jones
    Aquila 60, 61
    Azuila 60
    Benjamin 119
    Breton 84
    David 96, 101,
        104, 107,
        110, 117,
        119, 121,
        122
    Elizabeth 100
    Evan 120
    Fanning 67
    John 51, 68
    John H. 108,
        117, 118
    Joseph 108
    Samuel 100
    Thomas 120
    Thomas 151
    Willis 163
Jones
    Willis 165,
        169, 172,
        175-177

Jordan
    Benjamin 122
    Benjamin 165
Jordon
    John 165
Joslin
    Benjamin 63
    Benjamin 1
Joyce
    Patrick 208
Karr
    William 52, 67,
        72, 74,
        75, 78,
        79
Karr
    William 143
Kearney
    Henry G. 185
Kearney
    Henry G. 186,
        188
Keeling
    James 49
    Leonard 4, 8
Keesee
    George 64
Keisee
    George 58
Kencaid
    Joseph 132
Kenneday
    Dempsey 37
Kennedy
    Abram 57
    Dempsey 6, 9,
        55
    John 157
    Robert 8, 59
Kerr
    Samuel 146
    William 49, 55,
        56

Kethley
    John 21
Kethly
    John 49, 51
Kieff
    Thomas 134
Killebro
    Buckner 95, 110
Killebru
    Buckner 156
Kincade
    Joseph 55
Kincaid
    Joseph 62
King
    Edward 161
    James 181, 187
    Richard 145
    Robert 111, 115
    William 10
    William 170,
        181, 187
King, Carson & King
        181, 187
Kirkpatrick
    Alexander 1, 4,
        7, 10,
        11, 16
    Alexander 170
    John 37
Knox
    James 94
Krisel
    John 120
Lacy
    Thomas 140
Laird
    Alexander 117
Lancaster
    John 4, 7,
        9-12, 22,
        26, 27,
        30-33,
        35-38,
        40, 50,
        57, 102,
        123
    John 158, 163
    William 25, 96,
        101, 104,
        105, 109,
        117, 119,
        121, 123
    William 160,
        161
Lancaster
    John 165, 197
Lancastor
    John 49
Landers
    Edmond 22
Lane
    Robert 34
    William 133,
        136-138
    William 145,
        146, 158,
        160, 161,
        163, 169,
        172,
        175-177,
        186, 189,
        191, 194,
        197
Lanes
    William 165
Latham
    James 160
Latimer
    Griswold 103,
        104, 106,
        110, 117,
        119, 123,
        135
Lauderdale
    James 21, 23,
        26, 27,
        30-32,

　　　　　40, 68,
　　　　　133,
　　　　　135-138
　　James　145,
　　　　　146, 157,
　　　　　160, 161,
　　　　　163, 165,
　　　　　169, 172,
　　　　　175, 177,
　　　　　186, 189,
　　　　　191, 193,
　　　　　197
　　James, Sr. 13
　　William 106
Lauderdale
　　James 176
Laurance
　　John 24
Lawrence
　　John 166
Leachey
　　James Woods 92
Lee
　　Braxton 8
Legate
　　William 186
LeGrand
　　Peter 142
LeGrand
　　Peter 154
Lemmonds
　　Joseph 105
Lemmons
　　Peter 170
Lemonds
　　Joseph 35, 91
Lenior
　　Herbert 9
Letner
　　Eley 205
　　John
　　Christopher 205

Lewis
　　James M. 17
　　Joel 1, 4, 5,
　　　　　7, 9-11,
　　　　　16, 17
　　Joel 204
　　Seth 59
　　William T 7
　　William T. 19,
　　　　　48, 101,
　　　　　145
Lewis
　　Joel 146
　　William Terrell
　　　　　145
Ligate
　　William 187
Liggett
　　Charles 8
Liles
　　Hugh 9
Linton
　　Ezekiel 119
Lintz
　　William 37
　　William 174,
　　　　　176
　　Wm 117
Lird
　　Alexander 189
Litten
　　Jeffery 150
Litton
　　Jeffrey 44, 46
　　John 44, 46
　　William 44, 46
Lochia
　　Peter 84
Lockhart
　　Thomas 100
Lodge
　　Matthew 2
　　Matthew 161

Lofton
  Thomas 133, 135
  Thomas 143, 159, 162, 167, 168, 171, 173, 186, 189, 191, 194, 197
Long
  Samuel 154
Looney
  Peter 49, 95, 110, 113, 118
Love
  James 171
  Joseph 33
Lovely
  William L. 115
Lowe
  Marvel 6, 8-12, 69
Luma
  Peter 6
Lynn
  Joseph 203
Lyon
  Henry 68
  John 52
Lyon
  Henry 145
Lyons
  ~William 179
  Patrick 134
  William 133
  William 143, 158, 159, 167, 171, 173, 174, 178-182, 184, 185, 188, 190, 192, 197

Lytle
  Archibald 22, 113
  William 7, 11, 31, 43, 44, 60, 113
  William, Jr. 193
Mabion
  Charles F. 75
Mabius
  Charles F. 68, 70, 73, 77
Mabry
  Seth 13, 68
Mabury
  Francis 74
Macky
  William 34
Maclin
  James C 9
  John 118, 124
  Sackfield 26
  William 26, 27
  Zackfield 26
Maclin
  John 188
Macob
  John 28
Macon
  John 28
Madlock
  William 76
Magnees
  Jonathan 63
Magness
  Jonathan 38
Mairs
  Joseph 186
Mairs
  Joseph 165

Maliegin
    John 185
Mallard
    Joseph 53
Malloy
    Thomas 159
Manifee
    Jonas 49, 64
    Jones 176
    Nimrod 131
    Nimrod 156
Manifee
    Jonas 191
Maniffee
    Jonas 125
    Jonas 174
Mannifee
    Jonas 58
Mansell
    George 48
Mansker
    Kasper 2, 13, 68
Marchbanks
    William 30, 101
Marlin
    John 173
Marr
    George W. L. 109
    George W.L. 163
    James 55
Marshal
    John 62
Marshall
    James 33
    John 55, 132
Martin
    James 31
    Jesse 78
    John L 26
    John L. 21, 27, 31-33, 40, 44,
        49, 57, 68, 75, 78, 79, 103, 107, 117, 119, 121, 122, 134, 136, 137
    John L. 30, 104
    John S. 38
    Samuel 133
    Thomas 12, 35
    Winney 31
Massingale
    Thomas 138
    Thomas 158
Masterson
    Thomas 93, 107, 122
Maston
    Thos. 144
Maury
    Philip 161
Maxel
    Jesse 194
Maxey
    Edward 170
Maxwell
    James 8, 41, 56
    Jesse 56
May
    John 125
Maybury
    Francis 74
Mayfield
    Stephen 149
Mays
    James 78
McAllister
    James 63
McAnutty
    John 67

McBride
    James 121
    Samuel 154
McBride
    James 175
    Sam'l 147
McClain
    Sackfield 56
McCleary
    Samuel 154
McClung
    Charles 77
McConnel
    John 37
    John, Jr. 39
McConnell
    John 68, 125
    John P. 184, 185, 194
    Robert 204
McConnell
    Robert 205
McCormack
    George 118
    George 176
    Laurence 163
McCrabb
    Alexander 131
    Alexander 156
McCrary
    Nathaniel 176
McCreary
    Nathaniel 7, 64
    Nathaniel 174
McCruston
    James 103
McCuen
    John 107
McCuesten
    James 135
McCueston
    James 142
McCuistin
    James 142

McCuiston
    James 112, 125
    James 145, 146
McCuston
    James 142
McCutchen
    Samuel 100
McDanial
    Roger 104
McDaniel
    Roger 208
McDonald
    John 96, 101, 104, 106, 110, 113, 123
McElyea
    Elizabeth 127
    James 127, 128
McEwen
    William 193
Mcfersin
    James 63
McGaugh
    Matthew 193
McGavock
    David 14, 15, 17, 18, 125
    David 138, 182, 203
    Randal 14, 15, 26, 54, 73, 80, 82, 90, 96, 100, 103, 115, 124, 126
    Randall 42
McGavock
    David 167
    Randal 203, 205, 209

McGuire
    George 107
McIntosh
    Lackland 189
    Nimrod 161
    Zacklin 117
McKain
    Joseph 118
McKean
    Joseph 63, 64
    Joseph 185, 193
McKey
    William 188
McKinley
    Daniel 6
McKinney
    John 131
Mckinny
    John 162
McKnight
    William 147
McKnight
    William 186, 187
McMahan
    Daniel 186, 187
McMorn
    John 63
McMurry
    James 1, 4, 11, 16, 34, 40, 60, 113
    John 160, 161, 163, 165, 169, 175-177, 197
    Robert 171
    Samuel 78

McMurry
    John 184, 185, 188, 190, 192
McNairy
    Andrew 86
    John 17, 46, 98, 99, 110
    John 168, 172
    Nathaniel A. 36, 118
    Robert 133, 135
    Robert 143, 159, 173, 174, 178-182, 184, 185, 190, 192, 197
McNairy
    Nathaniel 174
    Nathaniel A. 141
    Nathaniel A. 141, 170
    Robert 159, 162, 167, 168
McNamee
    Peter 128
McNeely
    Hugh 192
McNeely
    Hugh 190, 191
McNight
    Lemuel 28
McQuerry
    Micajah 71, 76
McRaynolds
    Elizabeth 104
    Robert 104
McRenolds
    Archibald 42

McReynold
    Archibald 44
McReynolds
    Archibald 41
McWhirter
    George 44
    George M. 17, 46
Mear
    John 62, 132
Meeker
    Samuel 54, 93
    William 53
    William P. 53
Meeker, Cochran & Co 54
Menees
    B. 82
    B., Jr. 81
    Benjamin 89
    James 7, 34, 60, 88, 89, 107, 113, 123
    James 160
Menees
    Benjamin 202
Menes
    James 40
Meness
    James 51, 76
Merrit
    Benjamin 33
    James 107
Miles
    Charles 121
    John 150
Miller
    Reed 154
Milligin
    John 184
Mills
    John 68, 106

Minees
    John 9
Minor
    Golfin 126
Mitchel
    John 24, 63
    Thomas 52, 72, 74, 75, 79
    Thomas 143
Mitchel
    Mark 154
Mitchell
    Michael 68
    Thomas 49, 56, 57
    Thomas 153
Mitchell
    John 145
Mitcheson
    William 86
Mollow
    Thomas 209
Molloy
    Thomas 43, 45, 104, 114, 136
    Thomas 179
Monroe
    David P. 125
Montflorence
    James Cole 133
Montgomery
    Michael 115
    William 6
Moore
    Adam 128
    Alexander 129
    Amos 147
    Evans 37, 115
    Israel 107
    James 180, 182
    Sommerset 49

Moore
- Alexander 154
- James 180
- William 145

Moors
- General 93

More
- John 178

Morgan
- James 82
- William 81

Morris
- Andrew 20, 34
- Andrew 176
- John 44, 46
- John 151, 163, 173
- Josiah 173

Morrison
- Hugh 24

Morton
- James 31

Moss
- Thomas 24

Motheral
- John 33, 36, 61

Mott
- Joseph 175

Muherrin
- James 159

Mulheren
- James 17

Mulherin
- James 29, 43, 45

Mulherin
- James 209

Mulherin's
- James 181

Mulherren
- James 136

Mulherrin
- James 49, 58, 64, 83, 104, 114, 136
- James 204

Mulherrin
- James 179

Mullen
- William S. 146

Mullin
- William 75
- William 182

Mundine
- Charles 109

Murphy
- Michael 58, 63

Murphy
- Michael 141

Murry
- Thomas 27, 28
- William 34, 40, 60, 65, 66, 113
- William 182

Myrick
- Richard 20, 42, 116

Nance
- Bird 122
- Isaac 122
- William 31

Napier
- Richard C. 134

Nash
- Francis R. 7, 166
- Travis? C. 147
- William 17, 67, 68, 118

Neally
- William 173

Neeley
- James 6
- James 157
- William 143, 159

Neelly
    William 159,
        162, 167,
        168, 171,
        174, 179,
        180, 184,
        185, 188,
        192, 197
Neely
    James 97
    William 178,
        179, 190
Neilly
    William 181,
        182
Nelson
    Robert 21, 39,
        46, 49,
        51, 86
    Robert 160,
        161
Nevell
    Joseph Burgel
        86
Nevil
    John 87
Nevill
    George 87
    J. B. 87
Neville
    G. 87
    George 6, 54,
        86
    George W. 54
    John 131
    John 156
Nichols
    John 5, 17, 18,
        25, 32,
        50, 87
    John 191
Nichols
    John 193

Nicholson
    Elisha 75
Nolen
    John 11
Nolin
    David 171
Norman
    James 154
Norrod
    Jeremiah 158
Nowlin
    Abram 56
Noyes
    Levi 120
Nusam
    Francis 71, 76
Nusum
    Francis 30
Ogilvie
    Harris 194
Oldham
    George 171
    Moses 186, 187
Oliphent
    Samuel 147
Oneal
    Timothy 63
Ore
    James 48, 72
Orr
    David 106
    James Robert
        178
Overton 4, 21
    John 13, 14,
        20, 25,
        26, 30,
        34,
        43-46,
        52, 53,
        57, 74,
        83, 84,
        95, 104,

113, 114,
131, 136
John 159, 179,
193, 209
Thomas 64
Thomas J. 118
Overton
Jno 208
John 199
Owens
Edmond 135
Edmond 143,
159, 167,
179
Edmund 133
Edmund 159,
162, 168,
171, 174,
178-182,
184, 185,
188, 190,
192, 197
Edward 173
Oxberry
Christopher 138
Pace
William 115
Page
James 56
Robert 107
Robert 171
Paine
Greenwood 158
Parchment
Philip 6, 27,
28, 30,
101, 123
Parchment
Philip 202
Parker
Charles 116
David 157
John 119

William 174,
203
Parks
George 72
John 112, 134
John 165
Ruben 178
Parr
William 13, 68
Parris
James 149
Parrs
Mary 22
Parsons
Harrison 19
Parvis
Barnet 102
Paton 120
Patterson
Francis 150
Patton
Alexander 26,
95, 110,
136-138
Alexander 156
John 26
Tristran 122
Paxton
Nancy 198
Thomas 198
Payne
Greenwood 182
John 182
Josiah 107
Payne
Josiah 148
Payton
Ephraim 82
John 4, 11, 16,
22, 26,
27,
30-32,
34, 36,
37, 39,

40, 68,
70, 73,
77, 81,
82, 107,
111, 119
 John 140
Payton
 John 178
Pendares
 William 151
Penny
 William 152,
  155
Perkins
 Daniel 127
 Lewis 7, 59
 Nicholas 10, 74
 Nicholas T. 17,
  74
 Nicholas Tait
  74
 Thomas H. 49,
  58, 64,
  139, 141,
  193
 William 146
Perkins
 Daniel 206
 Lewis 143
 Thomas Harden
  141
Perry
 Nathaniel 24,
  25, 88,
  123
 William 186,
  187
Peterson
 Isaac 87, 89
Pettiweay
 William 132
Pettway
 William 33

Petty
 Henry 178
Phifers
 Capt. Martin 1
Philips
 Benjamin 37
 Bennet 122
 Isaac 160,
  162, 178
 Joseph 17, 49,
  58
 Joseph 193
 Merrel 77
 Merril 70
 William 105
Philips
 Joseph 207
Phillips
 Andrew 149
 Benjamin 65, 66
 Isaac 133,
  135-137
 Isaac 143,
  159, 167,
  168, 171,
  173, 174,
  178-182,
  184, 185,
  190, 192,
  197
 Joseph 63
 Joseph 204
 Merril 73, 75
Pillow
 Gidean 9
 Gideon 37, 38
 Gideon 145,
  146, 158
 William 80
 William 165,
  193
Pinkley
 Abraham 78

Pinkston
    Majer 33
    Peter 60
Piper
    Abram 6
    Samuel 6
Pipkin
    Philip 63
Pipkins
    Philip 189
Poe
    George 165
Poe
    Rhodin 193
Polk
    Col. William 57
    Richard 113
    Richard 171
Pollard
    Reuben 89
Pollock
    B. William 87
    B. Wm 19
    Barkley William 86
Porter
    Joseph 70-72, 75, 76
    Joseph 208
    Joseph B. 122, 165, 193
    William 203
Porter
    Joseph 208
    William 195
Powel
    Ambrose 186, 187
Prewit
    Elisha 58
Price
    Winney 31
Prince
    Robert 86, 87, 136-138
    William 127
Probart
    William 190
Probat
    William 192
Probst
    William 191
Pryor
    Norton 92
Puckett
    Richard 96, 101, 104, 106, 110, 119, 121, 122
Purtle
    George 96
P' Pool
    Wittshire 175
Raines
    John 173
    William 7
Rains
    John, Jr. 7
    William 125
Ralston
    Joseph 171
Ramsey
    David 58
Rasee
    George 49
Raulson
    David 61
Rawlings
    Aaron 49, 52, 55, 56, 60, 64, 72, 74, 75, 78, 79
    Aaron 143
    Benjamin 69

John 128
Rawlings
    A. 148
    Aaron 143
Rawls
    Shadwick 120
Raymond
    Nicholas 143
Read
    Alexander 112
    John 20, 85, 86
    Major John 87
Reader
    Jacob 143
Reaves
    Robert C. 59, 65, 66
Redich
    William 56
Reed
    John 122
    John 165
Reed
    John 147
Reeves
    Jack 68
Reid
    John 126
Renolds
    Gay 150
Reybourn
    Henry 202
Reynolds
    James B. 142
Reynolds
    Gay 155
Reynolds,
    James B. 142
Rhodes 28
    Captain Joseph T. 29
    Joseph T. 16
Rice
    Elisha 137

Joel 103, 119, 135
    Joel 175
Rice
    John 164
Richardson
    James 149
Richmond
    John 20, 36
    Mark 5
    Mark 145
Rickman
    Joshua 105
    Mark 51
    Nathan 51
Ridley
    Beverly 9
    George 9
    Vinson 68, 70, 73, 75, 77, 105
Riggs
    Joel 193
Riter
    Nicholas 203
Roane
    Archibald 94
Robbins
    Samuel 78
Robert 104
    Peter D. 45
Robert Stothart & Co. 42
Roberts
    Isaac 2, 3, 7, 8, 10, 11, 16, 38
    Isaac 204
    James 2-4, 7, 9-12, 16
Robertson
    Charles 7, 19
    Hugh 63

James 17, 19,
    51, 100,
    101
Jas 102
John 39
Jonathan F. 56
Joseph 87, 88,
    120
Joseph 161
Sarah 89
Stephen 57
Thomas L. 186
Robinson
    Moses 122
    Thomas L 187
Roe
    Richard 24, 39
Rogers
    Isham 161
Roper
    William 1-3, 20
Rowing
    Alexander 119
Russell
    Philip 9
    William 20, 35
Rutherford
    Griffith 4, 5,
        7, 11, 16
    Henry 6, 21,
        23, 26,
        27, 32,
        34,
        36-38,
        40, 107,
        112, 119,
        122, 128,
        135
    Henry 165,
        169, 172,
        175-177
    Thomas 116
    Thomas 173

Rutherford
    Henry 163
Rutland
    Blake 123
Sale
    William 161
Sample
    Robert 65, 66
    William 118
Sanders
    Adam 33
    Edward 12, 59
    Francis 56
    Francis 182
    James 13, 19,
        61
    John 89
    John 150
    Obediah 33
    William 12, 13,
        44, 46,
        103
Sanderson
    John 153
Sappington
    Roger B. 179,
        182-184,
        195
    Thomas 126
Sappington
    Roger B. 184,
        185
Sawyers
    James 21, 23,
        26, 27,
        30-32,
        35, 40,
        120
Sayers
    Foster 37
    Foster 190,
        192
    James 33, 35-38

Sayres
    Foster 117
    Foster 175, 191
Scales
    Nicholas 76
Scoby
    Joseph 113, 118
Scott
    Jacob 161
    James 150
    William 59
    William 146, 182
Scott
    James 151
Searcy
    B. 42
    B. 28
    Bennet 3, 9, 11, 22, 26-29, 34, 35, 38, 42, 43, 59, 60, 65, 66, 70, 72, 78, 90, 92, 93, 100, 101, 120, 121, 124, 134
    Bennet 146, 163, 173, 174, 191, 195
    Bennett 44
    Reuben 27
    Robert 26, 77, 89, 94, 95, 110, 124, 134
    Robert 156, 160, 161, 165, 168, 169, 172, 176, 177, 197
    Rueben 169
Searcy
    Bennet 161, 164, 172, 175, 176, 190, 200, 201, 205
    Reuben 170
    Robert 145, 158, 176, 177, 179-182, 189, 191, 194
    Rob't 174
Searcy & Carvin 177
Seawell
    Benjamin 84
    Joseph 68, 107
    William 77
Sedgety
    John 158
Sevear
    Valentine 87
Sevier
    John 88, 89, 94, 123
Sevier
    John 202
Seypert
    Robert 149
Seyport
    Francis 149
Shannon
    David 55, 62-64, 132
    Samuel 25, 63

Samuel, Sr. 76
Sharp
    Andrew 27
Shavers
    Michael 85
Shaw
    Basel 2
    Bassel 1
    Bazzel 14, 22
    James 19
    Robert 4, 7, 11, 13, 16, 68
Shelby
    D. 169
    David 12, 19, 68, 106
Shepherd
    Adam 51
Sherrer
    Godfred 151
Shouse
    John 9, 40
Shumate
    Benjamin 122
Shute
    John 71, 76
    Thomas 56, 71, 76
    Thomas 157
Siglar
    John 161
Simpson
    Isaac 25
    William 118, 135
    William 150, 153, 184, 185
Sitton
    Jeffery 153
Skinner
    Nathan 182
    Willy 78

Slaughter
    Robert Smith 5, 6
    Sarah 5
slave
    Ben 64
    Charlotte 30, 101
    Doll 105
    Fanny 104
    Harry 169
    Jim 105
    Josh 125
    Mille 157
    Milly 118
    Nell 169
    Paddy 104
    Sal 30, 101
    Sam 169
    Tom 105
Sloan
    Archibald 44
Sloane
    Archibald 46
Smith
    Daniel 19
    George 129
    James 150, 153
    John 2, 3, 31, 103
    Martin 126
    Mr. 183
    Richard 147
    Robert 44, 46
    Thomas 27, 28, 133
    William 59, 83, 99, 125
    William 161, 173, 183, 184
Smith
    William 154, 181, 185

Smithson
    Samuel 12, 13
Sneed
    William 117
Snoddy
    Samuel 165
    William 134
    William 145, 146, 157, 163, 165, 168, 169, 171, 175-177, 197
Snoddy
    William 158
Soloman
    Jordan 171
Sommerville
    John 91
    John 173
Spence
    Peter 127
Spencer
    John 122
Squires
    David 165
Standley
    Martin 165, 186, 187
Stanley
    Abraham 44
    Abram 69
Stanly
    Abraham 43
Start
    Thomas 168
Steel
    Archibald B. 110
Stephens
    Lewis 122
    Robert 191
    William 122

Stephens
    Joel 186, 187
Stephenson
    Hugh 44, 46
    Hugh 150, 153
Stewart
    Thomas 43, 44, 46, 56, 57
Stockett
    Thomas W. 165
Stockill
    Thomas W. 122
Stone
    John 1, 14, 23
Stothart
    Robert 41, 44, 107, 122
Stothart & Bell 41
Stothart & Co. 44
Strain
    Thomas 7, 95, 110
    Thomas 156
Stratton
    Owen 139
Strother
    Richard 34, 40, 60, 113
Stroud
    Marshal 52
    Marshall 52
    Marshall Stroud 53
Struart
    Thomas 37
Stuart
    Duncan 103, 104, 106, 110, 117, 119, 121, 123
    James 9, 112

Thomas 4, 5, 7,
  11-13,
  24, 25,
  29, 30,
  33, 39,
  45, 57,
  59,
  61-67,
  73, 79,
  81-83,
  88, 96,
  101, 102,
  104, 106,
  109, 111,
  112, 114,
  118, 120,
  122, 125,
  130, 132,
  136, 137
Thomas 140,
  145, 146,
  168, 170,
  191, 200
Thos 28, 125
Stuart
  Thomas
    139-141,
    145, 159,
    161, 162,
    166, 167,
    170, 174,
    178, 181,
    186, 201,
    204, 206
  Thos 188
  Thos. 167
Stuart,
  Thomas 140
Stubblefield
  George 107, 131
  George 156
  Thomas 63

Stull
  Zachariah 13,
    59, 65,
    66
Stump
  C. 116, 182
  Christopher 11,
    20, 34,
    40, 42,
    60, 92,
    113
  Christopher
    139, 175
  Frederick 18,
    19, 50,
    64, 67,
    71, 76,
    101
  Frederick 143,
    163
  John 9, 50, 57,
    60, 63,
    67, 72,
    78, 79
  John 143, 204
  Jonathan 142
Stumps
  Christopher 18
Suggs
  Lemuel 94
Sullivan
  Lee 99, 104
  Lee 198
Summer
  Thomas Edward
    31, 32
Summerville
  John 195
Sute
  Alexander 67
Sutton
  Thomas 44, 46
Swanson
  Edward 193

Sweetman
    Michael C. 45
Swingley
    George 24
Sydner
    Anthony 68
Syms
    William 162
Tabb
    Col. James 108
    James A. 107
Tait
    Anderson 50
    Robert 49, 57, 72
    William 63, 89, 133
    William 143, 162, 167-169, 171, 175-177, 186, 189, 191, 194, 197
    Zachariah 182
Tait
    William 159, 182
Talbor
    Thomas 46
Talbot
    Matthew 33
    Thomas 17
Talbott
    Matthew 132
    Thomas 8, 48, 59
Tate
    Anderson 132
Tatum
    H 1, 2
    Howel 4, 9, 24, 63, 76, 80, 82, 84, 132
    Howell 23, 56, 63, 71
Tatum
    Major Asalom 164
Taylor
    Charles 122
    George 63
    James 33, 40, 60, 90, 99, 113
    Jeremiah 150
    John 203
    Joseph 34
    Joshua 36, 39
    Thomas 36, 37, 57, 60
Tease
    William 95, 110
    William 156
Thackson
    Zaddock B. 33
Thomas
    Hickman 64
    Mark 194
    Nancy 198
    Robert 16
    William 103, 112
    William 146
Thomas
    Robert 156
    William 203
Thomas Masterson & Co. 122
Thomas Masterson & Company 107
Thompson
    Daniel 50
    Joseph 147
    Neal 191, 192

253

Neel 57
Neil 79
Niel 79
Robert 17, 112
William 182, 190
Thompson
    Neal 173
Thornton
    Yancy 94, 131
    Yancy 141, 156
Thursby
    Edward 53, 54
Titus
    Ebenezer 62
    George 57, 64
    James 189
Tolbot
    Matthew 167
    Thomas 17
    Thomas 167
Tooley
    Henry 131
Tooly
    Henry 140, 156
Top
    John 63, 65, 105
Topp
    John 59, 66
Totten
    Benjamin 52, 74
Totton
    B. 100
    Benjamin 49, 55, 56, 60, 67, 72, 75, 78, 79
    Benjamin 143, 156
Totton
    Benjamin 202

Trigg
    Daniel 145
    William 68, 107
Trimble
    David 34, 38, 123
Trousdale
    James 12, 106
    Robert 106
Trousdall
    James 106
    Robert 106
Truet
    Henry M 2
Truit
    Henry M 2, 6
    Henry M. 3, 7
Tully
    Israel 133
Turner
    Arthur 9, 49
    Arthur K. 28, 57
    John 141
    William 68, 70, 73, 77
Turner
    Arthur 189
Turney
    Peter 7
Turneys
    Peter 151, 153
Tyrell
    William 45
Tyrrell
    William 43
Ury
    George 59, 65, 66
Valentine
    John 17
    John Easten 17
    John Easton 8

Vantree
    John 103
Vantress
    David 1, 14, 23
    Leveck 58
    Lovick 49, 52, 60, 67
Vaughn
    David 81, 119
    Susanah 81
Ventress
    Lovick 56
Ventriss
    Lovick 55
Verrell
    John 197
Vick
    Cooper 172-174, 176
Vick
    Cooper 168, 169, 175-177
Vincent 39
    James 39, 110
Vinson
    H. James 95
    James 156
Waddel
    John 96
Walker
    Abraham 122
    Henry 178
    John 55, 62, 71, 76
    Joseph 38
    Philip 62
    Phillip 132
    Samuel 156
    William 25
Walker
    Alexander 146, 158

Jenny 162
    John 162
    Philip 163
    Samuel 202
Wall
    James 80
Wallace
    James 151
    Joseph 13
Waller
    Thomas 79
Walthall
    John 96
Walton
    William 151
Waltons
    Col. William 152
Ward
    John 109
    William 71, 76
Warrington
    Woolsey 10, 114
Warron
    Thomas 194
Washington
    Gray 135
Watson
    Josiah 61, 87
    Thomas 65, 66, 97
    Thomas 172
Weakley 135
    R. 102, 135
    Robert 3, 17, 19, 74, 101, 112
    Samuel 33, 103, 131, 132
Weakley
    Robert 167, 202
    Samuel 146

Weathered
   John 145
Weatherel
   Francis 111
Weathers
   John 13, 68
Weatherspon
   John 14, 15
Weatherspoon
   John 15
   John 15
Wells
   Hayden 86
   Haydon 86
   Heydon 57, 102
West
   Griffin 38
   Hezekiah 149
   John 165, 178
Wharton 151, 152
   J. 130
   Jesse 11-13, 28, 30, 37, 38, 43, 44, 58, 68, 69, 72, 77, 79, 90, 108, 116-119, 124, 128, 129, 136, 137
   Jesse 141, 154, 159, 160, 177, 179, 184, 188, 192, 198
   Jessee 80, 84
Wharton
   Jesse 142, 168, 170, 171, 173, 178, 180, 187, 194, 201, 203, 207
Wharton,
   Jesse 138, 141
Wheaton
   Charles 161
Wheaton
   Calvin 184, 185
White 1
   Chapman 2, 3, 7, 9-12, 16
   Chapman 161
   H. L. 6
   Hugh 2
   Hugh L 1, 4, 8
   Hugh L. 15, 17, 19, 21, 49, 113, 131, 206
   Hugh S. 39
   James Taylor 87
   John 112, 119
   John 178
   Robert 21
   Robert 203
White
   Chapman 160
Whiteside 26
   J. 64
   J. 8, 104, 113, 121, 126
   J. 20, 133, 158
   Jenkin 1, 2, 27, 32, 36, 67, 73, 77, 111, 129, 137
   Jenkin 139

256

Jinken 72, 135
Whiteside,
    Jenkin 139
Whitesides 34
    J. 40, 117, 126
    Jenkin 2, 56, 67, 75, 105, 120
    Jinkin 84
Whitsett
    Laurence 170
Whyte
    Robert 140, 195, 203
Wiggins
    Henry 84
    John P. 65
    John P. 66
Wilburn
    Daniel 45
Wilcox
    Thomas 50, 117
Wilkinson
    William 189
Will
    John 151
Willet
    William 193
Willets
    William 122
Williams
    Caleb 7
    Ethelred 204
    John 63
    Joseph 94
    Joseph 140
    Joseph J. 64
    Joseph S. 49
    Joseph T 6
    Joseph T. 58
    Mathew 116
    Matthew 8, 36, 41
    Matthew 190-192
    Nathaniel Washington 96
    Oliver 158
    Sampson 6, 33, 46, 74, 75, 108
    Sampson 143, 150, 151
Williams.
    Sampson 152
Williams,
    Sampson 153
Williamson
    John 12
    Thomas 7, 96, 101, 104, 106, 109, 113, 117, 119, 121, 122
    Thomas 204
Williamson
    John 165
Wills
    Benjamin D. 184, 185
    James 60, 64, 66, 91
    William 161
Willson
    William 162
Wilson
    David 36
    George 3, 14, 23, 53, 54
    James 105
    James C. 104
    James S. 96, 101, 105, 110, 117,

　　　　119, 121,
　　　　123
　James S, 145
　John　165
　Samuel 33, 122
　Samuel　193
　Thomas 33, 132
　William 36, 37,
　　　　113, 133,
　　　　135
　William 159,
　　　　167, 168,
　　　　171, 173,
　　　　174,
　　　　178-182,
　　　　184, 185,
　　　　190, 192,
　　　　197
　Zacheus 64, 95,
　　　　110
　Zachias 49, 58
　Zachius　156
Wilson
　John　161
Wilson & Eastin 53
Wimberley
　Joseph 120
Winchester
　James 134
Winfrey
　Valentine 38
Witherspon
　John 17
Woods
　Adam　154
　John　145
Woodward
　Micajah 49, 52,
　　　55-57,
　　　67, 72,
　　　74, 75,
　　　78, 79
　Micajah　143

Woodworth
　Asa 34, 40, 60,
　　　113
Woolfolk
　Joseph 1, 4,
　　　11, 16
Wooton
　Daniel　194
Wootton
　William 131
　William　156
Work
　Andrew　182
Wormack
　James 45
Wren
　Randolph　151
Wrenn
　George　171
Wright
　Jacob　162
Wyne
　John K. 11
Yandle
　William 34, 113
　Wilson 40, 60
Yardley
　Thomas　154
Yates
　James 95, 110
　James　156
Young
　Adam 50
　Daniel 8, 17,
　　　36, 37
　Daniel　204
　John L 7
　John L. 8

www.ingramcontent.com/pod-product-compliance
Lightning Source LLC
Chambersburg PA
CBHW070729160426
43192CB00009B/1374